Rethinking US–Soviet Relations

For America's 'Gorbachev' of Tomorrow
in memoriam HJM

We say: let us search and act together.
This applies to the Iran–Iraq war, the
Central American crisis, the Afghan
problem and the situation in the south
of Africa and in Indochina.

Mikhail Gorbachev, February 16, 1987

Rethinking US–Soviet Relations

George Liska

Basil Blackwell

Copyright © George Liska 1987

First published 1987

Basil Blackwell Ltd
108 Cowley Road, Oxford, OX4 1JF, UK

Basil Blackwell Inc.
432 Park Avenue South, Suite 1503
New York, NY 10016, USA

British Library Cataloguing in Publication Data

Liska, George
    Rethinking US – Soviet relations.
    1. Soviet Union—Foreign relations—
    United States   2. United States—
    Foreign relations — Soviet Union
    3. Soviet Union — Foreign relations—1975–
    4. United States — Foreign relations—1981–
    I. Title
    327.47073   E183.8.S65

    ISBN 0-631-15511-2

Library of Congress Cataloging in Publication Data

    Liska, George.
    Rethinking US–Soviet relations.
    Includes index.
    1. United States–Foreign relations–Soviet Union.
    2. Soviet Union–Foreign relations –United States.
    I. Title.
    E183.8.S65L57   1987   327.73047   87-5175

    ISBN 0-631-15511-2

Typeset in 10 on 12½pt Sabon
by Alan Sutton Publishing Limited
Printed in Great Britain by T. J. Press Ltd, Padstow

Contents

Preface

The essays collected in this volume interpret US–Soviet and West–East relations along lines suggested first a decade ago. They add both substantially and in policy-related specifics to subsequent writings even as they borrow from a more fundamental larger work yet to be published. Each essay is self-contained while complementing others either topically or conceptually. The amount of repetition that results from the incremental mode of producing the essays is, it is hoped, redeemed by bringing the message home with progressively increasing clarity and force. Brief summaries in the Overview give an idea of the principal concern of each chapter and, read consecutively, of the work's overall thrust.

The introductory essay was written for an issue of *Social Research* (Winter 1981) devoted to the work of Hans J. Morgenthau. Chapters 1 and 2 appeared in *Foreign Policy* (Spring and Summer 1986); reprinted with permission from *Foreign Policy* 62 [63] Spring [Summer] 1986. Chapter 3 and what is now the first half of chapter 9 were commissioned by the Johns Hopkins Foreign Policy Institute, a research branch of the University's School of Advanced International Studies (SAIS), which has also sponsored preparing this collection for publication. Chapters 4, 5, and 6 appeared between 1981 and 1986 in *SAIS Review*, a periodical brought out by students of the School. Chapters 7, 8, the second half of chapter 9, and the concluding chapter 10 are new. All previously published essays are republished here, some under altered titles and all with mainly stylistic changes, with the permission of the original publishers.

Presenting definite views on a subject chronically beset by unavowed *partis pris* makes it mandatory to disclose the sources of one's bias. I will do so now before returning (chapter 10) to the issue when I review opinion-shaping influences and prejudices across a wider spectrum.

Born in 1922 in the Bohemian part of Czechoslovakia, I had been in the 'right' place at the 'right' time to experience Nazism and communism at first hand before, ending a diplomatic apprenticeship in the Beneš–Masaryk Ministry of Foreign Affairs, I left for the West. Once there, I chose from among the courses open to an exile the option of inquiring into the forces and impulsions that made the culpable acts and events possible. The procedure leads through understanding dangerously close to forgiving; however, it also allows a dissected past to play a part in mending the future, just as aimless lamentations merely help fuse the two facets of time in sterile repetitions.

The strongest psychic impulse behind an emotionally charged intellectual probing into the causal undertow of such repetitions has always come from a thwarted urge to act amidst and against the consequences – an urge more than any other contrary to academic dispassion nourished by suspicion of all forms of power and its exercise. This engagement was certainly true of Hans Morgenthau, a major formative influence and benevolent mentor, in whose honor the introductory essay has been written. In his role as pathfinder for the latest exiles from the center of Europe to the day's seat of world power, he brought the tenets of continental European statecraft to bear on the examination of American foreign policy. The task of those who followed in his footsteps has been to elude the changing fashions of a discipline searching in vain for a master key to puzzling 'reality'. When projecting pertinent past into likely future trends and possible outcomes, the object was and is a blend of theory and praxis sufficiently homogeneous to combine scholarly merit with social utility – and be incidentally of use to a future historian.

For one unsuited to seek direct influence on policy in the country of refuge, the remaining way of repaying the debt has been to help shape, from an unfamiliar viewpoint, the thinking of those who, studying international politics today, would influence events tomorrow and into the coming century. It is only a possible exception from the rule that this volume appears at a moment in East–West relations when such a sense of vocation is not incompatible with a more immediate impact. For myself the possibility, and its appeal, are being dramatically brought home by events in my homeland. As this text goes, in April 1987, through the last stages of printing, the spontaneous popular acclaim of a reformist Soviet leader walking through the streets of the Czech capital has given voice to the hope that yet another

Prague Spring, less ecstatic but more enduring than the first, was in the making. The appeal to Mikhail Gorbachev to help remove conditions that placed too great a strain on the historic ties of sentiment with the kindred Slavic nation to the east, without extinguishing the more self-consciously intellectualized affinity with the democratic West, had also a vaster implication: it highlighted the increasingly critical importance of controversies that delimit the academic discourse in the West on issues that will condition a range of developments among which future trends in Czechoslovakia play only a minor – if for more than one reason symbolically as much as strategically not insignificant – part.

As regards, first, the dynamic of reform in Eastern Europe, seeing the Czech developments as they appeared to take shape in the spring of 1987 through the prism of the Prague Spring's demise in late summer of 1968 has begun to validate the proposition that a gradual, guarded but also stable and sustainable, region-wide change was near-certain to presuppose a prior beginning and parallel unfolding of change inside the Soviet Union itself. Reasserting this proposition does not deny the value – stressed by the contrary thesis – of reformist stimuli originating in Eastern Europe proper, most recently in places like Poland and Hungary, and encouraged by privileged engagement with the West. The 'dialectic' is, for once, a beneficial one and can continue to be such, on two conditions: one, that western propaganda and semblance of policy are not aimed at encouraging a rate of change exceeding the absorptive capacity of either the Soviet or the local regimes; and two, that US grand strategy enhance Soviet receptivity to progressive change by opening up the prospect of a global environment that has decreased the military-strategic significance of Russia's security glacis while downgrading the ideological importance of uniform orthodoxy in the 'socialist community'.

The global requirement is at the core of the larger controversy. The Gorbachev reform drive has supplied a superficially plausible argument to those who believe that denying success to Soviet 'expansionism' and enhancing its cost will alone compel reformist change in the rival superpower. However, even before inviting the question whether such a policy is sufficient in the medium term and safe in the long run, its proponents have already cast doubt on their own sincerity when hastening to indict the ongoing reform effort as apt to make the Soviet Union more dangerous than it was before.

So to argue is to suggest that only such reforms would be welcome that reduced Soviet Russia to the conditions of a liberal-democratic polity of a kind that has historically evolved only in tandem with the secular decline in power of continental states, as distinct from insular-maritime polities. Anything that confirms this suspicion cannot but feed the related one that the American thrust in foreign affairs is directed not so much to the removal of a totalitarian system inimical to freedom in an endangered world, as to the reduction of a geopolitical adversary challenging American interests and influence in a resurgent world. Viewed correctly, such an unwitting admission of intrinsic equivalence is not so much revolting in itself as it is potentially promising in its implication, provided it helps remove the normatively framed key ideological obstacle to a realistic approach to superpower relations – freeing it to apply the contrary belief or thesis: to wit, that Soviet reform will be best sustained from the outside (and withstand reactionary opposition and regression within) by reducing US resistance to any and all significant manifestations of Russia's role and status as a coequal and thus coresponsible world, and foremost if not dominant European, power.

The ground for initiating such a policy when the American political system too has produced its Gorbachev has been prepared by the simultaneously growing concern, on both sides, to improve competitiveness as a way out of what has aptly been called their 'competitive decadence': improving chiefly economic competitiveness vis-à-vis the rising Asian economies (headed by Japan) in the United States and also economic next to sociopolitical one by the Soviet Union relative to the 'capitalist camp' (anxious to coopt China). Any improvement in Soviet economic efficacy carries with it the prospect that the Russian bid to transpose an effectively won and conceded military-technological into more than token geopolitical parity will be increasingly pursued by materially underwritten diplomatic means and decreasingly by military means alone or primarily – a recourse as typical of upthrusting continental powers as it has been serviceable in discrediting also harder-to-contest substantive objectives on procedural grounds. Conversely, anything that would extend parity to the means and instruments of policy cannot but ease the certain pitfalls and mute the exaggerated terrors of any movement toward substantive superpower parity overall.

The latest, Gorbachev-style, Russian revolution from above has dramatized the gradually surfacing choice for American statecraft. One scenario consists of an increasingly traditional or conventional autocracy whose latent drive for enhanced efficiency entails inevitably because requires unconditionally a measure of controlled liberaliz-ation at home, while the conservatism innate to an established great power is fostered by satisfying the no less natural claim to a share in managing an international system that is prone to random upheavals locally and is globally once again fraught with the recurrently experienced major power shifts. The other scenario is latent in the supposedly 'conservative' American policy that, far from shifting to the promotion of genuinely conservative gradualism, would continue to press Russia into one more repetition of aborted ultra-radical reforms as either a prelude to empire-wide disintegration or its expected consequence, on pain of triggering unpredictably defensive–offensive Soviet behavior abroad.

The choice between the different hypothetical rewards and actual risks is still open at a time and in a world that need more than ever a stable and strong, internally ever more liberal because internationally both safely and rewardingly conservative, Russia if they are not to impose ever more strenuous tasks and debilitating burdens on an organically weakened because operationally misguided America.

Should it come to pass that the sequelae of Mr Gorbachev's springtime visit to the Czech capital helped remove the East–West division from the heart of Europe, because they strengthened the belief in real – ever deeper-reaching and wider-ranging – change in and around Russia, the role of Prague-centered events in awakening the Atlantic West to the need for self-defense in 1948, and alerting it in 1968 to the changing balance of long-term opportunities and immediate dangers, would soon find a fitting consummation. Begin-ning with the renewal of independent Czech statehood in 1918 and its loss in 1938, the oddly repetitive series of dates has linked the resurgence of Russia to the falling off of Germany's. As the unfolding rhythm interlocked with both highs and lows in the West's latest encounter with the East, the coincidences did more than punctuate a perennially troubled national destiny; they also reconfirmed an assur-ance the state-renewing philosopher-statesman had bequeathed to the nation's psyche, while updating its meaning: that the nation's lot was enmeshed with matters of larger significance – that the 'Czech Question' was universal in nature and bearing, intermittently in historical time ever since the Hussite bid for spiritual freedom and, in so far as political issues of the highest order are likewise timeless, *sub specie aeterni.*

It is on the strength of beliefs such as this that a small and exposed people can compare its own failings with the fallibilities of mightier powers without giving way to terminally maiming despair. And it is because such a people's separated offspring enjoyed the precious right to speak freely from the hospitable haven of a foreign land, that they have incurred again and again the duty to labor in the anguish of self-doubt when attempting to give the sustaining myth an interpretation that would fit best the changing times and tides. When the fit is there, it is not necessarily a self-delusion to believe that the interpretation is not inimical to the true interests of the country of refuge and a still larger body politic.

Note

1 Two of the original articles now forming chs 1 and 4 have been reproduced in a US Department of Defense publication *Current News* (Special Editions Nos 1454 and 1515) and what is now ch. 2 in similarly targeted *Current* (January 1987).

An Overview

A discussion of method in the broadest meaning of the term, the introductory chapter establishes the overall intellectual framework and perspective informing the subsequent discussion. The principal concern is to define a practically viable balance between the core dynamic of power politics crucial for a statecraft pressed to address immediate problems, and the more elusive modifiers of the narrowly action–reaction model to be taken into account by provident statesmanship that would reach beyond the ad hoc pattern of decision making. Of special interest is the controversial status and the unevenly helpful use of historical analogy as a basis for projections from past to future, on which much of what follows rests. Equally pertinent, and a recurrent theme in the essays that follow, is the relationship between history-conscious realism and conservatism as an intellectual outlook and social philosophical mindset, significantly distinct from liberalism, in its contemporary American as distinct from the classic European version. Stressing the historical dimension in the uneven mix of continuity and change amounting to evolution, and preparing the ground for the stress on geopolitical space as the arena for interaction among territorial states within differing time spans, the overall approach is best described as geohistorical. It restores an appropriately expanded notion of what constitutes political realism to its traditional connection with authentic conservatism.

Chapter 1 lays out the structural basis of principal kinds of strategy and particular policies. In the widely contested choice between domestic, ideological, and structure-centered systemic determinants of policy, it opts unequivocally for the last. In that respect alone the conception differs basically from the view underlying 'anti-Sovietism' in general and related US policies in particular, which favor the first two determinants. However, the chapter's bias in favor of international system dominance mediated through the configuration of power departs also from the structuralist views that stress bipolarity vs. multipolarity pure and simple as critical. It does so in favor of a pattern that is not only triangular but, more importantly, qualitatively differentiated in terms of the historically persistent distinction between primarily land and sea, or continental and insular, powers. The difference from either of the dominant approaches does more than revise the basic analytic framework. It supplies an altered view of (1) the continuing validity of the US–Soviet contention in terms of particular stakes and (2) responsibility for the US–Soviet conflict, a normative foundation for rethinking policies and revising the hierarchy of perceived threats.

Chapter 2 proceeds beyond the discussion of structure to a more explicit and detailed analysis and advocacy of strategy. The so far minimized 'revolutionary' changes in international relations are now called upon as potentially sufficient to expand, with assistance from past experience, the attractiveness of the previously least common, but potentially most creative, strategy of the three main ones corresponding to the tripartite land–sea power pattern, outlined in the first chapter. Discarding rigid containment of the Soviet Union in favor of its radical relaxation is propounded as most likely to deepen the 'mellowing' effects of the original policy and preclude the obverse result of continuing and escalating the denial approach. In so arguing, the chapter returns to the interplay between domestic and foreign politics, but mainly to reverse the determinative impact in favor of the external on the internal environment. In keeping with the postulated relationship between foreign-policy efficacy and regime legitimacy, the chapter outlines and illustrates a guardedly collaborative US–Soviet approach to emerging threats to world order within the framework of a flexible equilibrium, one exerting a more spontaneous or self-imposed restraint on extreme behavior than does mechanical balancing of power through outflanking alliances. The necessary tentativeness in moving beyond speculative generalities to policy-related specifics is also prudent when the risk is to invalidate the former by failing to be sufficiently persuasive when articulating the latter.

Shifting the ground from self-conscious emphasis on political issues and concerns, 'From Deterrence to Defense?' (chapter 3) integrates geopolitics with the consideration of a critical contemporary nuclear arms issue – that of strategic defenses in space. In so doing, the discussion remains faithful to the critique of the narrowly military-technological approach to the US–Soviet conflict and goes beyond the lip service once again commonly paid to the principle of the primacy of the political. The emphasis on the political aspect leads beyond the obvious interconnections to the consideration of differences in political cultures that condition not only the uneven disposition to use nuclear weapons in defense of key values and interests but also greater or lesser tolerance of the ensuing material and human costs along a West-to-East geographic and cultural spectrum. The greater likelihood that the 'statist' Soviet Union might initiate a first strike under specified conditions than the more 'societally' oriented United States is fitted into this larger perspective more firmly by emphasizing the ambiguity of the distinction between offense and defense in the behavior of states in past and likely future settings. The point leads, again, to the question of ultimate responsibility when deterring the adversary gives way to impelling him to uphold his constituent self-perception at the risk of suicide through mutual annihilation.

Chapter 4 deals with the geopolitics of regional conflicts in the perspective of a US strategy that would extend containment to eliminating Soviet influence in areas of the Third World now open to it. Within a general framework of two competing sets of doctrine: the political Monroe and Brezhnev doctrines reserving the right of intervention by one or the other superpower in the sphere of its special interests and influence, and the juridical doctrine of nonintervention, the chapter stresses the actualities of the superpowers bargaining with each other over the balance of immunity in their own and access to the other's sphere, as part of the overall problem of geopolitical parity and inter-regional global equilibrium. One general point – the difference between the strategic importance generously assigned to a regional position in peacetime and the position's quite possibly lesser real utility in a war partly due to the previous exaggeration – is counterpointed with another proposition, suggesting the utility of differentiating between the priorities of the Soviet Union as a world power and those of its local surrogates or allies as only regionally concerned actors. The underlying choice is one between the superpowers subverting one another (and one another's standing) in their respective spheres or moving closer to practicing elementary solidarity as an endangered species *qua* imperial core powers, in the interest of minimal world order and only gradual redistribution of power and influence both intra- and inter-regionally – an issue developed with reference to the pertinent 'rules of the game' in chapter 5. This and the following chapter 6 elaborate upon many of the principal points made before, even as each echoes the general thesis that permeates the entire work. In that 'In the Wake of Afghanistan' reacts more than any other chapter directly to issues salient at the moment of writing, it illustrates the possibilities and limitations of exposing live problems to a crises-transcending perspective on policy. Addressing this crucial facet of foreign-policy scholarship from a different angle, the second half of chapter 9 (preceded by a summary restatement of the main thesis) sets the stage for the concluding chapter by dissecting the conceptual frameworks and underpinnings of three major contemporary academic, but explicitly policy-related, discussions of US–Soviet relations as they differ from each other and the positions taken here.

In keeping with the increasingly speculative tone, the issues focused upon in chapter 7 are two major ones of international relations: war, as the culmination of competing efforts to deal with rival interests, and empire, as the consummation of expansive drives and urges leading to conflict. Instead of implicitly bypassing the possibility of a US–Soviet military engagement, or treating defeat in war as the recurring prerequisite to substantial reform of any Russian political system, the chapter reviews once more the reasons for, as well as the likely forms and directions of, a major war if the present policies of encircling the Soviet Union continue not only on the two fronts (European and Asian) but also the two levels (geopolitical and military-technological or -strategic), and the two powers' competing efforts to shape world wide developments are not viewed in a larger historico-philosophical perspective that denies full success to either party in favor of erosion of creedal authority for both and incidental aggrandizement for third parties. And, instead of ignoring it, the essay takes seriously the possibility if not probability that the Soviet continental empire, far from being the last, is not necessarily the worst imaginable. To substantiate the proposition, the chapter does that which is done only rarely if ever in either academic or bureaucratic analyses: it identifies the likely consequences of the Soviet imperial system being dislocated by the successful application of effective political or also military pressures from the outside.

The conceptual altitude of the discussion of war and empire in chapter 7 is accorded, in 'A West with Russia' (chapter 8), to the basic phenomena of a statecraft devoted to stopping short of – or averting – both: balance of power and diplomatic pre-eminence, in their interrelationship. While elucidating this issue, the emphasis on the US–Soviet conflict shifts to the troubled partnership between the United States and its European allies, prefiguring the more fundamental relationship of a problematically Europeanist America to a Europe of which Russia is incontestably a part. While US foreign policy is stalemated by the seeming impossibility to meet the requirements of either empire or equilibrium as the organizing principles of policies, the dynamic of European history has unfolded creatively through the tension between the two complementary sides of equilibrium politics. The situation points to either an eventual parting of the ways among the Atlantic allies or the balance–pre-eminence duality being imaginatively applied to both the European and the global theaters within the enlarged scale of things. In the last analysis, if the choice lies largely with the United States and the direction of its policies toward Soviet Russia, the policies themselves must somehow address the question of questions, to which they will largely supply the answer: is even a sovietized Russia part of the West in its broadest scope defined by fundamental affinites as well as differences from the traditional East, or is it not? And, if not, what will be the distribution of costs and benefits on the globally extending West–East spectrum of a mutually erosive conflict prevailing over the so far realized degree of US–Soviet convergence?

Matching the introductory chapter on method, finally, the concluding one (chapter 10) tackles the more difficult task of identifying the different kinds of thinking that underlie US foreign policy and that might conduce to rethinking it beneficially. The competing thought patterns are approached from three complementary angles: one, the institutional constraints and inducements that keep elective politicians and professional foreign-policy experts from articulating radical policy alternatives; two, the speculatively dialectical thinking mode as a neglected corrective to the prevailing one that helps perpetuate the frozen policies; and three, the collective American mind yet to take definite shape on the Soviet issue so as to contain the excessive influence of extraneously motivated particular viewpoints. Insofar as the favored procedure for rethinking US–Soviet relations can profitably draw upon the facets of the method outlined in the initial chapter, the two methodological discussions complement one another and, shaping the substantive content of the policies as rethought, are instrumental in unifying intellectual procedure with both political process and policy product.

Introduction

Theory, History, and Social Philosophy

No school of thought or theory concerned with international relations is closer to history, and more fully committed to the utility of historical antecedents for policy analysis and prognosis, than is political realism.

Yet stating the closeness merely opens up a wide range of questions. What aspect of realistically conceived international politics is most intimately wedded to the historical dimension: its dynamic or mechanistic side, or its evolutionary or organic side? What kind of historiography is most congenial: one stressing the complex individuality of phenomena that makes them unique or one uncovering continuities through cyclical or other recurrence that makes them meaningful? What slice of historical reality is most useful: a short or a long one; one narrowly political or a wider one? And, finally, what is the legitimate role, if any, of historical analogy?

Realists will easily agree on the character of the central dynamic of conflictual politics related to power and interests; they will find it more difficult to agree on how historically evidenced trends modify this dynamic or its implications for policy. The longer the envisaged time span, the more will the structural dimension be matched in importance by the synchronic dimension: that is to say, the more will the question as to how configurations of power and interests constrain policy choices be equaled in importance by the question how to employ the residual freedom of choice in order to orchestrate relatively shorter- and longer-term outcomes on concurrent stakes and threats into a best possible (provisionally) final outcome.

The temporal dimension ranks with the domestic-political dimension as a (desirable or actual?) co-determinant of policy alongside immediately perceptible and compelling external inducements and constraints deriving from the environing structure of power and configuration of interests. The internal factors tend to weigh upon (and, from a narrowly realist viewpoint, to derange) the thrust of the external configurations in the short run and on issues with a relatively low crisis component most of the time; ignoring the temporal factor will place at risk long-term outcomes and deflect them from the optimum on issues with a high crisis potential. Factoring in the domestic variables is more congenial to the liberal outlook, while the evolutionary ones are more germane to the conservative viewpoint so long as they are not confused with linear progress. Insofar as this is so, the issue is also one of the role the two discrete value systems or social philosophies play not only in the realist's view of power (his emphasis on its controlled or its more fundamentally creative or coercive use),[1] but also in his related choices in regard to high policy and grand strategy.

Interacting Forces and Evolving Powers

It has been a commonplace objection to realism that it likens states and relations among them to intershocking billiard balls; that, by ignoring the internal constitutions of actors and time-related change, it reduces interstate relations to an endlessly and unchangingly repetitive game of skill and chance. The point is well taken if it is not forgotten or ignored that such an interplay *does* constitute the central dynamics of interstate politics at any one time; that it *is* the essential hard core of such politics whenever it operates at a level of more-than-moderate crisis or tension. Only with this reservation is it theoretically legitimate to go beyond the inner-core mechanics of interstate relations; only then is it also practically useful to modify the rationally controlled and constantly motivated play of force and counterforce, pressure and counterpressure, for individual advantage by introducing concern for and with the organic factors of evolutionary change within and among states.

   In the short run, such organic factors are barely perceptible, and are wholly distinct from only marginally or provisionally influential variations in internal impulses and in adventitious external inducements or constraints. In the long run, however, the changing power distribution among rising and declining social groups or classes (rather than anything like a fleeting public opinion), and among ascending and decaying political communities, are ultimately determining for the postures of states and state systems alike. Yet just as only the most rudimentary realism can ignore the organic-evolutionary dimension with its both operational and normative implications, so concentrating on this dimension alone would risk losing contact with political realities as they are in favor of ideal states or imaginary utopias as they ought to be; vulgar pragmatism or actualism is then replaced with quixotic potentialism.

The line is thin between a correct simplification of the interstate dynamics being vital and being insufficient. It is crucial when keyed to, as well as in principle assuring, immediate survival in crisis situations; its application to policy is deficient when wholly pragmatic or opportunist and totally ahistorical. But, thin as is such a line, the intellectual space within which the various attempts at reconciling or fusing the mechanical with the organic aspects of total political reality can occur will be unavoidably wide. Attempting to do this is to be analytically stretched between the short run and the variably long run, between the simplicity of an elegant model and the complexities of the elusive change- and time-conscious mode. Spanning the two universes theoretically would still require conveying the synthesis by words which cannot but follow one another. The only recourse is to identify successively the elements in the compound of interactions and evolution. Even then it will be difficult for the maker of policy to integrate the insights and directives emanating from the long-term perspective into his short-term program of action in a way that is either self-conscious or rigorous; difficult, that is, to qualify the compelling simplicities of the billiard-balls model (or, put differently, of interstate mechanics as an aspect of political physics) by the nearly unlimited, largely hypothetical contingencies that can be subsumed under the organic dimension. Yet without the antecedent intellectual effort, the policy-maker's practical task is wholly impossible except where an inborn right instinct, a second sight, shows the way to statemanship.

The academic student who does not recognize that practical statecraft will always be about four-fifths a matter of instant reactions to immediate pressures and opportunities misses the analytical point and is useless to society. By the same token, however, a policy maker will be practically ineffective and be a danger to society if he is temperamentally or intellectually incapable of bringing to bear upon his routine stewardship a sensitivity to the remaining one-fifth of reality, or concern about reality, that transcends the workmanlike mechanics of daily business one way or another. Be he scholar or statesman, pedant or prince, the philosophical realist need not be for all that a full-fledged practitioner of the philosophy of history when he sets out to explore the historico-evolutionary aspect of a problem; nor, on the same principle, need he be a cultural anthropologist or country or regional specialist when exploring and attempting to assess the effect of cultural modifiers in the interaction- and evolution-related constants.

Such explorations will be nonetheless appropriate for the philosophical realist since, the more his doctrine directs him to abstract a simple model from the continuities underlying historical change, the more will he depend for verisimilitude on enriching that model by sensitivity to specific contingencies and variations. But again, just as the essential realist theory limits itself to supplying no more than a penetrating central insight into the dynamics, so the realist sensitive to history and cultural differences need not strive for a rigorous or coherent theoretical framework into which to fit the evolutionary and idiosyncratic variations. The only requirement is that he phrase the effort in terms that can be argued about with reference to identifiable assumptions and definable historical perspectives or antecedents; it is not necessary that the effort issue in a parsimonious theory or be sustained by elaborate methodology any more than by a sophisticated metaphysics.

Continuity beneath Diversity

An approach to international politics and foreign policy drawing on history must be sensitive to that which is uniquely constituted, but also point beyond it to that which is comparable and implies continuity; reach beyond that which is specific to what can be systematized. Its practitioner will have to take more than a hint or two out of Machiavelli if he is to assist those who walk in the footsteps of Guicciardini. A specific time or culture frame will, together with changing technologies and theologies, be among the givens that condition particular actions. But the distribution of space will be sufficiently persistent, and the configurations of power recurrent, to reduce the impact of such variables on what can or must be done.

In the search for patterns relating protagonists to processes, the evolution of salient state systems and of major powers – their rise, maturity, and decline – competes for attention with the course and contents of civilizations that encompass the smaller and can fragment the larger entities. One does not replace the other, however. There is a link between the three: states, state systems, civilizations. All are characterized by a growing capacity (and necessity) to act rationally and to innovate creatively, before the process of growth slows down and is reversed into its opposite. The rationality is empirical in foundation and mundane in function, inasmuch as it aims at relating the most efficacious means to intrinsically feasible goals. It has little, and need have nothing, in common with the postulate of a transcendental Reason that unfolds within and through a particular state, system, or civilization. However, just as the exalted claims of systematizing metahistory can be sidestepped, so must the opposing limitations of strict historicism be relaxed when it narrows down the perspective to unique individuality.

Uniqueness cannot be treated as absolute for purposes of policy so long as means–ends rationality necessary for the minimum goal of survival is deployed within a field of multiple forces. The environing structures of power and interests are sufficiently determinate to be constraining, and sufficiently constraining to compel adaptation. They are also sufficiently comprehensive to partially submerge any one individuality (or correlation between isolated factors) in the dynamic of the larger setting.

The need to behave rationally – or functionally – within a determinate setting makes for a variable but definite measure of compelling necessity in interstate relations. This fact alone reinforces the tendency for patterns to recur, restricting the freedom of action and the room for innovation through initiative or imitation. A varying residue of leeway for revising interstate norms and practices remains, to be sure; nor does necessity rule out uniformities being modified by the agency of values peculiar to a civilization. Being aware of this uneven mix reconciles the caveats of historicism with the tenets of systematizing (meta-) history.[2] It saves history-conscious inquiry into politics among states from two pitfalls: one, merely recording drearily repetitious interactions among culturally or otherwise neutral and unevolving units of power; another, thinking or acting as if anyone's goodwill, skill, or resolution alone could transform the world at any one point in the cycles of crisis and conflict.

Making history, viewed as a record of recurrences, act as a counselor to the statesman for purposes of high policy and grand strategy will carry with it the use of historical analogy. Contested by methodological purists, the use of historical analogy is commonplace in the state papers of the greatest practitioners of diplomacy. One reason is that the circumstances in which statecraft operates are sufficiently opaque, the nature of specific initiatives and responses unpredictable, and available information inadequate, to make reference to already completed actions and reactions, and their consequences, indispensable. The valuable aid to analysis is, moreover, a reassuring psychic support for what is at best a problematic speculation or action with portentous social implications. Because of the great possible benefit, it is necessary to accept the risk of a wrong analogy or even of a misleading use of analogy in the wrong hands.

Closely related to the reassurance analogies give to the formulator of strategy is their capacity to enhance his authority, difficult to establish by other means. Propounding a strategy is intended not only to illuminate a problem but also to persuade a public; not only to devise an approach but also to encourage its adoption. It is important that the effort inspire confidence, not only by the quality of the proponent's insight, but also on the strength of a quality easier to assess — his professional expertise. Since the validity of strategic thought is difficult to judge and nearly impossible to agree upon widely in a highly competitive market of ideas, there is no surer evidence of expertise, even in intensely technology-conscious times, than a demonstrated mastery of pertinent history. Indeed, its authority increases above that of technical know-how as the stakes rise to concern 'high' policy or 'grand' strategy. The kind of preferred history will vary: panoramic history will attract the speculative, the episodic variety the active, strategist. Yet statecraft and history are in either case as closely linked as is social science and, say, the participant observation of small-group behavior.

The all-important requisite is that historical analogy be not formal (dwelling on outward forms or appearances) but functional (focusing on adaptive reactions to comparable structures). In the formal analogy, actors or events are compared or equated outside explicit patterns of action and analysis identifying that which is comparable and equivalent. Yet, absent a disciplining framework, it is impossible to segregate the essential from the accidental and the significant from the trivial, making both similarities and differences in either protracted processes or dramatic events irrelevant. Thus little is gained by citing the Balkan antecedents to World War I in connection with this or that contemporary regional turmoil as the 'cause', or this or that isolated event as the precipitant of, a possible World War III.

A way to illustrate the difference between formal and functional analogy is to consider the position of France before World War I (functionally equivalent with Western Europe's today). It was highly significant in the realm of pre-World War I events, but of secondary importance in the scheme of analogical interpretation that highlights the critical interplay of key powers on a geopolitically defined persistent continuum. Whereas France had been a key actor in its own right in an earlier triangle, before being superseded by Germany as the 'central' continental state with naval-overseas ambitions facing one way toward the pre-eminent insular–maritime state (England) and another way toward the rival rear-continental power (Habsburg), by 1914 France was functionally significant mainly as Britain's extension into the continental balance of power, to be kept in stalemating equilibrium as a means of distracting the resources and ambitions of Wilhelmine Germany from its global bid. Nor is Austria-Hungary (and its Balkan involvements in rivalry with Russia) of interest, except as one of the precipitants that brought the Anglo-German conflict to a head. Russia looms large not as a regional actor in the Balkans but as a growing threat to Germany's world policy from the eastern-continental rear, setting a time limit on *Weltpolitik's* chances to bear fruit.

Seeing events before 1914 – and comparable contemporary (US–Soviet–China) interactions – through the prism of an interpretation reaching still farther back (to the initiation of the triangular land–sea power pattern in the sixteenth century) permits discounting the difference between a multipolar structure then and a bipolar one now. However, if it also permits downgrading the importance of actors and events hightly salient in a factually historical perspective, projecting tendencies from past occurrences does not spell the capacity to forecast future events in their particulars and, least of all, timing. It will merely point to possible-to-probable outcomes if policies similar to the earlier ones are applied in the context of comparable configurations of powers, the powers' geopolitical and other situations, and, therefore, fundamental interests and typical roles.

Such hypothetical predictions based on projection can serve best as a basis for a corrective strategy that withstands the tyranny of reflexive responses to a transient configuration of power and inferred interests, without contravening the primacy of a system's structure in conditioning state policies. If projecting from the Anglo–French–Austrian and Anglo–German–Russian triangles points to a major conflict escalating from its first (e.g., Bourbon and Wilhelmine) to the second (e.g., Bonapartist and Hitlerite) phase, a policy to counteract this trend in the interest of appeasement would have to differ from the British policies instrumental in promoting the trend and facilitating the outcome.

A mere mention of 'appeasement' automatically summons the image of Nazi (or Hitlerite) Germany, overshadowing the period before 1914. However, fitting a corrective policy prescription into a longer historical perpective will require seeing the 1930s as not at all comparable with the 1980s and beyond. The two periods differ in all of the critical respects ranging from basic power structures (or polarities), functional (economic and military) characteristics, and the distribution of threats, to the prevailing equilibrium system's elasticity in reacting to disturbances to be absorbed through the agency of readily activable centers of power and policy. Specifically, the Britain of the 1900s is no more the Britain of the 1930s than either one matches the United States of more recently; Soviet Russia differs significantly from Nazi Germany as principals in the escalating bid of the late-ascending middle power to be accorded parity and partnership with the dominant maritime-insular wing power. Reinforcing the differences which make a different outcome possible are those between pre-1914 and the present, including the contrast between tsarist Russia and contemporary China as pressing or only potential, immediate or only remote, threats to the 'encircled' power in the middle. The assumption underlying the Munich analogy has meanwhile been that what is more recent is or must be more relevant. The contrary belief is that several periods preceding World War I are more significantly comparable with the present and that the prelude to World War II will become increasingly pertinent if the 'lessons' from the earlier antecedents are not heeded or are misapplied.

Conservatism and Realism

Just as historical perspectives of uneven lengths affect ostensibly realistic policies, so do different possible widths of the interpretive grasp. Analysis can stay within the boundaries of intra- and interstate factors or move beyond them to the murkier area of political cultures or civilizations; prescription be vigilantly observant of narrowly defined competing interests or concerned also with the more grandly defined roles of (great) nations in the drama of their rise and decline. Thus, bona fide political realists could differ deeply over the war in Vietnam in the context of the empire issue, just as they will increasingly differ on the issues raised by the conflict with Russia in the context of equilibrium. The same is true when the determining outlook is shaped by social and political philosophy, reflecting a different conception of the relevant 'ism'.

Conservatism on domestic issues has by and large traveled more comfortably in tandem with realistic foreign politics than has liberalism. However, the attrition of the societal bases for philosophical conservatism, which has fostered selectively right-wing ideologies in the modern West and lately in the United States, may well have deranged the natural complementarity. In principle, the connection is strengthened by the conservative's sharing the realist's greater affinity for history and greater belief in the contemporary relevance of history than has been (since the rationalist Enlightenment?) the liberal's. Yet the affinity applies only to genuinely traditionalist conservatism, distinguished by its stress on the gradual unfolding and prudent managing of trends and forces which, validated by the test of time, became entitled to uphold their claim before the court of historic (as distinct from social) justice. Such conservatism will lift realist doctrine and strategy above the preprogrammed application of elementary textbook maxims of *Realpolitik*. It will encompass the routine devices of mechanical counterpoising of force by counterforce and the routine exploitation of momentarily advantageous ranges of options for tactical advantage. But it will not treat the technique as an unconditional strategic panacea and the tactic as the sum total of nonsentimental geopolitical statecraft. Instead, it will take into account the possibly adverse long-term consequences of short- and medium-term expedients for the stability of the international system and the survival of a civilization in the face of internal and external threats less easy to subsume under the categories of *Realpolitik* than is the conspicuous military power and political ambiton of the chief rival of the moment.

At the present juncture, integral anti-Sovietism does not

automatically confer the credentials of authentic conservatism in foreign affairs any more than it has an indissoluble connection with the reaffirmation of the values of family and faith internally. Nor will the marriage of a certain kind of realism and a particular brand of conservatism be blessed in its policy progeny if its foundations are flawed in two respects: one, if it rests on equating what is right with only one, procedural kind of freedom, be it that of the market in economics or of the individual in the political arena, to the detriment of other rights, including that of a national collective to realize itself in the present so as to leave an imprint on history; and two, if it advances the essentially liberal claim to providentially (as distinct from histori-cally and thus contingently) conferred entitlement in order to rebuke and restrain all competing adjustments of the freedom-related desiderata to power-related necessities. The vitiating presumption of superior virtue rests on a view of self as peculiarly free of the measure of guilt necessarily inherent in the element of tragedy that pervades interstate relations; on perceiving oneself as peculiarly adept at transposing utopia from an imagined national past into a future for all mankind. Both the presumption and the policies originating in it are profoundly ahistorical – and thus, even though they might be authent-ically liberal, at best pseudoconservative.

The argument points to a proposition and suggests a paradox. What kind of conservatism as a sociopolitical philosophy underpins realism (or *Realpolitik*) as international-relations theory (and actual practice) is all the more important because the erosion of the domestic bases of 'genuine' conservatism in industrial societies has made the hier-archically structured, role- and status-centered, gradually and spon-taneously evolving, international system into the arena of action best suited for the traditionalist conservative's values and outlook. As for realism itself, it is of all alternative approaches to international relations the closest to history, and profits most from the appreciation of history. Yet, paradoxically, the very intensity of the link generates divisions about how to use history, which account as much as anything else for discrediting allegedly realistic assessments and prescriptions for policy.

A randomly illustrative use of history risks conferring fallacious analytic depth on inquiry into the central dynamic of interstate relations; a philosophically thin conservatism risks distorting a polity's flagging involvement in the dynamic, even as it imparts a burst of ideological elan to the engagement. Richer drafts on history and history-conscious social philosophy entail other drawbacks. They will diffuse the stark simplicity of the interstate dynamic and decrease the analytical incisiveness and rigor of realism's central concepts. However, they will also enhance the saving claim of realism to social utility – the claim to cut through various obfuscations to the essential truth about a crucial predicament in international politics, making possible a policy that is shown wise in retrospect instead of merely impressing one audience as clever and another as caring in the present.

Notes

1   On this point among others germane to the subject of this chapter see my 'Morgenthau vs. Machiavelli: political realism and power politics', in Kenneth W. Thompson and Robert J. Myers (eds), *Truth and Tragedy: A Tribute to Hans Morgenthau* (Washington: *New Republic*, 1977 and 1984). I also noted Morgenthau's place in the study of international relations in 'The heroic decade and after: international relations as events, discipline, and profession', *SAIS Review*, Summer 1966.
2   On this distinction see Hans Meyerhoff (ed.), *The Philosophy of History in Our Time* (Garden City, NY: Doubleday, 1955) and R. G. Collingwood, *The Idea of History* (London: Oxford University Press, 1946).

PART I

Structures and Strategies

1

From Containment to Concert

Ponderously scaling the diplomatic heights at superpower summits, only to climb down again for the next spell of petty controversy, will simply lengthen the string of lost opportunities in US–Soviet relations. The makers of policy on both sides will eventually have to look beyond their immediate agenda to larger perspectives in space and time if they are to avoid mutual frustration or worse.

As increasingly also on the Russian, authoritative voices on the American side have called more than once for new ways of thinking about US–Soviet relations.[1] Yet genuinely novel thinking cannot emerge and the Russians will not settle peaceably into superpower status, until and unless influential Americans do more than discard the kinds of ideologically dogmatic views that have matched the Soviet counterparts in heightening tensions between the superpowers. Political and opinion leaders will have to transcend the ideas of today's so-called pragmatists – ideas that are little more than pallid versions of the dogmatic extreme. They accept in all essentials the assessment of the 'sources of Soviet conduct' that has held sway since George Kennan's landmark interpretation, under that title, appeared in *Foreign Affairs* just 40 years ago. Thinking differently means formulating intellectual foundations for American conduct that will do more than simply adjust containment to the fluctuations in American capabilities or will, and more than casually, reintroduce some elements of cooperation into the competition while retaining the flawed ideas that made the late attempt at detente so vulnerable to so many different indictments.

Varieties of Assumptions

As the term suggests, detente is not a strategy with a particular content, but only the possible consequence of a strategy designed to remove the causes of conflict. Even in the most favorable circumstances, partial measures will not begin to ease the conflict when they are not consciously related to the terminal goal of some type of far-reaching concert. The inability of Americans themselves to agree on either a definition or the prerequisites of detente suggests the inadequacy of partial measures. The suspicion is confirmed by the insufficiency of the limited steps toward Anglo-German accommodation before August 1914. In this perspective, attempts to place blame for the cold war or for detente's collapse help neither in judging the past nor in shaping the future.

The attempt to achieve far-reaching concert requires the development of positive assumptions about both the rival and the relationship that, if valid, would be capable of maturing into genuine concord. But if positive assumptions are to challenge effectively the negative premises that have always prevailed, they must be equally far-reaching and dramatic, no matter how skeptically they are greeted. They must do more than subject the extremist versions of the negative assumptions to a 'reasonable' discount by 'moderate' critics of either side. Only then can such assumptions begin to shift the public mood away from the picture of unprovoked and undeserved hostility that satisfies the mind because it simplifies matters.

Although not even the soundest redesign of assumptions will achieve rapid progress, there are strong reasons for starting sooner rather than later. It would not overestimate reformist tendencies inside the Soviet Union to observe that the emerging generation of Soviet leaders is asking how much and what kind of domestic change it needs to make and can safely make. Consequently, the new Soviet leaders will soon need to know how much elbowroom they can expect the United States to give them in what kind of international environment. Although rethinking must proceed on both sides, it is for the senior power and the more self-assured culture to point the way out of the deadlock of outwardly clashing but intrinsically similar – that is, equally messianic – world views and self-perceptions.

The best chance for successfully reconstructing US–Soviet relations lies in rerouting foreign-policy thinking in directions that are genuinely conservative. It will be impossible to heal creatively old wounds and chronic ills and to preserve truly vital values if a purportedly meliorist policy injects an objectively reactionary motif continuously into the rhetoric and conduct of foreign relations. Reconstruction means jettisoning attitudes and positions associated with pristine Reaganism, as well as precluding the re-emergence of Stalinist analogues.

Foremost among the American assumptions currently blocking progress is that the United States is in all respects different from Soviet Russia. This conviction has been fed since 1917 by analyses that stress an aspect of Soviet society and foreign policy that, superficially at least, is novel – an ideology of world revolution. It finds expression in the condemnation of anything approaching the suggestion of 'moral equivalence' between Moscow and Washington. Upon closer examination, this effort turns out to be ahistorical. In particular, it neglects ethically neutral geopolitical factors that over centuries have repeatedly led generically similar states into the same kinds of conflicts and alliances. In addition, for centuries before Karl Marx's birth these factors underlay and shaped chronic differences in domestic societies that ideologues with a short and selective memory view today exclusively as products of pro- or anti-communist leanings.

The geopolitical perspective provides a working premise far more useful for the purpose of exploring the two grounds on which the two rivals are essentially identical. One is schematic, in that both are imperial core powers that, having comparably expanded from a territorial nucleus, construe their security in terms of superiority within three concentric fields: an inner circle of contiguous client states, an outer circle of contingent actual or courted potential allies, and an outermost circle of volatile peripheral actors that need to be stabilized or subverted, depending on their dispositions. The other ground is dynamic. So long as it faces a comparable power, neither side can avoid erecting or seeking to erect in-depth defenses. But the forward bases of such defenses almost inevitably fall within either the outer or the inner security belt of the competitor. This essential identity commonly will be obscured by an existential difference that has repeatedly flowed – and still flows today – from fundamentally different geographic situations.

Historically, the greatest situational disparities, and those most likely to spark conflict, have been those between offshore insular powers and continental powers. The former are typically maritime-mercantile societies and cultures and the latter tend to be militaristic and either agricultural or newly industrializing. Relative economic backwardness and inherently vulnerable land borders require the continental state to rely heavily on coercion for economic solvency and military security, and consequently, both to act and to appear threatening to neighbors. Yet what this state must struggle for at home and abroad with might and main is conferred almost automatically on its insular rival through a combination of benevolent nature and favorable accident.

This good fortune has hardly been a recipe for peaceful behavior, however. One need not accept uncritically V. I. Lenin's theory of capitalistic imperialism to note that in the rivalries between Athens and Sparta and between the Anglo-Dutch so-called Maritime Powers and Spain, the first powers in each pair were the more aggressively expansionist and, in moments of truth, just as coercive as their continental adversaries. Only when the more plural sociopolitical orders have possessed themselves of a commanding margin of advantage do they resort abroad to markedly liberal policies or doctrines. The liberal policies are sufficient during periods of dominance to secure major goals. During periods of decline, the corresponding 'internationalist' doctrines are even more than corresponding policies the only remaining means of preserving the benefits of previously conquered positions and assets.

Patterns of Rivalry

The inner and outer security–superiority zones of Russia and the United States intersect most prominently in Eastern Europe, Southwest Asia, and Central America, and less intensely in Western Europe and East Asia. The outermost zones of both powers overlap haphazardly in the peripheral regions of the Third World. Just as the different techniques used by Moscow and Washington to accomplish their aims in these regions are not procedurally indistinguishable, neither are they qualitatively different. They are about equally rooted in those characteristics of the two rivals that are identical and those that differ. Therefore, it will only pointlessly aggravate the competition to attribute its causes to only one party.

But there is another geopolitical factor at work here, separate from the continental–insular dichotomy but just as surely underlying today's superpower rivalry. Its primary feature is the graduated shift in values and institutions that one encounters as one moves from the

English-speaking Atlantic isles, through the French and German zones, to the Russian sector. Traveling west to east, one passes methodically from outposts of liberty to strongholds of authority, from individualism to corporate collectivism, from societal pluralism to statist power, from free to directed economy, and from politics and economics to military power as favored forms of external self-assertion. And these differences were apparent long before the Bolshevik revolution. East of Germany's Elbe River, in particular, pressures and intrusions from still farther east retarded evolution and constricted opportunities for the more directly exposed societies.

These differences become acutely relevant to contemporary policies in the nuclear age, the first era in which the chronic efforts of nation-states to impose abroad different versions of only social or also historic justice can threaten human survival. Indeed, the waning moments of the West's Europe-generated ascendancy have been filled with always frantic and often misdirected attempts to right all kinds of real and imaginary past wrongs around the world. Ironically, however, the West has overlooked Europe's east in its search for history's victims. Given the possibility that these societies have unwittingly stood guard over and served as a feeding ground for their neighbors' prosperity and foreign ambitions, relaxing the definition of what constitutes offensive conduct stands out as a richly deserved reparation that is essential if reconciliation is to replace rivalry.

The liberation of both the Russian and the other East European peoples from the weight of the Soviet state and empire will no doubt strike Westerners as a reciprocal accommodation that any type of concert should include. Yet this may be asking for too much and offering too little in return. It was precisely the early decline in East-Central and Eastern Europe of great-power ensembles in the same league with emergent West European powers that opened a gap between the two regions. By the same token, it is difficult, in the context of a superpower concert, to imagine a closing of this gap unless Eastern Europe is headed by an authentically indigenous great power. And it is unlikely that any Russia-centered great-power complex (and there is no conceivable substitute) could perform the task without also embracing external policies nearly identical with Moscow's today. As long as Westerners fail to accept the fact that only gradual, Moscow-sanctioned change is possible in Eastern Europe, deepening East–West divisions will continue aggravating and obscuring the underlying maritime-continental schisms and resulting conflict.

The specific configuration of the Euro-Asian spectrum of types and sizes of territorial powers, extending from the Atlantic world through Eurasia to its insular appendages in the east, has given particular shape to a recurrent pattern of rivalry of which the US–Soviet conflict is but the latest manifestation. Each pitted insular against continental powers and each outcome contained the seeds of new conflict. Once England replaced amphibious Spain (and the briefly dominant Dutch) as Europe's strongest naval power in the seventeenth century, it found itself locked in struggles with a succession of continental challengers, each of which was located farther east than its predecessor. Thus France was followed by Germany and Germany by Russia, by which time the United States had displaced Great Britain as the dominant insular state. Also shifting eastward was the location of the third, rear-continental state that played a critical role – namely, pressing against the continental power that had developed amphibious ambitions – in each conflict. Initially, one of the principal Germanic powers (mainly Habsburg Austria) pressed against France, then tsarist Russia beset Prussia-Germany, and today, the People's Republic of China is straining against Soviet Russia.

A three-time occurrence of the same fundamental conflict is enough to confirm a regular pattern. And regularity implies that something about the common denominator is largely responsible for the problem. The recurrence of conflicts involving offshore insular, would-be amphibious continental, and rear-continental states makes even more sense in light of geopolitical logic.

At the core of this problem has always been the difficulty – if not the impossibility – of keeping inviolate the security–superiority zones of the two chief rivals. Each rival found itself strongly attracted by its adversary's sphere of influence for a variety of reasons: those that concern intangibles such as status and prestige and those that flow from material and strategic considerations; those that are defensively preclusive in nature and those that are brazenly predatory. These strong temptations turned into irresistible and continual conflict when the impossibility of keeping each sphere off-limits to the rival was combined with the fact that neither party could defeat the other single-handedly. The insular sea power acting alone was never able to neutralize the premier continental states by military action on land. It needed to encroach upon their continental security–superiority zone through alliances. Similarly, the continental states never managed to neutralize the insular state's reluctance to share access to the oceans on 'fair' or 'equal' terms by assaulting it successfully in its island fastness or life-giving overseas dependency. They had to reinforce themselves by expanding their land base through conquest or coerced cooperation – actions that inevitably helped the sea power gain allies on the mainland. The enlarged continental domain – from France's in the Rhineland or Northern Italy through Germany's in Middle Europe to Russia's in Eastern Europe and Southwest Asia – could serve as a springboard for or, when necessary, as an alternative to expansion overseas.

The effect of this expansion on the sea power was as provocative as was the effect on the continentally pre-eminent state of the insular power's determination to buttress nature's gift of physical immunity by contriving political alliances with smaller land powers. Not content with the clear diplomatic advantage and overwhelming maritime–mercantile superiority made possible by technological prowess and free-wheeling enterprise, insular or quasi-insular powers (beginning with the Dutch) invariably have tried to cage in their continental counterparts in Europe, touting the stalemate they have hoped to achieve on the mainland as a 'just equilibrium'.

The basic pattern has held in the case of societies as different and differently fragmented as France under the *ancien régime*, Germany during the reign of Emperor William II, and Russia then and since. And it has held during different evolutionary stages toward greater centralization within societies and more forceful self-assertion abroad – think of Germany under William II and Adolf Hitler, France under King Louis XIV and Napoleon I, and, a less clearly defined because so far unconsummated sequence, of Russia under the Tsars and the Soviets. The same failure of particular differences to nullify similarity in basic foreign policies has held for Great Britain and the United States. It becomes as unpersuasive in such a perspective to blame Soviet totalitarianism for aggressive expansionism as it is to relieve space and time, geography and history, of blame for its existence.

The Operative Stakes of Conflict

The repetitions reduce automatically the significance not only of the particular character of domestic political systems but also of the specific stakes of conflict. The depiction of Soviet expansionism as adventurism extrapolating its totalitarian essence implies conversely that the liberal–pluralistic American system is inherently self-restrained and pacific abroad. Americans therefore find it easy to overlook the extent to which the demonic view of the adversary may also be the reassuring result of the projection of their own unacknowledgeable drives and flaws onto the rival. Skirting the ethically neutral geopolitical factors, the dogmatic view obscures a potentially significant perception: after the initial conflict over who would fill more of the Central European power vacuum after Germany's defeat in 1945, the US–Soviet conflict has been progressively depleted of significant particular stakes. As it underwent the usual displacement from a stalemate at the strategic center to maneuvering along the lower-pressure periphery, the rivalry was fed primarily by its own momentum and, at bottom, by the timeless asymmetry between land and sea powers. The latter in particular has made it difficult for Moscow and Washington to identify the terms of mutually acceptable equilibrium.

A steady diminution in the specificity of the stakes of international conflict is nothing new. Compared with the concrete and precisely divisible material stakes of the Anglo-French conflict over commerce, over vast and wealthy possessions in the New World, and over command of the sea in the era of mercantilism and the sailing ship, the stakes of the subsequent Anglo-German competition – primarily a struggle for prestige – were already devalued, despite the new importance of overseas support-and-supply facilities for coal- and steam-powered navies. They reflected the political psychology of 'world power' as much as the realities of national and world economies. The attribution of the contemporary conflict to rivalry between socioeconomic orders and ideologies proves that ever more intangible factors are called upon to rationalize the competition's innate momentum.

The more specific and tangible stakes perceived today – geostrategic in places like Angola, with its alleged bearing on South Atlantic sea-lanes, or even relating to strategic minerals in places like the Persian Gulf, with its oil – do not in and of themselves propel the competition. It is rather the competition that gives these remote places and resources the appearance of vital importance in the context of planning eventual military engagements. It becomes immaterial that a military clash is improbable and, if it does break out, is highly likely to bypass the areas and to downgrade the assets concern over which helped spark conflict in the first place.

The vicious circle of genuine structural causes and operationally contrived stakes of conflict can begin to be relaxed only by acting on two considerations. First, although it is true that all geostrategic positions will assume exaggerated importance in a bipolar world, the conflict is further intensified by pitting an insular possessor of privileged security against a continental rival jealously seeking equality. Were the United States surrounded, as is the Soviet Union, by potentially threatening, if individually weaker, powers, the international situation still would be structurally bipolar. But the more similar respective positions of the two superpowers would encourage each prudently to limit interference in the other's orbit.

Second, two major powers that constitute a bipolar setting are likely to be large and about equally resource-rich. This makes it less than necessary for them to target policies on strategic materials outside their frontiers. Moreover, the fact that they are only two would make it prohibitively costly for either of them to try curtailing the rival's access with a view to outmatching it decisively. The situation differs when a global system is genuinely multipolar. Then, the individual powers – which would by definition possess less natural wealth – would have greater need for strategic materials from outside their boundaries. Just as important, each could reasonably seek to enlarge its access without fear of accumulating so much usable resource that any other state – or other states taken together – would feel forced to respond militarily. Thus the fact that bipolarity involves two states cannot by itself explain the tendency to exaggerate the inherently limited value of individual geostrategic stakes. But it does explain why it is too dangerous for either polar rival to try to deny the other truly vital material resources – an insight that undercuts one of the narrowly geopolitical rationales for US–Soviet competition.

The unavoidably provocative effect of insular America's geographically derived security suggests that the United States also bears significant responsibility for particulars that intensify the US–Soviet rivalry. Similarly, the actual or suspected advantage accruing to imperial, nautically supreme Britain fueled global competition over increasingly valueless colonies in the late nineteenth century. The issue of natural wealth imparts an ironic twist to the contemporary competition when American neoconservatives place a quasi-Leninist emphasis on the significance of strategic raw materials whenever the rivalry's basic structural foundation seems insufficient to maintain the competition at white-hot intensity. The irony, if not dealt with in time, could turn a latent into an enacted tragedy in one setting, should the relatively resource-richer Soviet Union come to depend on resources controlled by Washington while being denied access to them, either by American fiat or by shortage of hard currency. A similar danger might develop if present strategic nuclear forces and related postures were wholly superseded by ones requiring the dispersal of weapons over vast oceans and territories. Either of the two changes would necessitate stepping up the currently moderate rate of Russian peripheral expansion, designed primarily to achieve only symbolic goals or to score tactical points, not to acquire resources or territories essential to survival.

The Organic and Nuclear Factors

Many will no doubt object that nuclear weaponry has revolutionized international politics and that therefore little of the foregoing analysis is especially useful. Specifically the nuclear revolution is thought to have made thinking along traditional lines irrelevant because it makes major war unthinkable. Yet in the face of contrary trends, beginning with the conspicuous feasibility of minor wars likewise deemed inconceivable in the aftermath of Hiroshima, it seems clear that nuclear-wrought changes have been evolutionary, not revolutionary. The challenge faced by policy makers is to identify the extent to which these changes have modified – not negated – the bearing of historical patterns. What nuclear weapons basically have done is to remove some of the basis for intense US–Soviet conflict while monopolizing too many of its surface manifestations. The nature of these changes constitutes the prime reason for approaching the conflict conservatively and nursing potentially positive trends rather than seeking surgical shortcuts to heal secular distempers.

The most important nuclear-induced change involves the sharply enhanced decisiveness of organic as opposed to operational factors in shaping the international disputes that are managed as if the two factors were still comparable in importance. Even before the nuclear age, the relative growth and decline in a state's material capabilities and moral energies over time – the organic factor – was the key long-term impulse behind and determinant of major-power rivalries. Yet the operational plane – the force-supported diplomatic maneuvers and transactions – had a more direct impact on the immediate outcomes of conflict and, through them, the organic factor than can be and is the case today.

Great powers cannot resort to a major war as easily or readily as before, any more than they will effect sudden and substantial changes in alliances, for the purpose of readjusting policy pretensions to actual capabilities. Nonetheless, foreign policies continue to be transacted *as if* they could achieve significant results along the traditional lines, using various instruments and forms of leverage to promote what can be only glacially slow changes in relative capabilities and related alignments. The seemingly frivolous reason for this behavior is that there is no other way to conduct the business of competition and cooperation so long as some conflict is inevitable in a plural system of territorial actors either not yet willing (the rising and 'developing' countries) or not immediately able (the declining and overmature ones) to cease behaving like states – creatures of power – and to start behaving like inwardly focused societies. The deadly serious sustaining reason is that major war, and a dramatic change in alignments, remains available as a regulator of last resort.

The situation is replete with paradoxes, all deriving from the central paradox that a conflict profoundly real in its geohistorical foundation is also largely fictitious, if not imaginary, in the specifics ostensibly at stake. The paradox in the operational dimension is that arms-related substitutes for war, such as deployments, competitive arms races, sales of arms, and even arms control negotiations and related transactions, tend to multiply to compensate for the dearth of opportunities for effective diplomatic action backed by force. These substitutes contribute to the impression of prenuclear international politics and diplomacy as usual. In the process, they unwittingly increase the salience of territorial or geopolitical issues and stakes while making it easier to abstain from addressing these more intractable issues seriously.

With regard to the organic dimension, the allocation of attention and resources to contrived issues leads both competitors to waste scarce resources in a struggle for less important assets. The result ultimately weakens one competitor or another to the eventual benefit of third parties.

Attributing Soviet expansionism to its totalitarian base and declaratory ideology enables Westerners to minimize the extent to which the global conflict's ostensible stakes derive their importance from the ethically neutral dynamic of the land-sea power conflict. Incidentally obscured in the process is the ultimate origin of the Soviet system and its ideology in Russia's landlocked and eastern geopolitical location. Today's regnant analysis makes it unattractive to ask to what extent Russian probings in the global periphery – and notably in America's inner security–superiority zone in the Western Hemisphere – are unprovoked emanations from the doctrinal–institutional essence of the Soviet system, and to what extent they are procedurally reactive responses to both earlier and parallel US probings in Russia's own orbit. To what extent is Soviet 'aggression', reflecting inferior position and advantages, directed to securing a more equitable and effective bargaining posture with respect to America over the terms of mutual interaction inside each other's privileged oceanic or continental habitat? Finally, and pre-eminently, to what extent can a perennial source of conflict between offshore insular and mainland powers be turned into an opportunity for accommodation?

The supreme task of statecraft in these circumstances is to readjust the two facets of real evolutionary change – organic and operational. Needed above all is a de-emphasis of the military–strategic instruments that invest the US–Soviet competition with apparent meaning and create the illusion of significant ups and downs, gains and losses. The encouragement of long-term social, political, and economic organic change must be re-emphasized as a goal of statecraft. This will mean demoting the military instrument from its current role as a presumptive substitute for political process – as a potential savior from the consequences of malfunctioning statecraft rather than merely one of quasi-traditional techniques to accelerate desirable evolutionary and contain disruptively revolutionary developments. When the military–strategic dimension is seized upon as the one remaining type of meaningful superpower transactions – given the casual attention paid to truly critical geo- or real-politics – the neglected transformations will degenerate into crises unmanageable peacefully. Meanwhile, overrating the importance of nuclear technology in peacetime will have become a greater immediate danger than unleashing it in wartime.

As long as living dangerously is necessary to prevent dying prematurely from sheer moral or material exhaustion, the nuclear obsession must be exorcised, whether it takes the form of a pathetic faith in arms control or of an overly meticulous calculation of comparative arms capabilities. In the global arena this misplaced fixation has distracted attention from the necessary relationship between military–strategic and geopolitical parity. Once the Soviets were conceded strategic nuclear equality it became inconsequent in principle and virtually impossible in the long run in practice to deny them the kind of political influence in the Third World that would make their cooperation in monitoring and, if need be, managing local upheavals inevitable, as well as potentially fruitful. This consequence should have been foreseen and accepted or else blocked at its source.

In Europe, the analogous failure was not seeing the political side of the *furore* surrounding intermediate range missiles. The Soviet deployment of the SS-20s, undertaken primarily to modernize theater nuclear forces, had no real impact on the global strategic balance. However, up to a certain level, the deployment was an appropriate offset to Western Europe's and specifically West Germany's growing impact on sociopolitical change in Eastern Europe. Just as the economics of this development was accepted by the Russians for opportunistic reasons, so the military counterpart might have been accepted in the West for prudential reasons as a legitimate compensation for the disruptive potential of Euro-detente in general and West Germany's *Ostpolitik* in particular within the Soviet bloc.

Globally, it is simply unreasonable to expect the Soviets to possess nuclear-strategic parity without trying to use it to gain more tangible dividends around the world – especially before they could know that their probings would gain so little in the Third World periphery and would only increase US opposition to any kind of partnership there or elsewhere. By the same token, the Russians could not have been expected quietly to accept even peaceful Western penetration of their East European domain without erecting a barrier, however symbolic, to the abuse of this penetration and to the possibility that change will get out of hand. Had Moscow not so acted it might have seen the 'Euroglobal' power balance change in the West's favor without a shot being fired and without receiving worthwhile compensation.

The valid, even if not yet validated, place of nuclear weapons in the evolving mode of international relations is to encourage conventional strategic thought to explore diplomatic options that have proved unsustainable when they have been tried in traditional settings.

Whereas the real and indispensable basis of continuity in world politics is that major war between the superpowers remains possible, such a war becomes more likely when the rigidity of strategic thinking exceeds the degree of continuity in the system itself – that is, when strategy is not modified to take into account ongoing evolution. This failure is especially serious in conditions that recall the situation following the demise of the order associated with the Roman Empire: when embattled islands of civilized politics and polities survive again precariously within a sea of disorder that is only beginning to emerge as a coherent pattern of entities deserving to be called 'states', and the overall configuration of effective power harbors the ever less dimly apparent possibility of a shift in the center of gravity to East Asia.

The Strategic Paradox

Neither Russian nor American policy makers can be blamed for the existence of a conflict rooted in geographic and historical givens. But their responsibilities increase as they turn from identifying valid and viable stakes to choosing appropriate strategy. When two major powers view mutually incompatible concerns from unevenly propitious situations, the result is nonetheless a shared predicament. The solutions chosen by insular strategists of the past when faced with analogous situations ultimately destroyed both competitors. Failure to recognize the joint jeopardy had led again and again to calls for forcing the allegedly more aggressive continental state to abandon its principal aims – a posture that today's critics of Soviet 'adventurism' call 'prudent self-restraint'. These critics, like their historical predecessors, expect this abstention to be followed by a fundamental alteration of the expansionist state's domestic order, which, whether it has been absolutism in pre- and Jacobinism or Bonapartism in post-revolutionary France, militarism in pre-World War I Germany, or totalitarianism today, is considered the root cause of the assault on international order. Forcing the regime into reform by containing it abroad, in preference to facing it down in war, would release the triumphant insular protagonist for unimpeachably liberal methods of administering unchallenged global sway.

A more promising strategic posture would leave open the prospect of an eventual land–sea power concert that would contain overtones of a quasi-condominial partnership. This concert would also have the potential for avoiding the pitfalls of past failed attempts to master the conflict-prone configuration of offshore insular, would-be amphibious continental, and rear-continental powers. All of these previous attempts promised some kind of immediate advantage to individual parties. Instead, they polarized the state system ever more portentously as the location of the continental challenger moved eastward toward the spatially set terminus of the series of triangular conflicts centered in Europe. It has proved impossible so far to safeguard the vital interests of the parties, as they engaged in unavoidable competition, without derailing the evolution required to achieve world equilibrium.

Today, forging the links between the United States and NATO in the West and China in the East re-enacts the most common, encircling strategy. As it unfolds, this strategy risks creating a grand coalition in which the rear-continental power (now China) will be again valued as a passive weight but will actually be the ultimate regulator of the conflict. Conversely, the short-lived Sino-Soviet alliance represented (and could in theory again reproduce) an effort by the two main continental powers to translate a duopoly into co-hegemony on the mainland. Such an arrangement enhances, however unevenly, the capacity of the two partners to challenge the sea power or of one of them to pressure it into alliance on equal and favorable terms. When it confronts the reality or mere prospect of a continental bloc, the insular state will find it all the more urgent to extend the encircling strategy beyond the continental mass to an oceanic alliance with a fellow-insular partner – in today's circumstances, as before, Japan.

Because both strategies, for continental coalition and co-hegemony, push strong established powers into opposing camps, they heighten pressures to resolve the conflict in a climactic clash. By contrast, a condominial alliance of the dominant sea and land powers pits two strong, established, and relatively conservative powers against restlessly volatile but collectively weaker powers incapable of effectively challenging the 'Big Two'. Condominium consequently has the potential to appease not only the bilateral conflict but also the entire globe. Yet in the ultimate paradox, the strategy easiest to implement – the encircling grand coalition – has also been the one with the worst short- and long-term consequences.

The strategy's short-term consequence was a series of major wars. These conflicts ostensibly were provoked by the encircled central power – first France, then Germany – but were actually imposed upon each power by the prospect of being confined to continental Europe and then gradually demoted to second-class status as a land power. The longer-term consequence was to shift the focus of contention to a succession of states that had previously played the rear-continental role: Germany in the wake of France, and then Russia. Each new competitor was more potent and less congenial both to the insular state - after Britain, the United States – and to the dominant norms of the state system.

This role transfer and its attendant penalties reveal a hidden tendency for the rear-continental state to manipulate both the system's equilibrium and the insular state, commonly thought of as the master balancer. Being the one power seemingly equally available for alignment with both of the protagonists, this easternmost state repeatedly moved both while standing still. Its display of either actual or even seeming strength would press the central power westward and overseas for compensations, with the result of making the principal sea and land powers equally eager to win the third power over as a major ally. Real or apparent weakness shown by the rear-continental state would make the sea power look eastward with the aim of buttressing the last available or least vulnerable ally against the chief rival in the middle.

Co-hegemony by two allied land powers might in principle consolidate order on the continent and bring the premier continental power up to equality with its maritime counterpart. By undoing the insular power's near-monopoly on the seas, duopoly on the continent would transpose equilibrium to the global arena. But Franco-Austrian, Franco-Russian, and Germano-Russian attempts to collude all failed. The anticipated gains – on the seas for the central state and on the continental periphery for the easternmost power – were never commensurate. Moreover, they could be attained only unevenly and in sequence. Therefore, the momentary advantage gained by one partner over the other would quickly turn into one-power hegemony. Finally, any adjustments in control over territory located between the two proximate powers themselves that might be necessary to solidify the alliance would backfire once the alliance broke apart.

Land–sea power condominium, with a potential for ordering world politics greater than that of continental co-hegemony, could be most beneficial while being least common. It has been prevented by a different fundamental problem. Britain found it impossible to accept substantial oceanic activism by the continental counterpart so long as the island's territorial and resource base was weaker than that of its chief rival. In these circumstances, condominium would only augment the discrepancy by making the lesser continental powers adjust to the diplomatically and materially enhanced central power, thereby rendering the latter unchallengeable by an insular state that had become alienated for its natural allies. Britain consequently insisted that any continental partner accept a subordinate or junior role, performing delegated tasks in managing the continental balance of power in return for only minimal rewards in terms of oceanic access. For these reasons alone, movement toward accommodation could gather steam only if a third power were to present a challenge to the position of the sea power and the prospects of the premier land power at the same time and in equal degree. At that point, however, even combining the land and sea powers' resources might not suffice in the long run, and accommodating with the burgeoning power – as Britain did with Bismarckian Germany and tsarist Russia in succession, and also with Japan – would appear more profitable in the short run. Indeed, not since the Egyptians and the Hittites joined forces has such condominium materialized, and this thirteenth-century BC version was short-lived and sterile.

The problem posed by metropoles of unequal strength, critical for the British Isles when facing a succession of bigger land powers, does not arise between only quasi-insular continent-wide America and likewise huge Russia. Other traditional hurdles to accommodation are lowered by any development that blurs the disparities or removes a bone of contention traditionally pitting land and sea powers against each other. Thus, the autarkic nature of the Soviet economy all but removes competition in trade as major irritant. Also, both superpowers are sufficiently vulnerable to long-range missiles and bombs to render futile attempts to gain a decisive upper hand through the time-honored technique of competitive alliance formation. China is less imminently capable of triggering a conflict than was either of the Germanic powers or Russia in the earlier triangles. Moreover, the salience of sea- over land-based power is diminished as the principal maritime power finds it increasingly difficult to maintain clear naval superiority on the traditional basis of nautical prowess and superior naval technologies.

At the same time, the growing attractions of seaborne deterrents perpetuate the continental state's interest and stake in the oceans. And the superpowers still reflect their insular and continental characteristics faithfully enough in their strikingly dissimilar values and institutions to perpetuate the conflict. A potentially positive consequence of this condition is that, although the bases of irreconcilable land–sea power conflict are sufficiently curtailed to open a door to accommodation, the continental–maritime dichotomy has not been so radically devalued that combining the two powers' complementary resources would have little global effect. All in all, the concept of a zone of danger – only highlighted by the issue of defenses in outer space – also signals the arrival of an era of opportunity on the still vital plane of geopolitics.

Note

1   See recently George P. Schultz, 'Shaping American foreign policy: new realities and new ways of thinking', *Foreign Affairs*, Spring 1985. Also Richard Nixon, 'Superpower summitry', ibid., Fall 1985. Innovative pronouncements by Mikhail Gorbachev have been legion.

2

Concert through Decompression

Contrary to the reigning premises of the American approach toward the Soviet Union, the US–Soviet conflict is part of an ancient pattern rooted in geographical and historical givens. The resulting problems reflect an international reality in which traditional configurations of power, patterns of conflict, and ranges of available strategies are only partially offset by evolutionary changes in the relations of states and by the supposedly revolutionary impact of nuclear weapons. Obsession with arms-related issues and ideological differences obscures the perception and distorts the role of the vital geopolitical arena. There, organic trends governing the rise and decline of nations outweigh particular transactions in long-term importance.

In the past, states caught up in competition for world power have sought to contain the globally ambitious continental power through a grand coalition headed by the Western insular and Eastern rear-continental powers – for example, when Great Britain and Russia lined up against Wilhelmine Germany, anticipating the US–China 'normalization's' bias against the Soviet Union. On other occasions, the two continental protagonists have tried to combine their drive for duopoly against the insular power's contrary ambition to base its worldwide near-monopoly on confining a divisive stalemate to the Eurasian land mass – as when France or Germany had sought the Russian alliance against Britain and, most recently, China and the Soviet Union were arrayed against the United States. But neither of these strategies has succeeded; indeed, England's adoption of the former helped trigger a series of global wars ending in Europe's self-destruction. Then and since, most grievously neglected has been the potential for condominial concert based on parity. Never before has the triangular tension among insular maritime powers (in today's version, the United States), navally aspiring continental powers (the

Soviet Union), and rear-continental powers (the People's Republic of China), been resolved in this way. First an Anglo-French and, subsequently, an Anglo-German quasi-condominial concert proved either infeasible or impermanent as often as it was attempted. The two principals were never sufficiently tempted to make it impossible for the rear-continental third party, be it Habsburg Austria or Russia, to capitalize on its option between a grand coalition against, and a co-hegemonial alliance with, the continental challenger of the insular state's naval near-monopoly and global ascendancy.

Lately, the conditions responsible for the war-ridden continental–maritime schism have waned somewhat. But they have not defused a cleavage that has underlain much of the world's dangerous instability since the modern state system emerged. Moreover, ever since Germany superseded France as the prime continental challenger to Britain's world position (and to America's self-proclaimed right to succeed to it), the East–West issue has emotionalized the comparatively more pragmatic land–sea power contest. It has done so by injecting into it geohistorically rooted East–West value differences such as those between individualism and corporate collectivism, or between societal pluralism and statist power.

These issues are not simply academic. Minimizing the continental–maritime dichotomy in favor of the East–West conflict repositions Russia's German problem at the fulcrum of superpower diplomacy and contention. Germany must, in this light, either be seen as exposed to the opportunities and temptations of its centrist position on the European cultural, political, and social spectrum or, more even than Britain and France have been, be demoted to a position of secondary importance in the global context.

Adopting the global geopolitical perspective has an important extra advantage: it reveals where the boundary between East and West really lies. This enlarged view places Soviet Russia in a strategically central position and identifies this power culturally and otherwise with Europe. Adopting this view will lead to positive consequences provided that the organic growth of China in the East does not coincide with a Western policy of denying the Soviets compensating outlets elsewhere in the world. Otherwise, any incremental rapprochement between Beijing and Washington and its allies in the operative sphere of diplomatic intercourse would be quickly followed by Soviet attempts to escape forcibly the squeeze between a hostile East and an unreceptive West.

Alternative to Containment

This type of confinement is precisely what the West has sought, through a differentially rationalized and implemented strategy of containment. Yet the strategy has done its work and thereby outlived its usefulness if a Soviet 'mellowing' beyond totalitarianism is to be followed by a political maturation that points beyond authoritarianism. Containment prevented – if prevention from outside was needed – an elemental overflow of a Soviet-led communist tide. This tide might have sustained a revolutionary movement and ideology beyond its natural lifespan and, as Islam had centuries before, threatened the vital centers of the West. Failing to reach these dimensions, the Soviet system has been caught up in the routine tasks of self-maintenance in the face of pressing domestic problems and of noncommunist polities that have proved more attractive than yielding. As a result, it was bound progressively to shed its totalitarian straitjacket.

If the converse of compressing is to decompress the rival's policy environment, the related policy imperative is to replace containment with a strategy calculated to ease the Soviet system of controls by reducing opposition to all Soviet bids for influence. Confining a major continental power within its inner security zone inevitably will reinforce impulses requiring this power to tighten controls over the states within its orbit and maintain them at home. Control will always threaten to escalate or re-escalate into coercion in both arenas so long as the regime is driven to foreclose any internal softening that would undermine its capacity to repress the regional defections or revolts its control methods foster and the larger environment encourages. By the same token, both the core-state regime and its inner security zone are most likely to be relaxed only if expanding access farther abroad generates incentives for becoming more efficient at home. An intuitive sense of political dynamics matters in this regard as much or more than geopolitical logic, paramount in illuminating the reasons and outlooks for the principal strategies available to insular and continental powers. But the effect of different foreign-policy environments on domestic and regional orders of the principal continental power is no less critical as a result.

The policy of rigid containment rests on the belief that resisting the continued expansion or even threatening the previous gains of a crisis-ridden Soviet regime will force Moscow to choose between far-reaching immediate self-reform and retrogression ending in revolution – this time in a liberal direction. Pursuing US–Soviet concert would put into practice the contrary belief that relaxing US–fostered inhibitions on geopolitical outreach would tend to lower domestic Soviet barriers to policy changes necessary to improve performance at home in the interest of lastingly sustainable gains, independent of ephemeral opportunities, abroad. Whereas the more radical proponents of containment expect compression to dislocate the Soviet system as both state and empire in favor of an unavowed or unavowable alternative, the strategy of decompression aims prudently to continue raising the system above its burdensome revolutionary and totalitarian origins. Indeed, decompression is a strategy of appeasement, but appeasement in its original and etymologically correct connotation, meaning the pacifying effect of mutually reinforcing strategies that adjust equilibrium between two or more parties. This term should not be confused with the Munich-tainted connotation of one actor submissively placating another through uncompensated concessions of significant geopolitical or economic assets from a position of weakness.

History shows a high correlation between periods of external pressure on the Soviet Union – notably the post-1918 Western counterrevolutionary interventions, the interwar activities of the Anti-Comintern Pact, and the cold war – and the Soviet Union's shift toward or relapse into totalitarianism. Conversely, the liberalization that has followed Russia's wartime defeats or setbacks – from the Crimean War through the Russo-Japanese War to the two world wars – has been commonly shallow and short-lived. It has given way quickly to a reassertion of authority at home and re-engagement in adventures abroad, in Central Asia, the Balkans, or worldwide, weakening when not negating much of the argument based upon such precedents. External failures often destroy the power bases of one-man dictatorships but not those of more socially pervasive autocracies. The dynamics of the French Second Empire under Napoleon III, entering a liberal phase after it was thwarted in its international ambitions, are profoundly different from the dynamics of the Soviet empire. The Soviet ruling elite is far less dependent for internal authority on foreign triumphs than was the modern Latin caesar; nor does the Soviet political and economic system resemble the economically primitive, predatory Roman and Ottoman empires in depending on continuing expansions for inner vitality. Yet – and the difference is as crucial as it is subtle – a measure of success abroad creates the latitude necessary for risking domestic reforms. Failure or contraction will induce a tightening of internal controls and may prompt a return to traditional forms of coercion – but does not necessarily set off irreversible decay.

Thus the United States may be well-advised to tolerate more Soviet wooing of the West Europeans and occasional winnings in the Third World. This is not to say that Washington's tolerance need be unlimited or unconditional. Indeed, for the relaxation of constraints to produce the desired results and disarm critics, the otherwise haphazard and often unconvincing differentiation of expendable secondary from vital interests must be firmly and visibly rooted in a grand strategy reflecting explicit premises and an implied long-term objective. It is immaterial whether adaptations take the form of unilaterally altered American conduct or of formal US–Soviet negotiations. The latter rarely are useful without first changing priorities and perspectives, but may be worth attempting in a sufficiently structured but locally stalemated setting such as the Middle East. What matters is that the principle of US–Soviet geopolitical parity, matching the accomplished reality of military–strategic parity, is conceded as a goal which, though distant, informs present behavior pointing toward a mutually agreeable world order.

In this scenario, Soviet geopolitical gains from US-sanctioned decompression would be limited by a concurrent devolution of influence to qualified regional powers such as India or Brazil as well as China. Their promotion would increase the superpowers' incentives to conserve role and status by acting in concert. But if the third parties' interposition would decrease the scope for anything like a two-headed dictatorship, two-power concert is historically the sole alternative to sharing decline relative to third parties, regardless of how distant this prospect may seem at any one time.

An American policy that accepts the risks implicit in the strategy of decompression will have to elicit a reassuring response if it is to continue and deepen. Moreover, the Soviet response will have to take place soon enough to vindicate a strategy that, taking off from a considerable US geopolitical advantage, inevitably entails an initial investment in anticipation of future returns. But one caveat implies another: more than casual response can be forthcoming only when the

American change of heart is shown to be a matter of considered strategy, not a product of transient confusion or passing weakness. When both sides perform accordingly, solid detente can ensue from a process that is both 'comprehensive' and 'reciprocal'.

The major test for the decompression strategy will come in the Third World, where the two superpowers' outermost zones of security overlap haphazardly. Unquestionably, the development of a condominial partnership will require the Russians to tone down their support for local upheavals representing themselves as revolutions. Washington's challenge will be to tolerate levels of Soviet support that meet the Kremlin's residual need for ideological legitimation of conventional great-power practices. For US policy to make the required concession to long-term evolution means forgoing reflexive support for ostensibly counterrevolutionary responses to equally sham local revolutions that have opened the gates to Soviet influence. The new version of liberation strategy is no more likely to advance its purported aims – the orderly enlargement of individual freedoms and social justice – than was its forebear, espoused by the late Secretary of State John Foster Dulles. Indeed, American initiatives in, say, Angola promise to be as frustrating as the conversely idealized and equally questionable interventions in South Africa that seek to close off opportunities for Soviet meddling, before they arise, by engineering a radical revision of the existing social order at short notice.

For third-party forces to reduce US–Soviet competition effectively, they must be more immediately compelling than the abstract, hypothetical threat of mutual assured destruction. Sufficient dangers to the superpowers already are present in the international system and are not confined to the material costs and military risks of an accelerating arms race. They inhere in a range of wholly possible scenarios in which Washington and Moscow steadily lose various forms of leverage to important third countries. Yet the most conspicuous immediate threats, ranging from the particulars of state support for terrorism and religious fanaticism defying conventional state power to a general tendency for protracted conflict repeatedly to lure one or both of the superpowers into a costly pursuit of marginal objectives in a secondary theater, are located in the Third World periphery. Whether patent and immediately unimpressive or latent and more serious, the perils suggest the benefits of de-emphasizing US–Soviet contention in the Third World in favor of jointly overseeing the long, unavoidably crisis-ridden process of forming viable national and regional orders there.

These yet uncrystallized areas can evolve best, and might evolve only, when local powers respond to locally relevant issues and interests and when the resulting transactions articulate regional balances of power. The larger outside powers can usefully set only outside limits to the attendant upheavals by preventing the strongest local actor from suppressing the turmoil prematurely. Outside powers can also help ease, if only guardedly, excessive stress within the individual countries. But, in principle, the process should be restored to the parties directly concerned. Only in this way can viable states be identified, can governments be disciplined to act responsibly, and can the masses be impelled to develop the larger loyalties without which both political and economic development will remain for many backward countries a slogan denoting a chimera. The more developed societies can best help their unevenly developing counterparts – and help themselves in the process – if they not only withhold the military and economic assistance the recipients are unable to absorb constructively, but also abstain from extending to the conduct of the 'new' states the kind of constraints that prevent them from developing autonomously and, if need be, catastrophically. Insofar as assistance is either offered or demanded to repair flagrant injustices, it only compounds any past with a more insidious fresh injury. It interferes with the birthright to enjoy at least some of the latitude that a more free-wheeling environment automatically offered the earlier-developing societies while they were evolving the normative shelters for their maturity.

The prescription for a self-denying ordinance in the alternately turbulent and stagnant parts of the world defines the scope of a US–Soviet condominium by limiting it. It is within thus narrowed confines that President Ronald Reagan can be said to have taken a step in the right direction, in his speech to the UN General Assembly amid one of the spells of pre-summit euphoria, in October 1985, when he advocated joint superpower efforts to address local conflicts in the Third World. But if this type of initiative is ever to survive beyond a first step, the readiness for joint action must not be hypocritically confined to areas of embarrassing Soviet involvement and transparently disguise the wish simply to end it at little or no cost to Washington. On the contrary, the Soviets must be effectively present in an area if they are to be able to help. And the various regional orders must be defined so as to legitimate this effective presence, not least in the eyes of the American government.

Once the superpower accord was under way, it would quickly reveal the absurdity of the view that great powers no longer are strong enough to shape events in the Third World. In fact, any lack of superpower authority is largely the self-induced consequence of mutually frustrating competition. Do major powers still command influence over lesser powers? Surely they do to an infinitely greater extent when acting in tandem or along parallel courses than when backing rival proxies or clients. Lesser states will act irresponsibly when commensurate sanctions do not follow predictably upon actions that violate even the weak norms of the international system. Major powers can and do constrain irresponsible small-state behavior in two settings. One is an intense two-power conflict waged so ruthlessly as to scare any third power away from exploiting the resulting opportunities. The other is a hierarchical ordering of power that reposes hard-to-challenge authority in one or two paramount states. Neither condition is present today – with lamentable consequences. This situation can only worsen when the systematic irresponsibility of overly ambitious small-state governments converges with sporadic acts of terror by stateless agents intent on achieving often legitimate group ends by the only available if ostensibly criminal means, and when the presumably civilized powers blame each other for the results of a set of norms that has aroused all kinds of appetites under the rubric of the right to self-determination.

Toward a Global Bargain

A narrowly conceived balance-of-power policy is not in such conditions an appropriate device for combining a minimum measure of stability with the necessary degree of systemic evolution. Adding a quasi-alliance with China to the Atlantic and Japanese alliances meant parlaying the frustrations of a military effort in Asia into the diplomatic foundations of a less exacting version of containment. The 'normalization' met a seemingly pressing need. However, if adding a simple one-power counterweight did lessen the cumulative burden of worldwide activism, reducing the need to engage in minor wars in the near term increased the daunting possibility of a major war in the not indefinitely remote future.

Such an attempt to outflank the center has countless precedents. Unfortunately, it is also too crude a solution to today's problems. To make up for precipitously scaling down its unacknowledged imperial role, the United States will have to contrive a more subtle approach to a more complex equilibrium. The two superpowers now see their geopolitical momentum stalled to a roughly equal extent and face comparable domestic constraints on its reactivation. Thus they must assess realistically their possible gains relative to benefits to third parties of continuing entanglements in a competition bereft of meaningful stakes. Recognition that such a point has been reached has made itself felt in all major-power conflicts. The historically insurmountable difficulty has been to use this recognition to reverse mutually damaging policies.

The hegemonic wars that finally destroyed the European state system originated in the repeated failure to adapt the system's delicate mixture of multi-power balance and one-state diplomatic pre-eminence to a broader, global arena. Approximating the model in today's world means allowing Soviet diplomatic participation in European affairs to continue and expand conjointly with readjustments of access outside Europe; avoiding the model's corruption requires America's counterweight to prevent Russia's European pre-eminence from turning into dominance. Decrying this format as 'Finlandizing' or 'Hollandizing' Western Europe amounts to blocking potentially beneficial change for fear of its caricature. The logic of continuing the evolution of relations between Europe's latest – and now, in Russia's case, last – great power and her earlier foremost powers is revealed whenever the West Europeans assiduously avoid measures inimical to genuinely vital Soviet security interests and observe their stake in insulating their economic interests from Washington's political and military tensions with Moscow. The posture points beyond a mechanical balance to a more complex equilibrium.

In a complex equilibrium, instinctive checking and balancing by counterforce and counterpressure give way to restraint in exploiting temporary advantages. Shifting to complex equilibrium requires recognizing that the Soviet diplomatic presence in Western Europe cannot overstep definite bounds without frightening the West Europeans back into allying less conditionally with the United States and into joining wholeheartedly in extending the ring of containment eastward. Similarly, an unprovoked Soviet penetration into Third

World areas genuinely vital to US interests automatically would reduce American tolerance of the Soviets' European diplomacy. It might also lead to increased US military involvement with the Chinese or Japanese although, again, within limits set by a dissenting Western Europe's liability to neutralism out of fear of Soviet reactions.

Similar restraints apply to the West. If pressing the Soviets too hard impedes liberalization at home and moderation abroad, hasty and excessive European or American accommodation of Soviet Russia in Europe or in the Third World could convince China to incur the costs of reforging the Sino-Soviet alliance. This would augment Russia's bargaining power with the West, but only at the cost of decreased Japanese willingness to help either communist power modernize. Conversely, excessive US strategic or material support for China would risk undercutting US ties with Japan and the countries of the Association of Southeast Asian Nations (ASEAN). And such a policy would no doubt prompt Soviet efforts to placate Japan with one-sided territorial concessions and to win over the lesser Asian powers with increased trade and agreements for collective regional security.

How much US credibility is lost as a result of any of the possible Soviet gains will depend on whether the gains take place in spite of declared opposition or in the context of US policy of decompression that is tied to a longer-term strategic goal. The contrary policy of avidly seizing upon Soviet losses, next to blocking their gains, hardly represents a self-justifying plus for American interests or global stability. Indeed, automatic US assistance to help eradicate a previously invited but no longer desired Soviet presence in a Third World country will make other lesser actors more than ever irresponsible, tempting the Russians into efforts to exploit the indirectly US-inspired new openings. These same efforts can then be decried as evidence of innate Soviet adventurism.

The limit of US forbearance – that is, the line between indispensable and expendable positions – is not fixed in space. It varies over time with changing strategic priorities that reflect the perceived hierarchy of threats, itself depending on whatever international role or status is deemed feasible and judged necessary. By the same standard, the boundaries of strategically significant regions are determined less by spatial configuration and more by the constellation of antagonisms and alignments around focal stakes. Consequently, no position outside the physical borders of the United States is inherently indispensable nor interest in it inherently vital - not even an American monopoly of influence in Western Europe and Japan, should a sufficient external threat require US–Soviet cooperation 'at all costs' in the ultimate interest of all or most of the affected parties.

If the 'end' does not justify the 'means' in interstate policies, it is hard to see what does, outside normative abstractions that often disguise unavowed practical aspirations. National interests and specific stakes cannot be permanently calibrated as more or less vital or fictitious in themselves. Neither can they be traded off to mutual satisfaction outside an overarching strategic concept. It will be necessary to adjust national interests and reassess regional stakes if complex equilibrium, which is not wholly self-regulating, is to be implemented and if the principle of geopolitical parity, the actual shape of which is not self-evident, is to be applied so as to sustain a gradual transition from a strategy for conflict to one for a *modus vivendi*. Determining what each side can legitimately do within the different regions is part of defining a strategy capable of generating a comprehensive global bargain. To this end, leverages applied competitively as a means to equalize access to or exclusion from particular regions must become subsidiary to consensually evolving 'fair' compensations.

When this happens, mechanical item-by-item matching and attempted counterbalancing of particular gains and losses in more or less arbitrarily linked regions can give way to aggregating the gain–loss equations across several regions into an essentially equivalent global outcome for the two sides. In the case of competitive bargaining, the Soviets will tease the United States in its inner security–superiority zone – for example, Nicaragua – as a counterpart to America's probes against the Soviets in Poland or in post-invasion Afghanistan; Soviet-backed suppression of 'pro-capitalist' forces in Angola or Ethiopia (as part of Moscow's outer zone) will be matched by US-aided subversion of 'pro-socialist' forces in Chile and of the Soviet-leaning neutral regime in pre-invasion Afghanistan. Under the comprehensive bargain, by contrast, the two world powers would pair off regional gains and losses by virtue of less minutely rigid and schematic criteria. Thus, say, US or NATO gains in Southeast Asia or Eastern Europe, and reduced stresses in the Middle East and Central America, might be seen as compensating for Soviet advantages elsewhere in Asia and in the Caribbean. The actual procedure might include de facto US–Soviet co-guarantees shaped so as to diffuse the repercussions of regional trouble spots and distribute the costs and benefits of neither superpower seeking to remove or significantly diluting the local influence of the other as a means of introducing its own.

Such an arrangement could mean associating the United States with the Soviet guarantee of Vietnam's security against China as part of US–Vietnamese normalization of relations. But it also could mean that the United States would countenance a Soviet underwriting of a socialist regime in Nicaragua so long as this great-power guarantee served both of its normal functions: to protect a small state against a nearby great power while controlling and containing any disposition on the part of the client to disturb local conditions with actions inimical or provocative to its powerful neighbor. US tolerance of 'socialism in one [small] country' within its inner security–superiority zone would, on these terms, be warranted by the confident expectation that, even should the event be independently replicated in another small country in the region, the first Soviet-guaranteed socialist regime would have meanwhile faced material realities requiring it to resume productive relations with Washington.

Not only would local costs be contained but also globally dispersed compensations would become evident. A de facto US participation in the Soviet guarantee to Vietnam against China would defuse some of the risks of US–Soviet confrontation presented by excessively close Sino-American ties. It also would dilute the Soviet counterencircle-ment of China via Vietnam and go far toward removing Vietnam's reasons or rationales for military occupation of Kampuchea. The Soviets would lose their monopoly of access to strategic facilities in Vietnam, but US policy in East Asia would become more genuinely evenhanded toward the two communist giants, with the consequence of equalizing also the costs and benefits of the US–China connection for the parties to it. Removing an incentive from under Hanoi's present expansionism would not please its ASEAN neighbors less for this happening within a framework constraining China's in the future.

Yet the American gains in one area, the attendant Soviet renunci-ations, and the principle of geopolitical parity would all require that this approach apply also to areas of previously privileged US access. In effect repealing the Monroe Doctrine would not gratuitously demean a hallowed foreign policy tradition. It would reflect America's growth from a regional into a global power equal to managing the reform-revolution dynamic locally.

Such a move would also make it easier for the Soviet Union to endure the ongoing erosion of the Brezhnev Doctrine in its own inner security zone in Eastern Europe by a growing Western economic and political engagement there. The West, however, would have to do more than concede in return a more prominent Soviet involvement in West European affairs. Transcending any such particular barter, the global bargain would have to engender reliable Western self-restraint in exploiting the regionally centrifugal implications of East–West concert. In the past, radical would-be reformers in Eastern Europe have defeated themselves when, responding to platonic encouragement from the West, they undercut the more moderate and responsible initial leadership of an Alexander Dubček in Czechoslovakia or a Lech Walesa in Poland. Likewise self-defeating will be any policy that seeks to relax Soviet controls in the region without also devaluing its importance for Russia's national security and great-power self-esteem by expanding access to other parts of the world.

The Brezhnev Doctrine has merely sovietized the definition of necessary defenses against the West in Europe pioneered by the Pan-Slavic movement. By the same token, Soviet policy in Southwest Asia and, in particular, in Afghanistan, merely implements the nineteenth-century statesman Gorchakov's doctrine of self-protective expansion into Central Asia against threats from peripheral disorders then supported by Britain. Immemorial compulsions will not be stilled by isolated tradeoffs and linkages. Without adequate compensations across the board, the Soviets are unlikely to withdraw from strategically useful positions in Afghanistan in exchange for largely symbolic satisfaction there or elsewhere, or surrender the concrete leverage of radical Middle Eastern allies for the mirage of widening their peacetime influence in the region.

Indeed, Afghanistan illustrates the limits of strictly local trade-offs or joint guarantees that are not part of a wide-ranging accommodation keyed to long-term evolution. The best that Washington can achieve there is to record the change in regional power distribution since the days of the Anglo-Russian Great Game in Asia by getting the Soviets to match Britain's assurance against exploiting predominance in Afghanistan strategically.

In so far as a concurrent co-guarantee of Pakistan's integrity were implicitly or explicitly directed against interference by third parties, Soviet costs in relation to India probably would exceed US embarrassment with respect to China. After all, transforming Pakistan into a protected state, although symbolically formalizing India's pre-eminence in South Asia, would also block the already weakened neighbor's dismemberment in favor of the effective reunification of the subcontinent under Indian hegemony. More immediately, New Delhi's dependence on Moscow would be diminished if the threat of Sino-Pakistani encirclement were undermined concurrently with transforming the US–Pakistan relationship. All the while, Indo-Soviet strains would intensify if Soviet power, already projected toward India's northwestern frontier through military presence in Afghanistan, would extend to diplomatic entrenchment in Pakistan. At a minimum, a more evenhanded Indian foreign policy could be expected in relations with the superpowers. The longer-term cost to the Russians would more than match any more immediate prior cost incurred by the United States in Southwest Asia or in East Asia.

Vaster deferred advantages would follow if co-guaranteeing minor-power trouble spots in the Third World led toward upgrading more important regional powers as the products and future agents of systemic evolution. Just as direct exposure to Soviet power could be expected to force India to assume the once British regional responsibilities relative to the northwestern frontier, so would an even partially legitimated Soviet presence in Central America bring Mexico among others and in Southeast Asia, Japan, face to face with their 'vital' interests. All of the regional powers would forego the luxury of simultaneously protesting and profiting by an excessively protective and possessive US regional posture. Otherwise objectionable superpower collusions would be vindicated by their role in linking a wider range of national self-interests to the promotion of international stability for all states.

A strategy for concert would thus do more than decompress the environment of Soviet foreign policy and anchor global detente in localized superpower ententes. By defusing today's version of the land–sea power triangle and diffusing significant regional responsibilities, it ultimately would encourage flexible multipower systems to emerge, first in Asia. Inasmuch as it comprised the Pacific (US and Soviet) alongside integrally Asian powers, such a constellation would also prevent the depolarization of the Europe-centered East–West cleavage from automatically repolarizing the globe along the lines of still deeper racial and cultural distinctions. Much of the world's political transactions would gravitate eastward, possibly at a more rapid rate than had been the case before or would be true otherwise. But the level of intensity of conflict would be muted and, equally or more important, would not automatically entail a parallel gravitation of dominating power. Instead of US-fostered industrial and military potential migrating toward China and US-shielded economic and technological power continuing to grow in Japan – while superpower rivalry continued to erode the might of both America and the Soviet Union – China would both be free and be forced to develop innate resources and Japan to assume security responsibilities, as would India. The result would resemble previous transitional periods, such as the mid-nineteenth century, temporarily devoid of pressures from an active land–sea power triangle. The epoch exhibited relatively moderate and flexible international politicking among a number of (then only European) powers favorable to orderly changes in interstate hierarchy and equilibrium.

Releasing the Third World peripheries from the constraints and irritants imposed by today's superpower competition would not mean granting a license to native forces to behave irresponsibly. It would involve instead extending to the extra-European world a combination that was creatively applied in Europe for centuries – a pre-eminent role for the major powers within a quantitative balance of power. With a decompression strategy promoting orderly succession to the superpowers, while legitimating their residual roles and possessions vis-a-vis third countries, offering neither of them an intolerable threat or an irresistible opportunity, the superpower relationship itself would eventually find an internal balance. It would become largely cooperative – especially concerning the local trouble spots – but would remain competitive as regards the dispositions and alignments of the major regional powers. Both facets of the relationship would be sustained by valid strategic rationales and rooted in substantially revised reciprocal perceptions that would guard against exploitation by third parties.

In the meantime, the proven guarantee (including co-guarantee) device can serve as an operational technique for mediating the dynamic of organic transformations, which victory and defeat in major wars or major diplomatic realignments had effected more promptly and thoroughly in the prenuclear past. Concerting technique matters less than cooperating with trends. Yet properly combining process and procedure can shield any two principals from otherwise unavoidable frustrations. A positive evolution of the Soviet system can proceed only in the context of a complex world equilibrium encouraged by the decompression approach. The net effect of any strategy on the domestic Soviet arena can be measured only over a lengthy period of time, just as any particular geopolitical adjustments can be validly tried only within a global compass. The cause of US-Soviet accommodation will not be served by automatically condemning all Soviet attempts to retard the internal repercussions of decompression any more than by undermining all regional initiatives designed to force Washington to take seriously Moscow's global aspirations and worldwide interests. The subtle operations of complex equilibrium are safe so long as they do not threaten to substantially recast the pattern of military strategic assets to the unmatchable and irreversible advantage of either side.

What Kind of West?

As the farthest eastern rear-continental power, China is unavoidably the largest passive de facto regulator of the balance of power, pressing Soviet Russia westward when being or seeming strong, and luring a supportive US strategy eastward when weak. Yet China need not be encouraged in her growing and dangerous tendency to play the two superpowers off against each other. The foreign policy makers of four successive US administrations allowed China to determine, from its position of relative weakness, the moment of 'normalization' and have conceded China the lion's share in managing its mode and momentum ever since. It is not in the American — any more than the Russian — interest to let China control its relationship with the United States to the point where Beijing can manipulate the US–Soviet relationship. Yet this is the likely result of excessive worrying over a possible Chinese defection or, conversely, of staking too many hopes on the prospect of a stable, modernized, and self-restrained China voluntarily joining others in a multipolar balance of power for peace and order.

Thanks to the obsessive competition between today's principal continental and insular powers, China has been able to draw first on

Soviet and then on American material aid and may well move toward drawing simultaneously on both great rivals in an effort to combine economic growth with political independence. Thus did also rear-continental Habsburg Austria receive subsidies and expected territorial gains alternately from Britain and France in the earliest fully developed triangular setting. In the second, tsarist Russia was technologically and financially promoted first by Germany and then by France and Britain.

In keeping with the alternation between the two main priorities traditional to Russia, the present Soviet leadership's plans for the country imply a return from dramatic exploits abroad to seeking strength through internal consolidation and development. Only the United States, the least far-sighted of the three parties to the triangle, continues to strain its likewise finite resources in behalf of ambitious military–strategic and political designs. This failure to integrate the organic with the operational dimension of the total political process parallels dangerously the inability of both the Dutch and the English, at their peak, to scale down preoccupation with the premier continental state (France for the Dutch, mainly Germany for Britain) in favor of attending to other, internal and external, tasks and threats.

Such outcomes conceal portents and issue a warning against wasting energies and resources by continuing to fix on the Soviet threat while the American economic and technological lead slips away toward a Japan that now enjoys an earlier America's shelter from military exertions. The broad continental base of the United States may in the near future shield it from incurring the lot of comparatively miniscule Holland and only somewhat larger England as the leading liberal economy and a global force for political liberties. The United States, however, is heir no less than were the Dutch United Provinces and the United Kingdom to the weaknesses of pluralistic and capitalistic insular polities which, after a meteoric rise due to a propitious configuration of world politics and economy, are subject to an equally abrupt material decline and societal decay. The Soviet Union, meanwhile, is likely to exhibit for some time to come the sturdy resilience and capacity for resurgence – however undramatic – of the endemically crisis-ridden authoritarian land powers, from ancient Assyria and postmaritime Byzantium through the Spanish- and Ottoman-centered empires at *their* apogees.

Making wise strategic choices is difficult under any condition. It is especially taxing, however, when plausible inferences about long-term geopolitical trends, drawn from analogous past structures, clash with the need to adapt to immediate pressures and seemingly unique contingencies; when the hardest of all questions – which of two adversaries is rising and which declining in the medium- and long-terms – is not asked at all or is frivolously answered in favor of seemingly safe and superficially clever bids for momentary advantage. When targeted on the latter, US foreign policy making has not been particularly adept at the fine calculation of gains and losses required by the nervous oscillations of complex equilibrium. Yet the restraint built into such an equilibrium – its autonomous tendency to dampen and defuse excessive ambitions – can make its implementation easier so long as the strategy rests on a solid intellectual foundation and promotes fundamental interests.

In seeking to limit unavoidable risks while maximizing restraints and avoiding wasteful use of scarce resources, the strategy of equilibrium expresses genuinely conservative thinking when it points to concert between functionally complementary powers with a shared stake in the essential features of the status quo. The same is not necessarily true of the coalition strategy for balance-of-power schemes when it is anchored in divergently waxing and waning allies. Indeed, such schemes are inherently radical even as they seek stability, insofar as they purport to provide a simple total remedy to a threat perceived as the systems's single root problem.

Complex equilibrium can work as long as the West Europeans perceive a stake in staying out of the global continental–maritime dimension of the US–Soviet conflict and in defusing its East–West dimension, and so long as it is in the American interest to hinder the NATO allies from playing roles that demoted former principals have traditionally assumed: catalyzing the conflict by making the United States exaggerate the Soviet threat so as to keep wavering allies in line; or becoming jittery and soliciting destabilizing theater adjuncts to a global strategic balance that should crystallize, through an evolving combination of nuclear and conventional offense and defense capabilities, into a functional complement of the thrusts and restraints that make up the geopolitics of complex equilibrium. Just as imperative is the American stake in retaining control over the still undefined Chinese connection and the benefits from a developing shift of the economic center of gravity to the western Pacific. The fundamental corresponding interest of China and Japan is to avoid premature choices about international orientation and to stay on the course toward maintaining, in Japan's case, and achieving, in China's, economically dynamic and politically stable conditions.

In completing the potentially favorable circumstances, the Russians will continue to be more fearful of China than of the United States. No less enduring will be the Soviet stake in expanding access to a technologically and scientifically productive West, including Western Europe. If given the chance, Soviet neo-Westernizers will continue to hold their own against the anti-Western resentments of the neo-Slavophiles. To offer that chance would be the ultimate purpose behind a US policy that decompresses the environment of evolutionary change for the sake of narrowing, in due course, the gap between an aborted form of socialism and a no longer self-sufficient or sufficiently vibrant individualism. In the absence of an enlightened gradualism, one brand of ideological reactionaries will continue to equate the Soviet antidote to the anarchic individualism of old-style capitalism with irremediably regressive Stalinism, and the opposing brand will continue to insist on group conformism while unsuccessfully seeking a way out of corporate stagnation. Both sides will agree that either Russian traditions or Soviet techniques are incompatible with European-generated modernity and that the US–Soviet conflict therefore reflects an unbridgeable gap between East and West. A certain victim is the 'West' properly defined.

Receding as the West now is from millennial ascent, it can no longer afford mistakenly to group the Soviet Union among its truly Eastern neighbors. For with the end of the Stalin era Moscow shed the main features of oriental despotism: self-imposed isolation from the outside world and absolute centralization of all forms of power. As it continues to move away from these practices, the Soviet Union will continue to approach a range of regime types familiar to the West, provided that geographically rooted delays are allowed for and the international environment offers sufficient incentives and latitudes for change.

The Soviet Russian polity is assimilable over time not only because its dominant ideology is of Western derivation or because the regime originated in a revolution of the continental-European type, pioneered in contrast to the different Dutch and English prototypes by the French in behalf of enhanced national power as much or more than individual or group freedom. At its deepest level, the affinity is grounded in the fact that Russian and Soviet cultures have been subject to a constantly challenging and re-forming tension between the lower urges of expediency and various transcendent norms of religion or ideology. This feature, fundamental to the civilizations of the West since antiquity, differentiates even a sovietized Russia from the real East, which has been given to eluding this stressful tension in favor of a self that is immersed in an ineffable spirituality so that it may be free to act pragmatically – and, in fact, opportunistically – when dealing with the here and now.[1] This predisposition explains much about why contemporary China has been so ready and Soviet Russia so reluctant to renounce the principles of Marxist socialism to achieve greater efficiency. The ready turnabout has been pleasing for the moment; it is not necessarily reassuring in the larger perspective of chronically unstable world politics and economics.

Anchoring the evolution of the global system in a US–Soviet concert means graduating and spacing, not blocking, the worldwide dispersion of power and influence. America and Russia are the last offshoots of the West still questing for collective power as one way of fulfilling individual potentialities. For this reason alone, it is their duty to avoid bringing about the frivolous self-destruction of a common civilization. The preservation of America's constituent identity – no less than of the Russian identity of the Soviet Union – will require a supportive cultural setting of global scope. Without such a base, neither power will have even a fighting chance to absorb the growing mass of hard-to-assimilate ethnic groups. Originating for the United States in the regional disorders no longer amenable to imperialistic remedies, or in regression from the imperial experiment on a global scale, America's share of the problem of ethnic and cultural heterogeneity can be no more readily disposed of by the faded myth of the melting pot than its counterpart in the Soviet Union by the never plausible fiction of the new transnational Soviet man.

The impulse to see in the Soviets the barbarous enemy at the gates, bereft of any saving virtue, is equally specious whether it springs from fear or hatred of past or present Russian oppressors, from a doctrinal distaste for the Soviet order, or from attachment to a utopia befitting the American New Jerusalem. It renders a possibly fatal disservice to a West confronted with perils and disarray not wholly unlike those of its beginnings, but lacking now the sustaining authority of an unspoiled faith as much as the bracing urgency of material needs and palpable threats.

Notes

1 For a seminal discussion of the oriental attitude, see F.S.C. Northrop, *The Meetinq of East and West* (New York: Macmillan Company, 1946), pp. 380–1.

PART II

Issues and Interrogations

3

From Deterrence to Defense?

With the emergence of space-based defenses as the chief subject of military–strategic debate, the United States stands at the threshold of a new technology whose political implications will extend well into the next century. If these long-term effects are to govern choice among present options, the debate must transcend purely technical questions and seek to anticipate a hypothetical future. Unavoidably tentative at this stage, an inquiry into the implications of SDI, the Strategic Defense Initiative, for political policies will achieve little if it does not aim for the 'big picture'. It must not, therefore, be intimidated by the greater rigor of the exact sciences and specificity of technological data but must scrutinize the laws of politics which, while less reliable and compelling than the laws of physics, nonetheless indicate the range of the probable on the strength of historical evidence.

Correcting for biases that stress operational efficacy and technical feasibility is nowhere more important than in the American culture, including the political subculture. It is a culture that typically favors a strictly defined perspective but now faces a question with far-reaching implications for societies with a radically different orientation and hierarchy of values. Embracing a technology such as the one underlying defenses in space in the alleged interest of humanity at large requires taking into account the human factor in its many facets without, for all that, getting mired in pacifist or any other sentimentality.

Stability in Nuclear and Prenuclear Settings

The effectiveness of mutual deterrence in creating strategic stability can be ascribed to the great uncertainty of the outcome of a nuclear exchange. The uncertainty, and its relation to stability, reflects the fact that there is and can be no reliable identification of the requisites of stability in terms of numbers of weapons and kinds of technology alone. Between major adversaries, one man's or side's stability is another's instability just as, as between the United States and its principal allies, the same deployment can be viewed as coupling or decoupling the two theaters of the Euro-American ecumene. Even in the prenuclear military context, the existence of equilibrium (another word for stability or its foundation) could be established in most instances only by inference from the restrained behavior of the main actors, not by counting muskets in one era and mortars or machine guns in the next. In fact, the impossibility of quantifying 'power' was the precondition that allowed the balancing mechanism to work as well as it did. If the outcome of a military conflict could be predetermined by precise measurements, the marked initial advantage in ready capabilities that will prompt a state to challenge the existing order would make resistance decidedly unpromising and, therefore, in many instances less likely.

For strategic stability to be more than contingent – to rest on more than uncertainty revealed in cautious conduct – it must reliably inhibit states from employing military means to do the opposite from exploiting a real or imagined advantage: to wit, counteract a radically worsening political situation. Within a halfway rational universe of action, such total or absolute stability obtains when unleashing a military conflict means signing the death warrant of the attacker himself. A 'balance of terror' of this kind has been fading, and with it unconditional stability, as the technology of counterforce has progressed to the detriment of strategies targeting populations as the first or last resort. By once again making war thinkable (because it is escalation-resistant even if not escalation-proof), the increasing efficacy of both nuclear and conventional weaponry has reinforced the shift from total stability to one highly susceptible to pressures from the political arena. The importance of that arena increases also insofar as a major power is most likely to initiate war for objectives more psychological or diplomatic than military. To the extent that they intensify political stress while reducing destruction, partial defenses against ballistic missiles are apt further to weaken stability on the nuclear level. A failproof protection of not only retaliatory capability but also population would go one better and, in effect, restore the traditionally unstable conventional military balance.

Without the threat of assured self-destruction, the issue of war as a practical resort returns to its habitual context as a 'continuation of policy by other means', to be analyzed by reference to general principles of statecraft. When the future is at stake, the inquiry must reach beyond actually transpired behavior and consider underlying motives and determinants of action. If certain inferences can be drawn from the observed absence of conflict (for example, existence of equilibrium reflecting widespread satisfaction with the status quo relative to the costs of changing it forcibly), what are the commonly operative incentives to conflict? What will make a major power resort to substantial military action against another great power? Immediately at issue is rationality in statecraft, as distinct from the reasonable person's common sense. Moreover, where narrowly pragmatic or strictly military–strategic criteria would stamp certain conduct as irrational, a particular value system growing out of a specific political heritage might not. In particular to be considered is the hierarchy of values generated by a system (such as the classic European) stressing the absolute primacy of corporate autonomy and by a culture (such as the continental European) that is state- rather than homocentric. A social ethic emphasizing sacrificial heroism, as distinguished from essentially hedonistic needs, will further reinforce the primacy of the state; and this primacy will be portentous in its implications when coupled with a political culture (such as the East European ones, including Russian) whose tendency is to project menacing trends pessimistically into a future jeopardy to be forestalled in the present from still available strength.

Even before the nuclear age set in, great-power regimes had gone to war increasingly for essentially defensive (or preclusive) rather than unqualifiedly offensive (or predatory) reasons. They acted militarily not so much to aggrandize themselves further as to survive as great powers according to the standards of the age. The last purely acquisitive war, Prussia's mid-eighteenth-century conquest of Silesia, was initiated as a means of becoming a great power, whereas Austria's diplomatically aggressive counteraction was designed to recover the lost province in order to restore the empire's standing in the Euro-Germanic theater. Similarly motivated was France's self-assertion on the continent and globally, then and increasingly after 1815 and 1871. All parties to World War I acted for reasons they thought to be, and that largely were, defensive. In a state system that was itself aging, the fear, well-grounded or not, of irreversible decline could not but produce a deep insecurity in an increasing number of regimes, a condition that made an offensive enactment of an essentially defensive posture more or less compelling. For the British, the threat came from Germany; for the Germans, from Russia; whereas for Austria-Hungary and Russia, and increasingly also for France, fear was largely generated from within, from the prospect of instability in the short run or also organic decline in the long.

When pre-World War II conditions and perceptions are given due weight, even the aggressions of Hitler's Germany to a large extent fit the pre-emptive model, which finds a classic expression in the strategy of Tojo's Japan. Finally, actions calculated to keep open the path to world power by shutting out unacknowledged competitors, decried as unprovoked aggressors, can be considered defensive. In this category belongs US participation in the two world wars. It differs from earlier American wars waged for territorial aggrandizement within an essentially secure milieu under the banner of manifest destiny.

Notably on the part of the non-American polities, the political conditions of individual well-being and the material conditions of individual livelihood related only secondarily to the dominant statist value of corporate autonomy. They were of moment just enough to sustain the sociopolitical order against debilitating stress. Contemporary regimes may be said to remain all the more sensitive to status issues, the less they enjoy assured stability and security of tenure, while the state-centered ideal continues to predominate among the governed so long as the polity has not achieved the condition of material satiety. If true, even an ostensibly 'materialistic' ideology such as the Marxist-Leninist and a scientific–technological bias such as that of the Soviet regime and political culture do not significantly alter matters. Neither feature abolishes the greater-Russian-than-American propensity to respond forcefully to major threats defined by nonutilitarian criteria. Such threats include hostile denial of a still unrealized claim to national self-fulfillment conditioned by the geography and history of 'holy Russia'. The nuclear context has not altered the crucial equations any more than can or will any foreseeable implementation of strategic defense in space. In fact, the latter may restore them to fuller applicability.

Strategic (and Political) Stability and Strategic Defense

Exploring the policy implications of strategic defense requires distinguishing two stages of the scientific–technological progression: the condition of having arrived at a certain plateau and the process of getting there. In both stages, one must consider how far, if at all, one superpower is ahead of the other.

An actual defensive system is likely to extend in the foreseeable future only to the protection of strike forces, constituting terminal or point defense. Such a system, if in place on both sides about equally, could be said to maintain or even increase relative stability contingent on the uncertainty of the immediate consequences of a military engagement. However, such an assessment of deterrence will largely depend on ignoring impulsions from geopolitically focused competitive dynamics and its political–cultural context. When there is a sufficiently strong inducement, a first strike against the offensive or defensive capability of the adversary becomes more attractive than before: while the first strike partially cripples the retaliatory response (makes it 'ragged'), even a limited defense of the initiating side can be expected further to blunt the counterstrike. Stability is preserved only to the extent that the side that has been struck retains 'objectively' the capability and 'credibly' the will to intensify the exchange, on pain of setting off further rounds of retaliatory escalation. Such a retributory reaction becomes less likely the more one assumes that it would be the party initiating the first strike that was under greater pressure to defend itself offensively and was, therefore, more prepared to incur major damage and run ultimate risks. Under the same hypothesis the side receiving the first strike has less to gain from escalation because it faces the loss of no more than its prior geopolitical advantage. It can look forward to remaining or soon again becoming competitive in both the organic and the operational dimensions of 'national power'.

More effective defenses aimed at the boost and mid-course phase of enemy missiles are significant in the near future mainly as remotely possible developments. They are all the more threatening to stability if one side is lagging technologically and the technology can be used offensively against command-control–communications facilities. Given the high probability that in an uneven race for improved strategic defense the lagging side would be the Soviet Union, the situation risks enhancing any existing incentives for the Russians to act pre-emptively before the race was over. Should it by contrast be the Soviets who win a headstart in the higher-level defense capability, the incentive to use their advantage before it disappeared would be stronger than any comparable stimulus on the part of a similarly positioned United States. Since a Soviet headstart is apt to be both precarious and provisional, the likelihood highlights the risks implicit in any arms race when one party expends great effort to match or outstrip a resource-richer adversary only to see the nonrepeatable advantage fade and turn into its opposite unless it is used for a less reversible effect.

Thus, unless one is prepared to hypothesize a situation wherein the balance of both resource-related and geopolitical factors moves clearly from the US to the Soviet side, the Soviets will continue to be the party more strongly motivated to initiate a nuclear exchange. The seemingly optimal state – both sides having a foolproof bubble-like strategic defense over their populations – would only place the United States at a psychopolitical (next to military) disadvantage for a different reason, on the assumption that such a defense would restore the primacy of conventional military force.

Any deterioration in the Soviets' already adverse geopolitical situation would only fuel their urge to act. Since the United States is a saturated conservative power, it cannot be indifferent to the probability that the existence of limited, and the prospect of more advanced, US defenses would make a Soviet first strike more likely. Would the same military–strategic condition enhance US options for offensive (or counteroffensive) self-assertion in the world arena?

In principle, a US effort to exploit strategic defenses politically for a 'rollback' would merely increase the pressures on the Soviets to be more aggressive or subversive abroad and to repress or mobilize more intensely at home and regionally. In practice, an offensive US self-assertion on a significant scale would be 'rational' only if keyed to major strategic goals worthy of the attendant risks. Among such goals would be the elimination of Soviet dominance in Eastern Europe, using local disaffection from behind the shield of strategic defense. It is most unlikely that the mere possession of a capability would or could be used to push back the Soviets in peacetime. In a more likely contingency, deterrence would have broken down at least partially into a protracted conventional-military conflict. A serious threat to Soviet regional hegemony extending to the Russian homeland would then tend to elicit a matching assault on the territorial United States, a substantial escalation apt to either overcome less-than-perfect defenses of military installations or bypass them via countervalue strikes.

Comparable, if less drastic, scenarios can be envisaged with respect to other focal areas, such as those abutting on the Persian Gulf.

The hypothetical scenarios point to the real danger latent in partial defenses, even if these are on balance favorable to the United States. They could tempt the leader of the West into theater strategies that promised spectacular results, while being inherently unpredictable as to their military and political effects locally as well as globally on foe and friend alike.

At issue is fundamentally the relation of strategic defenses to offensive political or politico-military behavior at the peripheries of either of the superpowers or the global system itself. It can be (and has been) argued that both of the superpowers seek an advantage in defense sufficient to neutralize the adversary's nuclear capability. The difference begins when the aggressive–expansionist Soviets are said to equate stability with possessing the advantage as a shield not so much against a hypothesized US first strike (as they would claim) but for releasing superior instruments and techniques of lower-level violence for safe employment on behalf of an offensive self-assertion at their and the system's periphery. In the same interpretation the United States as a status quo power needed the advantage for retaining the ability to stage defensive political or nonnuclear military action abroad. Leaving aside the ambiguity of the distinction between offense and defense, the argument points to a glaring asymmetry between routinely limited geopolitical goals to be achieved incrementally and an imminent possession of qualitively upgraded military–strategic means. The question remains: Would achievable defenses in themselves impart a sufficient advantage to either side to alter substantially the cost–benefit calculations in regard to moderate, at best, gains in mostly inessential areas or on marginal issues? Would they sufficiently raise the nuclear threshold? Or would the peripheral issues continue to be approached and decided on the basis of locally available conventional capabilities and, if in terms of a balance, then one weighing the relative importance of competing national interests and the relative strengths of supporting communal will rather than high-technology military instruments?

Geohistorical Constraints and Extended Deterrence

Hypothetical scenarios will unavoidably proliferate so long as the US (or Soviet) security community is primarily interested in short-term perspectives on tactical or technical military settings of policy and continues to defy the theoretically conceded disutility of nuclear weapons for achieving results offensively. The presumption against usability is unlikely to be significantly altered by presently conceivable technological innovations. Moreover, to repeat, any conclusions or inferences drawn from purely military scenarios about the utility of this or that kind of defense will be flawed so long as they rest on assumptions about Soviet geopolitical objectives and behavior that, bemused by the imputation of a world-conquering goal, ignore the more real fundamental issue of survival in great-power role and status.

As terror oozes out of the deterrent balance via counterforce and defense capabilities, the weight of geopolitical (including geographically conditioned historical, or geohistorical) factors necessarily increases. And as the latest American defense initiative injects high drama into the US–Soviet discourse, the time span within which controversial issues and the relationship itself can be constructively addressed grows shorter.

An enhanced capacity to defend retaliatory facilities may well give the United States a diplomatic advantage over Soviet Russia. However, it risks inverting the larger psycho- and geopolitical equations to the United States' detriment. So long as Russia is exposed to confinement between the United States (and Western Europe) and China (and Japan), and especially if the encirclement shows signs of tightening and the comparative development ratios worsen (for example, by virtue of US-aided industrial buildup of China), the incentives will grow for the Soviets to arrest the adverse drift before it is too late. Moreover, just as the Soviets might acquire the stronger incentive to act pre-emptively by virtue of negative trends, they are likely to retain the greater positive capacity to absorb damage to population and other material assets owing to their communal culture and political system. A political culture that absorbed the loss of twenty million in World War II and was, if anything, morally invigorated by the bloodletting, is on the face of it psychologically fit to face up to a nuclear exchange. It may be better equipped for the ordeal than a society that has been spared any comparable testing throughout its existence, that recently lost its nerve under the stress of casualties in the tens of thousands, and that tends to be traumatized by terror- and accident-induced casualties in the hundreds or less.

By the same token, the temptation for the Soviets to act 'while there is still time' becomes an imperative once their options begin to narrow in relation to a neighbor (China), which, more hostile than is the United States and gaining in the capacity to inflict matching damage, exhibits a political and communal culture even more capable of absorbing human and material devastation than Soviet Russia. Tolerance for the loss of life increases along the West-to-East culture spectrum, while impediments to civil-defense preparations decrease. In such a setting anything that might set off a controlled nuclear exchange, only to risk degenerating into an uncontrolled one, constitutes an unevenly weighted deterrent working against the United States in the short run and against Russia in the long. It adds to the hypothetical cost of space-based defenses.

Less hypothetical are the political costs of enhancing US defenses insofar as the attendant dangers would need to be forestalled by appeasing the Soviets politically. To achieve the necessary calming effect in time to avert an impending crisis, the geopolitical setting would have to be reshaped both abruptly and drastically. In the likely absence of compensating Soviet adjustments, the entailed diplomatic revolution would affect adversely US alliances at the center as much as US containment policies at the periphery of the global system. Conversely, in the absence of one-sided 'appeasement', instead of staging a technological 'breakout' via an unmatched SDI equivalent of their own, the Soviets might more plausibly try to break out of the ring of geopolitical encirclement. They could do so in either direction: through China, possibly by way of a surgical or wider strike using Moscow's nuclear advantage while it lasts; or through Western Europe, most probably by means of a limited conventional thrust dramatizing the Soviet perception of the developing configuration as lastingly intolerable.

Short of such an extremity, the development of strategic defenses by the United States will still have a profound effect on its alliances and, equally important, on Soviet conduct with respect to those alliances. As the United States develops a more independent capacity to protect its own territory, its stake in extending deterrence to allies will decline even if its ability remains intact or grows — and it will be perceived as declining by ally and enemy alike. So long as Western Europe is less effectively defended than the territorial United States — a situation unlikely ever to change despite parallel defenses against shorter-range

Euromissiles – the Soviets will aim pressure or action in the direction of their nearer neighbors. Should such action take a military form, an effectively defended United States would be perceived as being able to defer a climactic confrontation with the Soviets indefinitely while buttressing further its extra-European alliances.

The temptation to sidestep irreversible decisions grows with the ability to defer them. This cliché cannot but impress, and its implications discourage, America's Western allies if US defenses grow faster than those of both the Soviets and themselves. Intra-alliance stress would only intensify if a raised nuclear threshold (due to inter-superpower defenses and/or nuclear force reductions) increased emphasis on conventional-military buildup and related expenditures. Unlike the United States, the politically weak West European governments and their strongly economics-minded publics would rather live dangerously under the shelter of mutual assured destruction (MAD) than slowly atrophy from the strains and costs of adequate conventional or any other defense. Increasing the role of air-breathing delivery systems, such as bomber-carried cruise missiles, in conditions of antiballistic missile defense would not fundamentally alter the intra-alliance equation. The long travel time of such weapons, which makes them susceptible to recall, multiplies occasions for exerting psychological pressure on US allies, which will be responsive to popular anxieties because they have representative governments and which will be free to respond because they are members of a noncoercive multimember alliance. This dual susceptibility augments the Western handicap in relations with an adversary not only comparatively immune to similar pressures but capable of manipulating the scope of military initiatives and the presentation of political intentions in ways calculated to sharpen dissent from radical deterrence or defense on the part of the more vulnerable side.

If extended deterrence is subject to weakening in relation to Western Europe, it is apt to fade in relation to China even before taking on a clear shape. To compensate, a partially and preferentially defended United States might soon see itself compelled to reassure a volatile eastern protégé as much or more than the more solid Western partners. The compensations might be no less military–strategically irrational for being seemingly reasonable (because necessary) politically. The most ironic consequence of upgrading China's military resources and militarily relevant industrial–technological potential might then surface only gradually. Whereas strategic defenses have been initiated against Russia, their development might be eventually vindicated against the furthermost Eastern power, positioned as the next challenger in the process.

Arms Control and Controlled Competition

It is conceivable that the danger of an uncontrolled competition over strategic defense could lead the superpowers to coordinate its development within the framework of a fresh approach to arms control. However, concerted progress in a militarily critical technology seems impossible without prior or at least concurrent movement toward political accommodation. The military–strategic competition, despite its superficially autonomous dynamics, remains a mere reflection and symptom of relations in the geopolitical base. This does not mean that pressures emanating from a dramatically new phase in the military–strategic sphere cannot extend into the geopolitical theater and create there new incentives and possibilities as well as accentuate existing perils. Any Soviet gains that would result from continuing to extend a previously conceded military–strategic parity incrementally into the geopolitical sphere would be marginal when compared with the adjustments that might be necessary to neutralize the explosive effects of disparate developments in strategic defenses. Moreover, barring a growing disparity of that kind, actual self-restraint would be apt to grow as the Soviets developed a stake in the consensually revised order, resting on a henceforth legitimized access to areas and transactions critical for the dispersion of material and military capabilities among lesser regional powers within an evolving international system.

Mutual confidence-building behavior in the sphere that counts most in the final analysis, that of geopolitical competition, would inevitably extend to arms control. The latter's principles and provisions could begin to de-emphasize quantitative levels of current weapons allocations and deployments. Instead, they would address primarily the middle- to long-term intentions of the superpowers in regard to research and development initiatives planned in support of their specific security strategies. Such long-term planning is inseparable from the aims pursued in the geopolitical arena. Consequently, a halfway serious attempt to coordinate weapons developments would not only reflect the degree of current consensus but also generate supplemental inducements to concert political policies. It might accelerate the convergence of more fundamental foreign-policy postures to culminate in the sharing of potentially disruptive scientific and technological innovations as they took shape and before they irreparably unbalanced political relationships.

Just as isolating the evolving military instruments from the larger context in the stage of preliminary planning may create new dangers, so conjugating arms development with corrective policy dynamics can open up new opportunities. Optimum defense technologies can mature only in the remote future. But they might still be focused upon now because intermediate improvements would not be sufficient to warrant diverting resources and attention from the eventual optimum. By the same reasoning, political strategies might usefully be keyed to the long-term best in US–Soviet relations, in preference to problematically enhancing questionably vital American interests at the cost of making the relations more antagonistic than they are, or need be, when judged by the standard of uncontestably valid stakes.

However far in the future the positive or negative outcomes might mature, the basic decisions are apt to be taken in the remainder of the present century and some at least in the present decade. The contingency to avoid most – by creating the impression of it being the unchanging US objective – is demotion of the Soviet adversary that compounds the risks from tactical rollback and strategic encirclement. Although the costs to the United States might be greatly deferred, they could still be more than materially devastating. The moral burden is greatest on a polity that has had the less immediate or compelling reason to set the stage for the military resolution of a conflict, should it come to pass for reasons not wholly free of its prior responsibility. In such a perspective, it would be reckless to proceed with the planning and development of defense technologies that (1) do not guarantee a substantial net increase of defense over defense-suppressant or offensive capabilities, and (2) are conceived and deployed in isolation from the largest possible psychopolitical context, one made up of divergencies in geopolitical situations and both communal and political cultures.

US preference is for technological and organizational shortcuts to the solution of political problems rooted in ambiguities spanning space and time, geography and history. The impatience has been saved so far from spawning a major catastrophe, let alone a terminal one. In fostering this immunity, the US margin for errors has exceeded the measure of foresight and the quality of design mobilized on America's behalf. It may be that if the latest of Pandora's boxes is opened recklessly too wide, it will disclose a hidden mechanism for evil stronger than the good fortune of history's most favored people. It would then not suffice that it was one of the luckiest political leaders ever who first set the challenge to Fortuna in motion.

Restatements and Elaborations

Basic to the US–Soviet relationship is the projection of each party's fears and ambitions onto the other, resulting in the mutual attribution of aggressive intent. In the Marxist view, 'internal contradictions' in capitalism make the West 'objectively' the aggressor. They will eventually induce – if not force – the leading Western power to strike out first to improve its ability to survive among the competing and less militarily burdened capitalist economies. The propensity of the American ethos to emphasize (material) damage-limitation in choosing between alternative strategies would not, in such a doctrinaire view, withstand compulsions from the military-technological advantage vanishing amidst accelerating fiscal or widening economic stress. However, ideological self-exculpation to the contrary notwithstanding, the Soviets, too, face conditions that make them susceptible to a first strike should threats from East or West undermine the chief basis for the regime's claim to internal legitimacy: Russia's position as world power. If the Western powers increasingly define survival primarily in quantitatively assessed human and material terms, the Soviet embodiment of Russia as a nation built around the state looks first and foremost to the qualitative factor of role and status. Yet again, despite differences in basic mindsets, either superpower could be impelled toward the abyss of war by a valid kind of strategic rationality, one that meets the test of minimizing loss rather than maximizing gains. The resulting calculations may well prevail under sufficient stress over the contrary counsels of a prudence construed as nothing more profound than risk-avoiding caution.

In terms of historical analogies, a Soviet pre-emptive strike – and the political culture motivating it – would replicate Japan's offensively defensive response at Pearl Harbor to the prospect of an unmatchable US naval buildup (combined with geopolitical and economic denial).

Future US behavior could be tentatively inferred on the same principle from the importance of economic incentives behind America's entry into World War I and World War II (interest in recovering Allied debts in the first conflict and in frustrating the German bid for succession to Britain's imperial assets and advantages in both). More pertinent is the analogy with the pre-World War I Anglo-German naval competition. Like the British dreadnoughts, defense in space raises military technology to a qualitatively higher new level, restarting the arms race, as it were, from zero and reducing the value of the previous generation of weapons. One perceived result is to elevate the two main competitors categorically over other parties, just as the Anglo-German naval race overshadowed the resources as well as the stakes involved in the receding Anglo-French and Anglo-Russian naval competitions. Another consequence, more galling for the Soviet Union than it was for Germany, lies in reopening the issue of military–strategic parity.

For the Russians, as for the Germans earlier, the purpose of achieving (or closely approximating) such parity was to advance, by one stroke, a twin goal: to deter the established rival for the sake of military self-protection and to exert pressure on it as part of an expansive design aimed also at geopolitical parity. The similarities may be potent enough to outweigh a difference. Rapid technological change endangers the effort to attain and maintain parity most for an Eastern power. Such a power tends to favor size and scale over versatility in weapons, more germane to the Western polity: to wit, specifically, Soviet missiles with superior throw-weight capacity, as against the US triad stressing seaborne and air-breathing deterrents. Thus also, before losing out to Rome, the eastern Mediterranean Hellenistic powers had futilely enlarged the Greek military instruments (four- to five-deck ships in lieu of smaller and more mobile three-deck ships, just as war elephants were used in lieu of only human phalanxes), while overly large and immobile Ottoman siege guns proved no match for the Western powers' mobile field artillery. Soviet gigantism in weaponry, too, would in the end prove much less effectual within an environment dominated by antimissile strategic defenses.

Meanwhile, the US–Soviet conflict parallels the Anglo-German pattern most alarmingly by stimulating fears and encouraging mutual suspicions of surprise attack. Yet the real surprise might eventually come, for better or worse, from the high-technology nuclear weapons that generate so much concern on both sides playing as small a role in actual combat as the dreadnoughts did in World War I. The impracticality of actually using the 'ultimate' weapon would then result in a shift to lower-grade weapons, such as directed conventional munitions, performing the substitute role of torpedo boats and light cruisers then.

Should strategic defense play a key role in decreasing the importance of nuclear weapons in favor of conventional forces, US–West European relations might face even greater political strains as more of the burden of matching Soviet conventional strength fell on the European allies. The cohesion of the Atlantic coalition, like that of any hegemonial alliance, requires that the protection provided by the leading ally exceed the ally's provocation of the enemy. The level of US protection of Western Europe might well decline if strategic defenses shielded mainly US territory while they reduced Washington's incentives to run the ultimate risk for Europe's defense. As for provocation, it might, in unbalanced conditions of defense, emanate not only from the US side directly but from related developments on the German side of Russia's two-front situation that makes Russia (and its clients) vulnerable to territorial revision. Even if the Soviets responded with nothing more serious than their own version of strategic defenses, it would substantially undermine the French and British nuclear deterrent forces, further aggravating the no-win situation for NATO's European members. Just as European military security and diplomatic status risked being substantially degraded in a peace that has been made more precarious, so the potential for physical survival would not be enhanced in a war that has become more likely. In these conditions, the Strategic Defense Initiative might well point less to a pot of gold at the end of the envisioned rainbow than to the end of the alliance itself.

On the extended East–West spectrum, China has begun to be for Russia in this century, and will be increasingly in the next century, what the Russian Empire was in the nineteenth for the Germans and Persia had been for the Ottoman Empire still earlier. When the more centrally located polity confronts the day's principal Western power, it typically interacts strategically with the Western party not least as an occasion and impetus for imitating innovative technologies. These are equally or more useful or necessary for dealing with the comparatively backward, but more directly threatening and instinctively feared, power still farther to the east. In the present setting, just as deploying intermediate-range missiles has been more important for the Soviets' undermanned Asian theater than the European theater, so current and future Soviet antiballistic missile defenses are likely to have a similar bias.

How explosive the eastward bias will be, and how intense the pre-emptively defensive Soviet urge in the western direction, will depend on the prospect for a cooperative transition to a defense-reliant world between the superpowers, attended by political accommodation. Just as any trade-off between US and Soviet assets and liabilities in various regions of the globe is impossible on a one-to-one basis outside an overarching global bargain, so arms control transactions can be neither individually satisfying nor cumulatively productive so long as they merely trade individual weapons or weapons systems against one another. The 'trade' must be the most comprehensive one possible if it is to link present capabilities to compatible concepts of the future.

Near-utopian correctives to competitive power politics become possible only when they are no longer necessary to forestall serious conflict. This truism was progressively revealed as a truth in connection with the League of Nations type of a collective security system. It applies equally to apolitical approaches to conflict and security, characteristic of single-minded arms control efforts. They threaten to elevate a mere procedure that is not even an ongoing process to the status of panacea, while in fact harboring a dangerous illusion insofar as the ostensibly neutral technique fails to relate military capabilities consciously to political intentions.

The issue becomes acute whenever efforts at arms control escalate to schemes for substantial reduction, nearing elimination, of strategic nuclear weapons centered on intercontinental ballistic missiles. In contrast to an incrementally evolving politico-military concert attended by weapons coordination, such a leap of faith into the unknown sidesteps the resulting imponderables for strategic stability – unless, of course, the military–strategic and military-technological turning point is recognized as entailing repercussions in the geo-political arena sufficiently far-reaching to actualize its symbolic significance. In the absence of wide-ranging political accommodation, the issue of possible bad faith and deception on one side or the other cannot but inhibit the implementation of a reduction-to-elimination design that equals totally effective strategic defense in transferring prime dependence from nuclear weapons to conventional military weaponry. Related concerns will almost certainly frustrate the benign expectations from curtailing strategic offense, as will the threatening asymmetry with regard to third parties that are likely to resist a self-denial matching the one bilaterally and (in third-party eyes) collusively agreed upon by the dominant superpowers. Even a partial failure to conform on all sides would require extending the degree of superpower accommodation sufficient to defuse their competition to a virtual co-management of the worldwide military–strategic chess-board. In brief, a thoroughgoing US–Soviet 'deal' on strategic defense and offense, to be militarily safe and politically stable, entails a multifaceted global bargain with selectively condominial overtones of truly revolutionary proportions.

In making a judgment whether the bargain is feasible and desirable, the first step is to grasp the nature of the US–Soviet conflict. Just as the United States does not behave as it does because it is, in Soviet parlance, imperialist, but rather because it is insular, so the Soviet Union is better understood as continental than as communist. It follows that the United States is not inherently aggressive, but acts expansively when it seeks to preserve the advantages of its position first across geopolitical space and now in outer space. The Soviet response aims to approximate and ultimately match the defensive advantage of the insular counterpart by all possible means. But whereas the insular power by nature employs the more discreet political–economic instruments of persuasion, the less favored continental power has to rely on more direct and dramatic politico-military means. Its appearing all the more assertive and expansionist as a result accounts in large part for the temptation to rationalize the need for hypothetically feasible defense by the fact of unchanging Soviet aggression. The imputation feeds readily into the Soviet suspicion that the initiative is but the latest medium for realizing an unalterable plan for undermining the peaceable Soviet state.

Similarly, in an earlier era, the Soviets branded NATO as an instrument for Western aggression impelled by resurgent German revanchism, when, in fact, the more plausible threat lay in NATO's politically offensive purposes aimed at the structural weaknesses of the Soviet bloc. By the same token, US proponents of SDI may rationalize the need for something like it (as, before, for NATO) by the need to prevent the Soviets from using an actual or asserted advantage in intercontinental ballistic missiles (as, before, in armored divisions and massed infantry) to possess themselves militarily or only politically of Western Europe and, now, also of much of the Third World. In reality, NATO was in all probability no more necessary to prevent a Soviet invasion of Western Europe than space-based defenses are likely to be required for precluding cumulative Soviet gains either at the Third World margins or the West European center of the international system. What NATO did accomplish – and it was not negligible at the time – was to impede a precipitate all-out 'Finlandization' of a war-shocked Western Europe, and to do this at a bearable cost in terms of intensifying the emergent conflict. SDI's object of forestalling a Soviet grab at geopolitical parity or more is likely to be fraught with greater risks for a lesser reason.

Productive Accommodation or Preventive War?

Why, it might be asked, and to what end pursue geopolitical parity? The simplest answer to that question is another query: Why else attain and for what other end seek military–strategic parity, a condition the United States previously conceded to the Soviets? Beyond that, geopolitical parity (combining increased Soviet presence in Europe with no more drastically decreased US pre-eminence worldwide) is both an alternative and a possible intermediate stage: an alternative to a contentiously prosecuted balance of quantitatively defined power, continuously raising the issue of one party's predominance so marked as to constitute hegemony; and a stage on the road to inter-superpower partnership, one that helps resolve the dialectic of defense and offense in the technological and strategic–military dimension and disposes of the offense–defense ambiguity in politically critical perceptions, while the parties embark on an evolutionary process pointing toward cooperation and convergence.

For evolutionary convergence to speed up and deepen has meant continuing to replace monocentric Stalinist totalitarianism with a political system that embraces functionally plural technocratic features in response to external opportunities and challenges that neither can nor need be managed militarily. The United States for its part would have to evolve toward modes of formulating and implementing foreign policy that impose longer-term and wider-ranging perspectives on the anarchy of individual and group biases. In that they make a society more flagrantly freewheeling in style than free in substance, the biases inevitably distort the manner of implementing the notion of the national interest. By playing upon the indeterminate content of the 'national' and maximizing the particularistic connotation of 'interest', they deform the thrust of the superficially similar but intrinsically contrasting norm of the 'Reason of State'.

As the key by-product if not principal goal of convergence, a mutually acceptable evolution of the international system cannot have as its goal a world order based only on American-type values. A more plausible goal is an environment that is congenial to the continued validity of the more inclusive – and essentially Europeanist – diplomatic culture shared by the two superpowers and supportive of their prolonged viability as major actors among emerging ones.

Within an evolving system, the offense–defense dialectic compounds the interplay between primarily land- and sea-based powers, each offensively defensive in its own fashion. Any provisional resolution of the offense–defense dialectic in the military–strategic sphere will take the form of an institutionalized mix of defensive and offensive technologies and strategic applications, conducive to the moderation of militarily achievable goals. The analogous opposition of insular and continental powers will be periodically dissolved into a multiplicity of more symmetric land- and sea-oriented – that is, amphibious – powers, a process already initiated in the transition from the sharp Anglo-German to the more qualified US–Soviet dichotomy. Thus the Greek and the Italian city-state systems, organized around the land–sea power cleavage, yielded in time to the Hellenistic and the early European pan-Mediterranean systems, composed of unevenly amphibious larger powers. Currently, the transition to a new offense–defense mix in military technology and strategy is already entangled with the initial stirrings of the other transition: from US–Soviet maritime–continental asymmetry, one that has carried the European antecedents forward into the era of continent-wide powers, to a more polycentric world of major amphibious powers.

The development entails some demotion of the Big Two to the profit of not only China but also other aspirants to expanded regional roles. For the superpowers to monitor and channel the diffusion of functionally diversified power into a pattern viable for both is, meanwhile, the alternative to the center of gravity in an updated as well as inverted land–sea power spectrum moving away from both. If Japan replacing the United States as the key insular power, and China supplanting Russia as the key continental power, is the scenario that comes first and easiest to mind in that connection, it is not the only possible one over time.

Replacing the land–sea power schism with a polycentric configuration of amphibious powers does not bring a guarantee of eternal peace. Nor would cosmic bliss result from transcending the continental–maritime disparity through outer space, a more fundamental modifier of the traditional cleavage than was air power beginning with World War I and transcontinental missiles since World War II. Least promise resides in outer space becoming the locus of permanent defensive or offensive military installations, conceived and emplaced competitively. For the two superpowers cooperatively to manage the dispersion of power on earth and jointly develop new resources in outer space has the more positive potential. More realistic, it is also a more inspiring goal than is one of merely denuclearizing an unresolved conflict. Space-based defense, notably when advocated in the millenarian version, bound to arouse apocalyptic visions on the Soviet side, injects an unnecessary irritant into an unavoidably precarious and protracted process of evolution. If the politics of such evolution are to contain the side effects of a multistage military-technological revolution, they must be nursed with the patience genuine conservatism owes to all organic change – not least when it involves bodies politic with constitutions that, markedly disparate in outward forms, are equally a historically validated outgrowth of distinctive conditions and situations.

The constituents and the promise of a strategy that promotes processes of change that heal old wounds, rather than opening new ones, must first assume a discernible shape on earth. Only then can any incidental benefits and the consummating reinforcements become manifest in outer space. There is nothing wrong with gradually developing a new defensive–offensive mix in both inner and outer space. On the contrary, such a development can be desirable if it promotes stability by enhancing the uncertainty of military outcomes, not least in regard to a first strike and a whole range of third parties that are harder to deter and penalize than either of the contemporary superpowers because they are hardier in either cultural or material makeups. The wrong sets in when military deterrence is outmatched by psychopolitical 'impellence': when one side is swayed toward running a more than hypothetical risk of annihilation in order to preclude a not necessarily greater possibility that the other side is alone about to achieve the capacity for strategic compellence, by virtue of developing complete invulnerability against the key weapon on which deterrence rests. The asymmetry deepens when the challenge offered dramatically in the skies combines with a policy designed to perpetuate also the geopolitical inferiority of an ambitious rival: when, that is, the objective is to make a fiat from the heavens consolidate the rewards of meritorious works performed on earth.

The problem of sin assumes a secular face in world politics when the quest for an abnormal measure of protection by one party spells unbearable provocation for another, inviting desperate reaction. In the guise of a preventive war, such a reaction is inspired less by the expectation of success over the rival party than by the urge to avoid surrender to an irreversible process. More fundamentally than on the probabilities of the immediate outcome, the question of expediency rests then on the predictability of larger developments over a longer period of time. Can prediction be based on the projection of current trends? Is a present generation either obligated or entitled to run the risks of violent death to ensure bearable living for the next? As political expediency becomes indistinguishable from moral validity, the arrogance of the party that strikes out consists of acting to prevent a future it cannot know. The yet greater conceit is of the side that, failing to ask itself similarly pertinent questions before creating the situation calling for the fatal choice, has presumed to take upon itself the very shape of fate.

4

From Restraint to Rollback?

A policy of active US support of forces challenging pro-Soviet or Soviet-supported regimes around the world has been the Reagan administration's addition to the long list of ephemeral presidential doctrines since Truman's, although one more ambitious and potentially detrimental to US–Soviet relations than most. The policy can be usefully examined in the light of enduring principles and past manifestations of the underlying impulse. Insofar as it was a dynamic version of traditional containment, it recalls John Foster Dulles's strategy of rollback-cum-liberation. Only this time the net was cast out wider: the theater is no longer limited to Eastern Europe but encompasses the Third World at large. The means, too, have been enlarged from propaganda only in the 1950s, to rhetoric backed by military assistance and 'humanitarian aid' in the 1980s. At the same time the ambition has dwindled: regaining Angola for a democracy it never knew does not rate liberating Poland from a communism it would gladly forget.

Neither is Central America worth East-Central Europe, when the criterion is the balance of world power and the impulse is more than parochial preoccupation with one's backyard. With attention focused on Central America, we are back in the strategic universe of the Monroe Doctrine. Although US power has grown well beyond dependence on Britain's Royal Navy for implementing it, a diminution is again in evidence: the globally imperial America, which fought Hanoi's regional imperialism in Southeast Asia, has shrunk to something resembling the regionally imperialistic United States of the nineteenth and early twentieth centuries.

The analogy of Vietnam has been invoked by both the opponents of the policy and its supporters. The former would see the Central American policy as fraught with the threat of escalating military involvement, the latter hail it as insurance against a deepening loss of political credibility. Both are incorrect. The comparison to Vietnam is not valid in terms either of the military risks or the geopolitical stakes. A military intervention in Nicaragua would be not another Vietnam scaled down but another Grenada scaled up. In the political and diplomatic equations, little Cuba is playing in the regional setting the global role of China as the third corner of a triangle.

There is a price to pay for reducing the ambition and the burden. Miniaturizing the volume of armed power deployed in Vietnam also meant demeaning what in concept and purpose had been (in President Reagan's defendable characterization) a 'noble' effort to repel regional aggression, and engaging instead in an attempt to subvert a local revolution. To bring the message home to an unfriendly Soviet client (Nicaragua) in America's traditional sphere of interest, the United States stooped to the methods of the pilloried rival after using disproportionate force on a threadbare pretext elsewhere in the region (Grenada). As the administration dug in and sought to show vigor, limited military demonstrations were supposed to fuel a worldwide 'democratic revolution'. In actuality, no attainable ends to the application of force were to be discerned in certain instances (Lebanon); in others (Libya) the stated objectives were so wide-ranging and varied as to preclude demonstrable failure.

Principles and Propensities

All major powers intervene at one time or another in their spheres of influence against disturbing developments or alien encroachments. Dating from time immemorial, this is practically an inalienable right. Such actions are routinely clothed in pious rationalizations that do not usually succeed in obfuscating the real reasons behind the intervention. The US incursions in Grenada and Nicaragua and the Soviet invasion of Afghanistan are similarly transparent in intent. Yet the question remains: Was the mode and the scope of the great-power action commensurate with the provocation implicit in the disturbance? The judgment rendered on this score will determine whether an intervention will eventually come to be accepted as an unavoidable – if perhaps regrettable – act, a natural phenomenon of the political world that, up to a point, is a requisite of minimum world order.

Unfortunately, the principle of proportionality is as flexible as the perception of local provocation is subjective. The right of the regional core power to intervene must be reconciled with its duty to show restraint. The balancing act between innate right, ready power, and self-imposed restraint is normally difficult enough; it becomes even more problematic when an extra-regional power is involved. Obviously, the threat to the regionally dominant power is real only when another major power fosters the local disturbance or exploits its consequences. It is nearly as self-evident that such outside interference is least legitimate if the affected regional power has itself kept out of the sphere of the extra-regional actor. And it follows that the right to intervene against a smaller nation located in the core power's sphere of influence is most indisputable when the aim is to remove the occasion for an unprovoked interference by the adversary. Such interference is unprovoked when it does not retaliate for a comparable, prior or simultaneous, action by (regional) power A in the sphere of (extra-regional) power B that can be construed as provocation. When interference is reciprocal, A's right to intervene in its sphere is not nullified, to be sure. But the right and the rationale for exercising it are weakened by B's entitlement to countervail in A's sphere.

Dilemmas attending the most sincere attempts to balance rights and obligations will be sharpened by the attempt being caught up in the age-old dichotomy between maritime and continental powers. Land-bound powers invariably seek direct access to the seas in pursuit of material prosperity, military security, or political equality. The navally and economically dominant offshore insular (or quasi-insular coastal) power will oppose this effort in the interest of preserving a monopoly of access to the sea-lanes and an uninhibited approach to the land masses. In these respects Soviet Russia is simply obeying the same impulse as the ancient Hittite and Persian empires, and the more recent German Reich; likewise the United States responds to the same forces that drove the Egypt and Athens of antiquity, along with the late British. The two kinds of powers have always found it difficult, when not impossible, to define the criteria of equilibrium. Such a parity would afford to each an equal measure of security, material sustenance, and status through unequal mixes of the strengths and liabilities deriving from the distinct environments they inhabit and try to master.

The problem is not eased by the fact that the United States and the Soviet Union are not only substantively different power types, being, respectively, insular and continental. They are also regional core powers and, in that abstract capacity, symmetrical. The result is a two-faceted setting that adds to the problem of parity the delicate question of reciprocity. Since parity bears ultimately on security, it is interference with the conditions of security that raises the issue of reciprocity most acutely. Prevailing degrees and modes of reciprocal interference (and noninterference) define the limits of minimum order in the international system; a related task for national strategies is to adjust the degrees and the modalities into a rough equilibrium through leveraged bargaining.

Thus the ancient practices sublimated as innate rights merge with a more or less orderly pursuit of equilibrium, itself operationalized by the ambiguous concept of parity. The difficulties of reconciling 'abstract' symmetry between the United States and the Soviet Union as regional core powers, with Russian bids for 'substantive' parity in conditions of land–sea power disparity, are so intractable that they invite evasion. Such evasion is apparent whenever the insular United States denies the Soviets equivalence, not only with regard to requirements of physical security but also in politically significant values.

Who threatens whom more by interfering in the other's security sphere depends on the ability to project military capability across maritime distances and continental land masses. The facility of such projection depends on how receptive lesser regional states are to being wooed by major powers from outside the region. Whereas the lesser states react to the different forms of control of insular–maritime or continental–military core powers, the degree of autonomy each of these is prudently able to concede depends on its sense of security. The technological ability to apply force over land and sea, together with the supporting economic system, makes the insular power more immune than vulnerable; the continental power, by contrast, because more often than not critically imperiled, becomes more directly coercive. Land-based military capabilities tend to elicit counterpoise from parties threatened by the continental or also incited by the insular power; their seagoing counterpart has the contrary tendency toward one-power superiority, verging on monopoly. That difference alone has throughout history provided near-absolute security for the insular–maritime power. Yet these insular states are often needlessly paranoid, regarding themselves as more physically threatened than psychopolitically threatening.

What was initially a historical experience soon becomes a feeling of entitlement providentially conferred, not to be matched or aspired to on the continent. The invention of air-borne military instruments altered but did not abolish traditional strategic equations and affected the more fundamental psychological ones much less, if at all (pending, perhaps, the conversion of outer space into a full-scale third dimension). The maritime power's pretension to total security renders it all the more sensitive to outside threats. Such threats symbolize a real or ultimate insecurity implicit in the fragile psychological basis of physical security once it has been equated with immunity and rooted materially in transient economic superiority – a superiority that is necessary if physical insulation is to be buttressed by wide-ranging political influence. So long as the moral–psychological aspect of vulnerability predominates, the controversies over parity and reciprocity surrounding the land–sea power cleavage will overshadow the latent threat to the economic dominance of the insular power from another ascending, provisionally allied, maritime–mercantile power. The fixation on the continental rival meanwhile distracts attention also from other and less clearly focused threats to the nation's integrity. It helps misapply, if not dissipate, resources required for anchoring domestic stability in sustained economic growth.

In the aftermath of the Anglo-German wars it was America's turn to assert the radically unequal worth of the values intrinsic to the American and Soviet Russian political systems. Yet taking the normative high road blinds the observer not only to the symmetries between the two imperial core states but also to the root causes of the discrepancies between their institutions and behavior: one entrenched and embattled, the other an enterprising and insulated polity, each subject to a different evolutionary rhythm and disposing of unequal potential to attract and compulsion to coerce. When this discrimination is unqualified by an understanding of the reasons for the differences, it will erect alongside the claim to total security the affirmation of absolute moral right to deny anything like it to the adversary, to the detriment of genuinely realistic policy.

Practices of Great and Small Powers

The foregoing general principles entitled (and related tendencies induced) the United States to invade Grenada. They have since given it the right to assist 'freedom fighters' in Nicaragua. However, just as being entitled is not the same as being well-advised, so affirming a right in principle does not rule out qualifying it in practice. The prior American interference in the Soviet sphere of control (Eastern Europe) or concern (Southwest Asia) could be considered as 'qualifying' in this sense. That interference gives the Soviets the incentive – and legitimates it as an imperative – to look for leverage that might serve to constrain such interference. Such points of leverage are to be found best in areas of US concern and presumed vulnerability. The result is tacit bargaining over the conditions of mutual restraint, possibly as a preliminary to effective or explicit understanding on that score.

America's involvement on the Eurasian continent amounts to an entrenchment with respect to Western Europe. It was bound to stimulate a Soviet urge to seek access overseas so as to equalize status and security and expand future options. The urge is no more to be found in the Soviet Union's ideologically Marxist-Leninist or organizationally totalitarian character than is America's opposition to be explained by its 'imperialist' or 'capitalist' political economy. But in the resulting contest only the American polity has disposed of economic assets and cultural attraction sufficient to avoid the need for military coercion in relations with dependents (or dependent elites) willing to trade an often unusable margin of autonomy for substantial material advantage (or security of regime tenure).

Within such a gravitational setting the dependent small country will obey the imperative of territorial statehood and assert its independence only in exceptional conditions, which temporarily extinguish the societal factors that account for the material or cultural attraction of the maritime core power. First among these exceptional conditions will be a revolutionary social upheaval. As the radically revised societal formula takes on a refurbished statist garb, the dependent polity will recoil from the near-regional to the remoter extra-regional great power in a dramatic reversal of alignments. While the outsider power will be expected to supply protective counterpoise in the nearer power's orbit, the smaller state will either be expected or will volunteer to reciprocate by acting there in the interest of the extra-regional protector. This hazardous division of labor pointedly demonstrates the protection–provocation duality that underlies so much of international conflict. Recoiling from the greater to the remoter power restores the affected small country to normal state behavior. More importantly, the defied insular core power's retaliatory response brings its procedural norms, if no other values, in line with behavior commonly attributed to the continental regional hegemon.

That the breakaway of a small country is exceptional in the orbit of a sea power is shown by the time lag between the original Cuban revolt and the subsequent Nicaraguan and Grenadan ones. But when the event does occur, the American response can be most revealing. The reaction of the United States diverged in this instance more from the ideal values and principles of the American political ethos than from the practices of the typical (including Russian) land power when dealing with the more frequent revolts in its sphere. The impression of similarity is increased when one considers the relatively wider latitude and array of tools available to the one power rather than the other for reversing defections or confining their impact. Any measure of convergence in behavior under stress points beyond routinely discrete procedures and regular instruments to the shared realities of raw power and basic political instincts. This hidden commonalty helps one to understand that the disparities in institutional strengths and flaws shaped by the different geohistorical situations of insular and continental states are potentially complementary. Once recognized as such, they might serve to offset the divergence in those fundamental values that aggravate conflict and prevent facing up to shared geostrategic dilemmas.

When the particular requirements of policy crowd out general principles in favor of generic predispositions, the dialectic of conciliation between conflicting rights and values narrows into the dynamics of contention over rival stakes. Innate tendencies are overlaid by flagrant attitudes, assumed to fit adopted strategies, once a specific issue of security has supplied the focus for diffuse anxiety and given rise to the problematic relationship between sufficient arms and unnecessary alarms. Thus, even if the Caribbean basin and Central America are strategically sensitive for the United States, it does not necessarily follow that they are acutely endangered by – or even vulnerable to – Soviet military–strategic designs. Nor is it imperative that the United States enjoy unqualified control over the areas in order to safeguard important American interests in peacetime (e.g., protection of oil supply routes and restraint of Soviet intelligence-gathering capacity) or, for that matter, in wartime (e.g., deployment of nuclear weapons, shipment of manpower and materiel to the

European theater, security of the Panama Canal link to the Asian theater).

Caveats from Past and Present

Here several caveats must be introduced. The first concerns US strategic theory and practice, aimed at upgrading maritime (offshore insular) in relation to continental (NATO-centered) strategy. Vertical escalation dominance along the ladder of increasingly lethal weaponry is to be supplemented by upgrading horizontal escalation, along the crisis arc of dispersed Soviet geopolitical positions. Before strategic defenses in space, vertical escalation dominance was pursued by installing the Pershing II missiles in Western Europe in retaliation for the Soviet SS-20s. However, the more directly vulnerable the Soviet (and protected the US) homeland is, the greater is the impetus for the Soviets to acquire access and assets in overseas areas, not least those adjoining North America. The parallel attempts under the Reagan Doctrine to roll back Soviet positions in the periphery have been an experiment in horizontal escalation, in delayed retribution for Soviet gains in the Third World during the 1970s. Yet the more pressured and occasionally dislodged the Soviets are on the periphery, the more reason they have to pre-emptively step up the 'adventurism' that so distresses the United States. Nor is this all. A prior or parallel Soviet expansion into gray areas outside the sphere of vital Soviet and American interests is necessary for horizontal escalation to work. The Soviets must be present in places where they can be pressed upon without being provoked to mortal combat.

Moreover, besides having short-term punitive thrust, it is desirable that the strategy have a long-term positive goal. A competition that simultaneously expands in scope and subsides in intensity as it becomes routine is the path to such a goal. Ideally, it will generate a shared stake in preventing local powers from embroiling the superpowers in unwanted conflict. Actually, horizontal escalation is only a tactic at the periphery of the system for managing the more basic strategy of horizontal encirclement of Soviet Russia via the West European–Chinese–Japanese trio at the system's center. It would foreclose Soviet attempts at counter-encirclement of either the West (in the Persian Gulf area) or of the United States (in the Americas).

While relating tactics to strategy as a part of designing and implementing the latter, to guard against is the psychopolitical tendency, under the influence of worst-case hypotheses and mental habits of total security, to exaggerate the threats to national security in peacetime. When war finally comes, most objects of peacetime concern become at best secondary strategic stakes; the undifferentiated image of integral security does not long survive the impact of operational priorities in the crush of battle.

The hysteria over the Russian advance toward America's underbelly in the guise of Cuban- or Nicaraguan-inspired revolutionary movements recalls an earlier episode: the excitement over the alleged German involvement in the Mexican Revolution of 1910–12. At that time, too, American attention was being drawn from the distant Pacific (the Philippines then, Vietnam today) to more proximate regions as America's own *Weltpolitik* waned in intensity and shrank in scope. It remained for later historians to determine conclusively that the Germans' objectives and means were almost wholly a function of indigenous (i.e., Mexican) needs and aspirations. The regional issue was not decisive in inducing the United States to join the war against Germany. Yet the initial assessment of clear and present danger had a part in planting in the American psyche an irreversibly negative view of the then pre-eminent continental European power, fitting into the larger pattern of the era's land versus sea power rivalry.

Nor did the Mexican and the Caribbean positions prove important in the war with Germany. In a future war with the Soviet Union, it is a hypothetical question how crucial might be comparable assets (ranging from Soviet missiles or brigades on Cuba to the Cuban-built airport on Grenada). It cannot be disposed of by inflating the means required for checkmating the Soviets' hypothetical capacity to project naval and seaborne nuclear capability to American shores in a total war or to interfere with the projection of American power to a limited conventional conflict in Europe.

When American global empire-building was at its height, the emplacement of Soviet missiles on Cuba shocked the United States into ending its long neglect of the region. There is no one explanation for the latest re-emphasis. The possible reasons are several: the US public is anxious to retrench, following disclosure of the costs of global involvement; or we are witness to a statesmanlike attempt to achieve a stabler balance between global and regional imperial policies; or the military transactions amount to the flexing of newly firmed-up muscles, calculated to impress a domestic constituency while making up for isolated setbacks elsewhere.

Hemispheric activism may condition America to emerge from the post-Vietnam syndrome into sustained reinvolvement worldwide. Alternatively, it may unwittingly prove America's incapacity to do so. In either case, when assessing the competitive dynamic between the United States and the Soviet Union in Central America as well as in other areas, it is useful to bear in mind how erratically US regional and global concerns can fluctuate. The result is an unstable, fluid setting for dealing with the more enduring superpower dilemmas. This is true regardless of whether the primary dilemma is internal to the superpowers' orbits of control (an aspect more critical for the Soviets) or (an aspect more problematic for the United States) is intrinsic to the most intractable issue of world politics, to wit: how to fashion a guarded relaxation of intra-orbit predominance while progression toward geopolitical parity is underway globally.

Presumptions and Probabilities

The United States' new-found interest in the Western Hemisphere is inseparable from wider US–Soviet relations. It is a truism that when viewed in the globalist perspective, governed by the East–West conflict, policy toward countries such as Grenada, Nicaragua, and El Salvador takes on a completely different aspect than when viewed in a regionalist perspective. In the latter, local problems are to be remedied through either pseudo-Marxist revolution or US-sponsored gradualist reform. However, American policy planners can employ the non-military regionalist approach only when the state of relations with the Soviet Union on the global plane frees them from acute, real or simulated, anxiety over the explosive reform–revolution mix.

US assumptions about the motives of Soviet involvement in the Western Hemisphere are critical in this connection. Is the Soviets' behavior part of a strategy of worldwide expansion for its own sake, independent of American policies? Or is Soviet interference primarily a means of gaining leverage over the United States, so as to make it abstain from anything that might undermine Soviet predominance in *their* sphere? Regional predominance relates to the objective of global geopolitical parity in two ways. First, even limited global gains enhance Soviet standing in their regional orbit. Specialized East

European elites can be diverted to outlets in Third World areas open to Soviet influence, while any related discouragement of revolts at the grass roots spares the Soviets the necessity to intervene forcefully. Second, as they make strides toward global parity, the Soviets will be under less pressure, for reasons of either psychology or prestige, to insist on absolute security (of the American kind) in the continental region adjoining their heartland. This could be considered a long-run strategic advantage for the United States and would be of undeniable benefit to the peoples concerned.

With regard to specifically military–strategic security, Soviet motives are subject to a further interconnection equally critical for American assessment and response. How much the superpowers reciprocate in keeping their hands off the opponent's regional interests, while controlling the rivalry in the intermediate zones, will affect what they perceive their military–strategic needs and goals to be. Consequently, how comfortable or satisfied the Soviets feel in the geopolitical arena will influence how much value they place on strategic assets in the Western Hemisphere.

Whatever else might be the Soviet incentives for mischief-making, it should not be hard to reduce them. If this entails, as an inducement, that the United States act with greater reserve in the Soviet sphere, it also presupposes enhancing US capacity to apply sanctions. However, the capacity to punish excess by denying access depends on first making the concessions apt to generalize Soviet stakes in parts of Africa, the Middle East, and Asia that lie outside both Soviet and American spheres of vital interest. Combining mutual self-restraint in regional orbits with a fair (if not necessarily equal) sharing of access outside them means that certain 'vital' interests will have to be downgraded to nonvital ones. Fortunately, these categories of variable content are flexible. Unfortunately for the American architects of the late detente, the Soviets will not observe 'restraint' outside their orbit in exchange for nothing more congruent than material or technological resource benefits determined by the United States.

To actually test the extent to which Soviet interventionism in the Western Hemisphere is self-generating, and keyed to objectives independent of American policies, would require painful adjustment in current US policies that would probably not be immediately or visibly rewarded by radically altered Soviet conduct. The United States would have to desist from interfering in such trouble spots as

Poland and Afghanistan, show greater reserve in its courtship of China, and demonstrate acceptance of the Soviets' drive toward the oceans and the wider world, which is historically determined or newly useful strategically, and may become materially essential for them in the future. The costs and risks of such testing can be limited and are reversible so long as the United States retains the power and the will to call a halt to flagrant abuses. In the absence of a test, the debate about Soviet intentions will continue to be stalemated. Some will attempt to read promising trends into cryptic remarks by Soviet officials, while others will extrapolate all sorts of menacing designs from overinflated estimates of Soviet capabilities. The alternative to testing Soviet goals has been to postulate a spontaneous drive for worldwide hegemony, implemented by means of 'national-democratic' (if not yet 'socialist') revolutions in the Third World, in the pattern of Nicaragua and Grenada. A largely speculative proposition, it is best dealt with on its own terms.

An authentic all-out drive for hegemony is not the same as enjoying the pre-eminence that naturally accrues to the strongest power in a particular diplomatic theater. Historically, the drive has invariably been a response as well as an initiative. It grows out of manifest structural weaknesses in the international system arising incrementally out of the decline of previously leading powers, and it is timed and propelled by a nearly inexplicable surge in the will to power of the would-be hegemon. The surge is always supported by a major technological or organizational innovation. The coincidence of external erosion and internal energy, and the interplay between exterior stimulation and innate drive, bring into the open different but mutually reinforcing surpluses (which permit expansive efforts) and scarcities (which compel such efforts). If this mixture of strengths and weaknesses is typically random, it is a deliberate policy that triggers the resulting conflicts. It expresses the ascendant actor's sense of present opportunity, heightened by grievance over past limitations and apprehensions about the future. Ultimately responsible is an incoherent system that generates both necessities and opportunities for individual self-help, only to impose constraints on how it is employed. The contradiction will repeatedly tempt a strong state to seize a transient advantage to permanently resolve the incoherence.

Leaving aside outside imputations of intent, none of these conditions are sufficiently present to justify assuming a Soviet hegemonial drive going beyond two wholly normal and intrinsically manageable objectives. The first is to assert the status of Russia as pre-eminent among the powers of Europe. The second is to translate a laboriously achieved (and, in effect, conceded) military–strategic parity with the United States into a corresponding reapportionment of geopolitical access outside Europe.

An ideological explanation for Soviet globalism is not convincing, either, whether alleged from without or within. Marxist-Leninist ideology does not bring forth a strong enough impulse to fuel the hegemonial drive. As a maturing power approaches and comes near to passing its climacteric, the inducements to bid for hegemony multiply and the drive's intensity rises. Conversely, a revolutionary ideology as the impetus behind policy declines quickly from its intial world-conquering appeal and thrust. Although the declaratory Soviet ideology utters dire predictions for the lot of the capitalist states and thus for the contemporary world system, its operative manner is keyed to a prudent calculation of the correlation of forces assessed intuitively and far from reliably. Since the creed failed to generate the elan that commonly infuses the hegemonial surge, and since the regime did not develop the crucial innovation, it was globalism itself that has had to compensate for the erosion of the strictly Soviet features of the Russian state – such as stress on labor discipline, technology, and economic rationality – instead of being able to draw on them. It remains subject to the Russian state's handicaps in the world, which make US fears for the Mexican and Persian Gulfs as exaggerated as Britain's had been for India.

The ideological apparatus is not totally devoid of utility. It contributes a medium for relating conventional objectives to the revolutionary aims of Third World insurgents, while offering the latter a tool for analyzing the resented social order and justifying the forceful means for changing it. However, the greater ability to relate to indigenous revolutionary movements does not remove the practical limitations on Soviet global outreach that have beset all continental states in the past. In fact, Marxism-Leninism will be more useful to the local revolutionaries than to their would-be sponsor, if only by placing a doctrinal gloss on brute coercion and providing a vocabulary for explaining – if not excusing – repressive violence. Small-country revolutionaries are either self-centered (witness a Castro or Qaddafi) or, when conformist, other-directed to only an ineffectual degree (thus the Grenadan 'Leninists' and their Nicaraguan analogues). In any event, a great power need not style itself revolutionary to foster rebellions embarrassing to a rival. The most conservative powers have been notoriously promiscuous in that regard at all times.

All regimes, democratic as much as authoritarian, depend on a varying compound of official ideology (or civic myths) and demonstrated efficacy for popular acceptance and support that constitute their legitimacy. In the Soviet case, the surviving ideological issues are located in the closely interlocking spheres of a supposedly proto-revolutionary world arena and a centrally managed socialist economy. Seeming to manipulate the two spheres is crucial for the Party, even as the regime's stronger claim on popular backing resides in achievements bearing on national security and great-power standing. Accordingly, it is a matter of concern for a Soviet leadership how to extend influence by promoting change abroad and relax deadening controls over the economy at home in ways that enhance efficacy without wholly discarding ideological rationalizations; how to orchestrate the visible costs and intangible returns from gains especially in the Third World arena and the uncertain material rewards and certain ideological and organizational risks of altering the practices of economic management at home.

The dovetailing US concern is to determine under what conditions the Soviet party–state regime might accept domestic reforms that cannot but weaken, along with the Communist Party's role in the economy, the state's nominal rationale and the Party's principal reason for being. Such a spontaneous retrenchment is unlikely to take place unless new sources of prestige, apt to increase latitudes for tentatively evolving the foundation for greater prosperity, are being secured – and are secured in ways that permit a lessening of emphasis on the revolutionary nature of the state's activity in the world arena as well as a less restrictive exercise of authority in the regional orbit.

Whether concession or denial of external gains would be more conducive to a beneficial evolution in Soviet Russia is the great unanswered question for American foreign policy. Contrary to the premise behind the denial strategy, prestige successes abroad are no more lifesaving for the Soviet regime than underwriting them is materially suicidal. Therefore, it is not the regime's existence and survival that are at stake, but the direction of its demonstrated capacity to change, to alternately mellow and harden. An ever more

substantially conventionalized foreign policy along a widening geographic perimeter is most likely to combine with a rationalized
domestic economy to produce ultimately a net shift toward a
'liberalized' application of Russia's traditional authoritarian model to
the Soviet polity. A global dynamic that stimulates internal development will incidentally increase the Soviets' capacity to project
influence abroad by economic rather than only military and
unconventional political means. America and Russia could thus
eventually move toward parity on an expanding plane, including the
methods and instruments of foreign policy.

Russo-American rivalry will not disappear overnight, and relaxing
it would generate a compensating increase in rivalries with or between
third parties. However, defusing the most dramatic and dangerous
global conflict of the present day in its several and changing sectoral
theaters would expand the latitude for dealing with regional, including
Western Hemisphere, issues on their merits. Applying appropriate
instruments to the solution of indigenous problems will not guarantee
a regional utopia any more than applying the right concepts and
strategies to the global matrix will automatically bring forth mutual
US–Soviet appeasement. The former goal is a liberal vision; the latter
desideratum is fundamentally conservative. In fact, these liberal and
conservative blueprints are interdependent in areas the severity of
whose internal problems exceeds their strategic significance and where
a truly stabilizing objective is dual: one, to enhance local-power
development by drawing selectively on the means and techniques
peculiar to the rival politico-economic systems; and two, to reduce
superpower conflict while the developmental process is underway.

So long as US world policy and US–Soviet relations stay as they
are, the globalist approach to the Western Hemisphere and most other
regions will have the upper hand over the regionalist perspective.
Socio-economic reform is normally too slow in producing political
stabilization when the attendant evolutionary upheaval is subject to
being inflected into a revolutionary course by externally supported
coercive force. Thus, if a US administration is incapable of restraining
itself in the matters of Poland and Afghanistan, in deference to the
Soviets' core-power dilemmas, then it must keep alive the option of
invading a Grenada and making war in Nicaragua. The same may
become true for the Middle East and beyond, if militarizing the link
with China goes hand in hand with keeping the Soviets out of the

Middle East peace process, impeding their turn at 'pacifying' a turbulent spot in Asia (Afghanistan as the Soviets' Vietnam), and waging undeclared war on their clients in Africa (Libya).

Giving the regionalist approach a chance to prove itself presupposes changing global policies in a more fundamental way than most proponents of the regionalist approach are prepared to concede, let alone advocate. Blending a progressive regional policy with an authentically conservative global strategy requires US strategists to first locate the golden mean between unqualified concessions to, and integral denial of, Soviet geopolitical aspirations in the larger world.

In the meanwhile, the United States might experiment with extending the strategy of differentiating between the Soviet Union and its clients (and among the clients) outside the Soviet sphere in Eastern Europe. Applied to the American sphere in the Western Hemisphere, the approach would aim at exploiting divergencies between the Soviet principal and a local surrogate such as Castro's Cuba and, down the road, Nicaragua's Sandinistas. That such divergencies exist was made evident by the more critical Cuban than Soviet reaction to the radicalization of the Grenadan revolution preceding its collapse.

The divergencies between principal and surrogate illustrate yet another facet of the global–regional dichotomy. The revolutionary local power will promote some relatively radical sociopolitical movement in the area. However, to relax more substantially its isolation, the revolutionary regime will sooner or later seek to expand its options to include rapprochement with the proximate (American) core power, while diminishing its dependence on the remote (Soviet) patron. This rapprochement will be essential if constructive achievement is to first supplement and then supplant the revolutionary creed as it wanes. To that end the regime must demonstrate a willingness and capacity to start acting as an agent for moderating the regional revolutionary process and circumscribing its bearing on global transactions. So long as US–Soviet competition continues unabated, the global perspective of the Soviets gives rise to a different pattern of priorities and behavior. It does not necessarily entail high-risk involvement in a remote region, but it does encourage a high-stakes diplomatic game.

In pre-invasion Grenada the Cubans would have settled for less revolution rather than lose all to reaction. The Soviets, by contrast, might well have preferred to see the local revolutionaries go all the way, because they themselves had little to gain by their stopping half-way. If a country converts to Soviet-style Leninist party rule, Moscow acquires more control than a charismatic–revolutionary leadership of local vintage offers, for example Maurice Bishop's in Grenada. The result of complete subversion locally is a small step toward geopolitical parity with the United States globally. Moreover, local radicalization induces the United States to intervene repressively. For the United States to act in its sphere as the Soviets do in theirs will add moral equivalence to the abstract symmetry between the two core powers. Further, the escalation attending the US intervention allows the Soviets to consolidate their hold on the local accomplice, in this case Cuba. It compromises Castro in American eyes as the participant, however reluctant, in the drive for an all-out Leninist solution (by the Coard clique in Grenada).

This does not mean that Soviet gains are without losses. The more cautious the Soviets are in backing a Third World client against American displeasure, the more often will they have to pay a real political price for conspicuous passivity. This will not do much for their prestige as an authentic world power. By the same token, however conservative they may be in conferring bona fide 'socialist' status and 'irreversible' membership in the socialist commonwealth, and in adjusting their protective guarantee accordingly, they will incur an ideological cost whenever they stand still in the face of a spurt of militant American energy. Even if they redefine ideological categories in order to avoid a prohibitively costly – and perhaps unwise – effort to underwrite the surrogate, it will hurt, insofar as such classification is one of the few remaining manifestations of the regime's ideological commitment and self-image. However, those liabilities do not in themselves warrant making US policy more ideologically committed and rigid than is the Soviet, not only with respect to the Soviet sphere but also the American. Being more pragmatic within a revised conceptual framework means displaying greater tolerance for local-brand revolutionary leadership and leftist initiatives, pending the radicals' submission to the facts of life as represented by local penury and America's pull as the only possible source of relief.

Polarization arises out of a revolution's initial need to distinguish itself from the past versus America's tendency to demonize the revolution's architects. But as revolutions run out of steam internally and are crowded out by more radical militancy in their neighborhood, the dynamic of polarization finds its counterpart in the dynamic of moderation. The sobering exposure of the Vietnamese revolution to the excesses of the Khmer Rouge is an extreme example of the interrevolutionary dynamics of decolonization in the Third World, set off by the seminal 'radicalism' of India's Congress. The Americans stand before the choice, then, of trying to master the revolution actively while it is in its ebullient infancy or waiting out (by practicing masterful inactivity) its mellowing into thermidorian middle age. The wait-and-see approach is safe so long as the duration of 'totalitarianism' in a country either too small or too poor, either too remote from the Soviet patron or too close to the American policeman, is unlikely to match even the finite lifespan of coercive Stalinist safeguards against reaction in the fountainhead of Leninist revolution.

By failing to be permissive or patient, the United States only reinforces the impression that it is unwilling to countenance any half-way radical social and political change or to allow it to evolve to maturity along either gradualist-evolutionary or violent-revolutionary paths. The possibility will have been finally lost of arriving at a tacit intra-regional understanding of the scope and mode of change in the Western Hemisphere that the United States will, because it safely can, tolerate. Such an understanding would have a good chance of proving more durable than any explicit Soviet–Cuban or Soviet–Nicaraguan alliance for the promotion of revolution, the means and extent of which can only lead to disagreement between the unequal and unequally situated partners in crime.

Whereas the Soviet Union cannot on balance lose when venturing into the US sphere, the United States cannot win while defending there its irreducible paramountcy so long as ideologically intransigent and practically uncompromising US policies are in force. If the United States does not forcibly intervene in spite of its known posture of unqualified opposition to anything smacking of revolutionary change, it stands revealed as impotent; if it does intervene with force, it stands arraigned as a falsely liberal tyrant democracy, a modern Athens consolidating an empire behind the façade of common defense against the day's Persia. Any immediate gain in either self-confidence or reputation for resolution is then liable to be gradually eroded, and eventually more than offset by deepened disaffection on the part of both the liberal-to-conservative and the reformist-to-revolutionary elites in America's regional habitat.

The Reagan Doctrine has been the latest turn on the twisting road to a new regional–global regime. It would be deserving of warrant if disappointing results of an untimely zeal laid to rest at last the ever-returning ghost of the Monroe Doctrine, while the lack of real accomplishment in the areas beyond America's habitat demonstrated finally the insufficiency of the neo-Dullesian approach to US–Soviet relations. If, as suggested at the outset, Angola does not rate a Poland as the reward for effective rollback, backing there a Savimbi in retaliation for Russian presence in, say, Aden, ranks with supporting a repressive regime in Pakistan as retribution for Afghanistan. The penalized Soviet transgressions have been among the factors that made it seem imperative to implement active containment by pitting no less questionably democratic Contras in Nicaragua against the Sandinistas. Yet, before the United States can forswear forcible coercion of revolutionaries through the medium of auxiliaries more reactionary than reformist regionally, it will have to relax containment with elements of US–Soviet concert globally. The price both inside and outside America's regional sphere is not negligible when calculated against the background of a supposedly unchangeable Russo-American conflict; it does not entail injury to national security when projected against the prospect of a reshaped inter-superpower equilibrium and enhanced overall stability.

PART III

Reappraisals and Refinements

5

In the Wake of Afghanistan

In Spring 1981 the Soviet invasion of Afghanistan exerted a mesmeric effect on American statecraft, lately also haunted by the specter of an off-again on-again Russian intervention in Poland. And the hypothesis of a Russian-induced or orchestrated oil cut-off in the Persian Gulf stimulated strategic and deranged political thinking. It was a good time for taking a step back in order to review immediate concerns from a larger and longer perspective.

Long-term Tendencies and Worst-case Thinking

After World War II, Europe was the laboratory for outright division of physical space between the superpowers. This state of things has been precariously yielding to interpenetration of influence: diplomatic Soviet in Western Europe, economic Western in Eastern Europe. Elsewhere, the region in and around the Middle East is poised between two divergent courses: it can travel the European path in reverse and move toward a fixed partition by way of an aborted spell of mobile interpenetration of superpower access and influence; or that part of the world can test further and vindicate the more dynamic and hopeful approach to regional and global stability. It can do so under certain conditions. One condition is that the local regimes remain impermeable to integral or irreversible control by either superpower, and defend their primacy in managing local conflicts and regional balances. The other condition is that the superpowers relax their fears and expectations relative to the region. On the Soviet side, these are rooted in the geopolitics of the vulnerable underbelly; on the Western side, in the geoeconomics of a vital resource. Neither of the resulting pretensions is fully valid and sustainable in full without grave dangers for both parties.

As for the West alone, so long as policies remain hostage to worst-case scenarios regarding Soviet intentions vis-à-vis the region and the resource, it will not be possible to experiment with the more dynamic approach to regional and world equilibrium. And it will be more than possible to derail irreparably a longer-term approach to the secular problem of Russia in relation to Europe and the West. That problem is intimately tied up with prospects for a steady and steadying approach to the longest-term issues, posed by the West–East cleavage within a wider compass than is currently in fashion – or, as now euphemistically phrased for chiefly economic purposes, the North–South dialogue. Within both its narrowed and the wider circumference, the East–West issue will have retained and may increase its importance well after the material parameters of the energy issue have been largely or completely changed. This is not the first time that international politics has been temporarily focused on one commodity or mineral – nor will it necessarily be the last. *Primum vivere . . .*; but, in order to survive into a livable future, it is also necessary to philosophize here and now.

It has been the ill-fortune of American foreign policy that it has rarely managed to find and lastingly occupy the ground on which both the mechanical and the organic dimensions of interstate relations – the first revolving around the dynamics of thrusts and counterthrusts; the latter concerned with the evolution of trends and potentials – meet and correct the opportunities and pitfalls each presents for statecraft. Instead, the tone and inspiration of American policy has found it easier to oscillate between pragmatism and providentialism, under the thin layers of tribal ideology or preachy sanctimony.

The alternation can be discerned over both long and short swings of the pendulum: the first, between the only thinly disguised realism of forcible continental or regional expansionism (thus the eras of Polk and McKinley), and the only deviously realistic illusionism of the initial venture in worldwide reformism (or world power-through-institutional reform: Woodrow Wilson); the second, most recently, between the early and pristine Carterism and the likewise not fully tried and tested Reaganism. Carterism stood for a species of reactivated American commitment to humanitarianism. If generalized worldwide, it would either convert or circumvent, infiltrate or isolate, Soviet Russia. The spokesmen for Reaganism have expressed their version of realism in the language of a species of American nationalism. It is one that finds nervous release from the many-faceted obligations of major power and dilemmas of world politics in indictments of Soviet imperialism, proxy terrorism, and indiscriminate adventurism. While they have filled the vacuum of strategic concept on the foreign policy stage, the indictments were as sweeping or even as diffuse (and on occasion, thus *in re* terrorism, unsubstantiated) as the proffered responses were concrete and the remedies specific.

Whereas the remedies have prominently included US military buildup and arms transfers, for example, in El Salvador and in relation to the Persian Gulf, the responses were enshrined in short-term tactical argument. The trouble with classic diplomatic reasoning of this kind is that it more commonly rationalizes a preconceived posture than it motivates action or inspires original thought; it can be readily turned upside down, and equally likely or hypothetical negative consequences can be opposed to the anticipated positive ones. Put forward in behalf of a self-consciously tough approach to the Soviet Union, the policy anticipated positive dividends in such realms as interallied cohesion in Europe and third-power orientations and alignments in the Middle East.[1] It is just as plausible to predict that the approach will cause interallied stresses and tensions in relations with Western Europe, and intensify local conflicts while disclosing the limited support for either local moderates or for American mediation in the Middle East. It is the contingent nature of apparently rigorous tactical or strategic reasonings that makes it legitimate and necessary to supplement them with patently hypothetical long-term perspectives, if only to counterpose to the anticipated short-term benefits of a hardnosed approach the probable long-term costs of a radically, and pridefully, ahistorical *Realpolitik*.

Diplomatic Sanctions and Sociopolitical Change

The consequence of the new right's self-righteous foreign policy attitude could be a replay of the cold war. This is not very likely. But it might be something still worse, because more confused, if the revival of the language of the cold war is not relieved by the degree of sophistication about inter-superpower relations that was gradually evolved in the course of the postwar competition. Thus, it can be argued that, as of early 1981, the threatened American or, more widely, Western reactions to a possible Soviet military intervention in

Poland exceeded the sanctions either contemplated or applied in the earlier cases of Hungary in 1956 and Czechoslovakia in 1968, when the 'right' of each superpower to retain control in its sphere of influence was (still?) recognized.

The implication of the later approach – to the extent that it was more than public grandstanding – seems to be that what was legitimate in the period of the cold war or soon after has become illegitimate as a result of the intervening period of detente. One possible underlying logic is that, from the Western viewpoint, detente in Europe was linked with Soviet acceptance of 'liberalization' in Eastern Europe, and a Soviet repression would renege on that acceptance even though detente itself has been declared passé (and the word itself became taboo) in the United States. However, it can also be argued, and perhaps with more powerful logic, that if detente is to be a 'two-way street' for both parties, its long-term liberalizing effect in Eastern Europe had to be coupled with Western understanding of – and, if necessary, support for – the immediately conservative Russian needs. This can only mean the Soviets' interest in preserving, by any means required, their essential positions in Europe pending a funda-mental recasting of world politics and great-power alignments as the consequence of a progressive transmutation of East–West detente into something like entente.

If this is a tenable view, then the only legitimate implication of the nexus between detente and liberalization, and only valid condition of detente, is that forcible superpower counteractions to social change do not occur lightly at the first provocation and without exhausting all alternative remedies short of force. The social change in question is likely to comprise turbulence from a presumably beneficial process of industrialization, patronized by one of the great powers and dominant ideologies: Soviet Russia and 'socialism' in Eastern Europe, as much as the United States and 'capitalism' in Central or South America, among other places. Instead of adopting this viewpoint, the appre-hension of some, including official, American observers seems to have been from time to time that the Soviet (or Polish) regime might find a devious way, short of overt invasion force, for rolling back the reformist-cum-rebellious movement without offering an unequivocal occasion for Western retaliation.

It is difficult to see in these circumstances how the Soviets could have had an inducement to respect Western interests in, say, Iran, had the United States displayed the power and the will to contain (as it had both reason and provocation to do) the reformist-cum-rebellious upheaval within its sphere of vital interests. It is equally difficult to see how the Soviets might retain an inducement to manifest understanding for future Western needs in either Iran or any comparable area and situation. A similar point can be made with regard to the refusal to see any connection between El Salvador and Afghanistan. More stridently even than the Carter administration, the Reagan foreign policy establishment has claimed a right to interdict and counteract the external, allegedly Cuban and Soviet, support for the 'leftist' forces for change within that part of the American geopolitical orbit. At the same time, both administrations indicted, and by implication vetoed, any Soviet entitlement to act against the ultimate consequences of a prior (and US-encouraged) effort by the Shah of Iran to effect in Afghanistan, with results that triggered the 1978 communist coup, a Westward and rightward change in the pro-Soviet orientation of Afghan neutralism that had endured since World War II.[2]

So described, the background to the eventual Soviet intervention is operationally more significant than one stressing a pan-Islamic threat to Russia, whether supported by China or not. If accepted as true, not only does such a scenario highlight the immemorial difficulty in distinguishing between offensive and defensive motivations and, therefore, underline the delicacy required in dealing with such ambiguities; it also points to the dangerous disparity between the illusory character of ingrained or ideological preconceptions (in this case positing unprovoked Soviet aggression) and the very specific possible consequences of monochromatic appreciations. There are concrete implications for policy to be considered in this connection (and they will be in due course); the immediately disturbing thought is that widely accepted, simplified representations and evaluations of events that verge on distortion can remain too long unchallenged before a sufficiently wide audience. When this happens in the liberal-democratic conditons of a formally free press, the consequences differ too little from the more obvious deceptions generated by the overtly controlled communications system of a dictatorship. A culture such as the American one, already divorced from both the historical and the conceptual perspectives by its preference for pragmatic solving of problems as they arise, is then denied even the contemporary perspective while it matters. The full truth about a critical policy matter is revealed only in retrospective revisions and re-evaluations by (an often overreacting) historical scholarship, and revealed then only to the few who remain attentive to policy issues without necessarily influencing policy while it is being shaped.

Sweeping Conclusions and Selective Containment

Whether or not a new round of cold war supervenes as a result of either misperceptions or misrepresentations and either commensurate or misguided reactions, it has seemingly been the immediate purpose of the Reagan administration to reinstitute a policy of strict containment, first and foremost in the Persian Gulf area. In that area, the attribution of hostile intention to the Soviets on the basis of a putative ability has reached an extreme form, one that could be grounded only in a view of the adversary as not only unqualifiedly hostile but also totally reckless. Thus, in his prepared statement to the Armed Services Committee of the US Senate, Secretary of Defense Caspar Weinberger declared on 4 March 1981, inter alia: 'That area, Southwest Asia and the Gulf, is and will be the fulcrum of contention for the foreseeable future. The Soviet Union will almost certainly become a net energy importer. This, coupled with their economic necessity for eventual access to the Gulf oil basin, is their long-range objective of denying access to oil by the West.'[3] For Secretary Weinberger (and many others) to deduce from a hypothetical Soviet need for access an automatic intention to deny access to the West – i.e., for him to rule out the possibility of a Soviet interest in no more than the capacity to negotiate shared access – is, at the very least, a non-sequitur. Such a worst-case scenario fails to explain the cost–benefit calculations that would plausibly induce the Soviets to resort to the extreme measure under any circumstances other than those of a war already under way.

The failure to hint at any but the vaguest premises of sweeping conclusions, or assumptions behind far-reaching affirmations, so that they might be tested for consistency with an articulable theory of interstate relations, was commonly not confined to any particular issue; it is equally manifest, for instance, in the failure to differentiate between what arguably motivates and defines an adventurous as compared to a merely assertive foreign policy. Once this academic point has been made, however, it may be conceded that the deviation of early Reaganism from the canons of any but a very shallow realism could be attributed to the tendency of all administrations to stake out an extreme initial position, to the left or right of its immediate predecessor, in order to look different. The administration was bound to move toward the center when its verbal overkill, partaking of bluff, had been made less risk-free by the Soviets having eased themselves out of immobilizing involvements, and the psychological need for verbal excess had waned with increases in US material, including military, resources for dealing with more reasonably defined contingencies and related risks. It is, therefore, more to the point for a discussion with speculative pretensions to examine the version of containment often described as selective, presumably in contrast with its strict or dogmatic version.

It is irrelevant for the purposes of such an examination where the auxiliary non-Western countervailing power is specifically focused: in the People's Republic of China or, as part of an all-oceanic alliance policy,[4] in Taiwan, among other such insular places (in a view seeking to integrate opposition to PRC communism with opposition to Soviet imperialism). It is also irrelevant whether the positions of Western material as well as political strength are to be built up by way of coordinating US with European and Japanese industrial and democratic potentials in something called trilateralism, or the West's ideological credentials are to be refurbished – and Soviet Russia's further dimmed – by association with either industrializing or revolutionary Third Worldism. What is relevant is that even moderate versions of selective containment are prompted by an essentially negative view of East–West or US–Soviet relations. Its proponents would relax opposition to Soviet expansion only where the stakes are not of significant importance for extensively defined Western interests or where it is no more possible than necessary for the United States to offer effective opposition.

Being essentially negative, the range of viewpoints that can be lumped together as a reasonable modification of a rigid containment strategy has also tended to be formalistic. Such viewpoints would oppose or condemn Soviet penetrations also in areas of Western disinterest or incapacity if their method was forcible, i.e., military. Thus, even if the invasion of Afghanistan did not materially change the Soviet threat to the Persian Gulf – e.g., because alternative penetration routes via Iran directly from adjoining Soviet territory are logistically superior and the shortening of the air routes from Afghan airports is not critically decisive – the intervention would still be intolerable because it entailed crossing an international boundary in force.

Yet, commendable as the implied ideal standard might be, it is also true that a doctrine in favor of a radical demilitarization of super-power behavior is potentially more disturbing to inter-superpower relations than has been or is likely to be their recent militarization (to use the critically meant expression of George Kennan). The doctrine is disturbing inasmuch as it is radically one-sided in concep-tion and would tend to perpetuate an imbalance in fact. Given the economic and other-than-military Soviet inferiority to the United States, the doctrine implies either an indefinite congealment of the status quo or its being changeable by other than wholly spontaneous processes only to the advantage of Western or third powers. As a result, it cannot but be unacceptable at the very least, and at worst be seen as provocative, from the Russian viewpoint. To adopt this exclusively procedural standard and related diplomatic and moral posture, while returning to cold-war rhetoric, is to execute an acrobatic overleap of cold war-induced realism. It lands one back in a species of legalism that was dominant in the period between the two world wars. Then, it is useful to recall, the campaign against 'aggression' in the League of Nations setting was to a great extent a means of covering up, in large part knowingly and in a smaller part cynically, for the inability of the satisfied – and, more truly, dispirited or even decadent – Western European (and the isolationist American) democracies to act effectively in the world arena and preside over changes within and among nations from a sufficient position of strength.

The more negative or formalistic they are, the more even the reasonable proponents of moderated containment will overlook or de-emphasize two aspects on which positions divide in the last resort. The first is that in the perspective of historically informed realism, the Soviets, while 'expansionist', behave in a way normal for an aspiring great power. They do so with the means available to them, as in the case of most or all past continental states facing an economically superior maritime power, with heavy emphasis on military means. The second, and more important, is that an expansive Soviet foreign policy could also have positive consequences, if in different ways and time spans, for both the evolution of the Soviet political system internally and the defense of the Western position and interests in the world system at large. It is possible to hypothesize the first-mentioned positive effect insofar as internally not-too-costly foreign policy successes help legitimize and thus moderate, while the functional requirements of foreign-policy efficacy in directly uncontrollable non-contiguous areas tend to diversify, and thus deconcentrate, the internal authority structure of a state that is not only authoritarian but also, in fact or aspiration, modern. Furthermore, on the supposition of such an internal development, Soviet Russia as an effective world power would be a useful partner in dealing with other sources of global disturbance. Many minor-power disturbances will be more directly or subtly subversive of Western values and interests. They will also be less easily manageable than expansion by the Soviets – as well as less manageable in competition with the Soviet Union than in a mutually reinforcing or even co-managerial way made possible by a more discriminating Western attitude to Soviet ambitions, intended to regulate rather than to repress them.

Without being ready to consider such a positive rationale, a merely negatively or prudentially motivated doctrine or strategy of selective containment lacks intellectual credentials. It may also lack practical viability as a centrist alternative to right-wing and left-liberal extremes on the American foreign-policy spectrum – to unqualified anti-Sovietism and illusionist pro-Third Worldism. Since it is only tactically opportunist, the selective-containment approach is no more authentically conservative than is the more radical or rigid one. It is not sufficiently preoccupied, in regard to Soviet Russia, with correctly assessing its historic memories, present force, and alternative future thrusts. Such facets of evolution are the necessary counterpart, suggesting politic concessions and compensations, to the mechanical checks employed to graduate the rate of consequent changes and moderate their impact on other states and interests – until, hopefully, their object has itself become instrumental in dealing with the next-in-line prime threat to rudimentary social and international order.

Yet insofar as the centrist alternative is not a viable one, the conclusion is stark. It is possible for events to belie the positive presumptions behind a conservative Western strategy that is aimed at decompressing the international environment of the Soviet global outreach and the internal and regional Soviet authority structures, and is committed to trying to do no more than control (but then efficaciously) the scope and rate and channel the direction of Soviet expansion toward the elusive state of not only nuclear-strategic, but also geopolitical parity with the United States. It is possible that even insufficient disproof of the premises would have to be treated as conclusive for practical purposes at the outermost boundary of risk that may be reasonably incurred in behalf of a bona fide experiment-ation with a Western strategy for accommodation or – replacing one untranslatable French term, *détente*, with another, *apaisement*. The disproof would be administered by the Soviets were they to reject the implied challenge to adjust, as their response, both global and regional goals and methods in ways permitting a yet more far-reaching readjustment and realignment in intra-European and global East–West relations. Then, following the failure of the experiment – itself a necessary preliminary to a widely sustainable defensive resistance in America and Europe alike – the alternative would be a militant and not merely moderate containment until such time as a new opportunity might appear.

The ambiguity of the relationship between offense and defense, the short- and the long-term, the simplified mechanics of balance-of-power interactions and the complex interweaving of that dynamic with multistrand evolution of trends and forces better described as organic, is something to live with or die by. It will not be resolved by the comfortable device of embracing middle-of-the-road policies that merely halve the difference between all and nothing on grounds of momentary expediency or inability to mobilize a nation's intellectual and moral resources for reaching out for more at greater risk.

Inter-Superpower Solidarity and Subversion

The relatively short-term and immediately critical issue concerns the attitudes of the two superpowers to one another as empires with spheres of influence; the longer-term issue, whose elements are already in the making, bears on the implications of the imperial spheres of influence being gradually loosened up, if not dissolved, into a more complex worldwide equilibrium.

At the bottom of the first, shorter-term, issue is the question of the 'code of conduct' between the superpowers. The effective relationship is not, however, between two great powers identical in kind, location, and endowments, and thus liable to behave identically in terms of procedure. It is a relationship between two powers with many differences, including their stages of development and degrees of satiation. They have one main similarity: they are both empire structures, for whose relationship the critical issue is whether their interpretations of events result in substantive policies that aim at inter-empire subversion or aim at a measure of inter-empire solidarity – however circumscribed the latter might initially be in scope and however diffuse its initial target.

Reverting to Afghanistan, it matters whether the Soviet intervention is condemned on procedural grounds or (without renouncing either appropriate counteraction or compensation) condoned on substantive grounds as, in the last analysis, a defensive response to the security risks emanating from the vacuum of internal authority created by the overthrow of the Afghan monarchy (in the 1973 Daoud coup). The intervention could be regarded as, on balance, defensive regardless of whether the chief subsequent threat came from Islamic fundamentalism (affecting the Soviets internally), from trends toward Westward- and rightward-leaning neutralism (affecting the Soviet strategic and prestige position in the region), or, after the 1978 communist coup, from US-encouraged trends toward Titoism (creating doctrinal and practical problems for the Soviets in Eastern Europe). It is immaterial in this view in what precise degree and context the Soviets had intially reacted to the increasingly likely consequences of the pre-revolutionary Iranian regime's effort to effect an Afghan realignment, and took the next step in anticipation of a US action against post-revolutionary Iran that would have consequences for the (by then radically changed) situation in Afghanistan. It is likewise immaterial that any such Soviet anticipation was belied by US inaction, so long as it was predicated on a correct reading of the inter-superpower (or inter-empire) rules of the game.

As evolved in the cold war era, these rules entailed the obligation of the superpowers to observe the de facto distribution of spheres of influence (as the provisional basis of a minimum global order); they also entailed the right of each to defend that distribution against attempts at change. Insofar as American policy makers encouraged the successive efforts to change the pre-existing situation in Afghanistan to Soviet disadvantage, and the Soviets were progressively drawn first into deeper involvement and then into a last-resort intervention in order to prevent the efforts from succeeding, it is not impossible to contemplate the thought that the Soviet behavior was more in keeping with the minimalist rules than the American – a balance of infraction and observance not altogether unlike that which can be applied to the 1973 war that marked the collapse in the Middle East, soon after they had been enunciated, of the more ambitious or maximalist rules for a US–Soviet co-management of regional conflicts.

In such a perspective it may be regrettable, but is not a reason for punishing the Soviets, that the American failure to act in Iran did not permit a conclusive test as to whether the Soviets continued to observe both sides of the rules – or observe the rules for both sides. As matters stand, America's uncoerced surrender of her sphere of influence in Southwest Asia (though not in Central America) has only given rise to invidious parallels between US restraint and Russian rashness. If it is not a Soviet transgression that American policy was unable to relate a clear intent to effective means in the Persian Gulf area, it would be perilous if the fortuitously recovered innocence (*in re* interventionism) were to be fired by resuscitated ideology (of anti-communism) into continuing to slant US policy toward an inter-empire subversion strategy.

Should this come to pass, it might become significant in the not very long run that there is after all a subtle, but operationally important, difference between the two empire structures – one that refracts the dichotomy between an association of equals and a tyranny over dependents. Unlike its regional antecedent and the Soviet continental rival, the post-World War II American world empire has been largely an accidental one of inheritance (from the Europeans, as were to different degrees most Western world empires beginning with the Spain-centered one of Charles V). Stripped of dynastic pride and principle, such an empire is subject to the temptation of accepting near-imperceptible, gradual erosion on the principle of easy come, easy go. It is subject – as was the late British – to the belief that the fortuitous circumstances that made the empire possible have been replaced meanwhile with differently favorable and less strenuous conditions that make it no longer necessary. Conversely, the continental–military empire by conquest and organic accretion will long find the strength to fight attempts at secession and to avert dramatic disintegration.

Were the American accidental empire to continue to unravel in the setting of ineffectual attempts to precipitate secessions from the forcibly acquired Soviet empire by a policy aiming at its subversion, matters might reach a critical pass soon enough. They would do so not least if the West Europeans, faced with a rising threat of violent Soviet reaction, were to conclude that they had little choice but to add surrender to the range of options no longer meaningfully comprising a stabilizing measure of inter-empire solidarity. Finlandization of Western Europe might then win in a photo-finish over Russia's Europeanization in the long-distance marathon between the two evolutionary trends, an Olympic event in European history that could not be canceled at orders from Washington.

Exclusive Spheres and Divisible Space

Important as it is in the short run, however, reciprocal respect for spheres of influence is only the necessary precondition of a process that would lead eventually also to US–Soviet appeasement. The intermediate stage involves relaxing the division of physical space by such spheres – a primitive and precarious balance-of-power technique – into a more complex pattern institutionalizing the divisibility of strategic space or, better put, of access to it. The process has already begun, not wholly and onesidedly to Soviet advantage. On the Soviet side, the mechanism has been that of a series of outflanking implantations of influence in the Middle East and eastern Africa in particular. In one interpretation, these threaten to strangulate Western access to a vital war-prone region and welfare-maintaining resource; in another possible interpretation, they represent counterencirclement moves in retaliation for Soviet extrusion from a symbolic and otherwise crucial role in a peacemaking process (between Israel and the Arabs) as well as the regional variant of and response to the US–Chinese global encirclement of Russia.

At least as important as the immediate reasons or rationales are the principles that would make such encroachments tolerable and productive in the long run. Among such conditions is that the reapportionment of access be reciprocal; that the extent and intensity of access be graduated to reflect the extent and importance of either superpower's stake in the different areas; and that access be used as a lever for bargaining over and, if need be, forcing admission to a share in resource or influence for the newly penetrating power rather than as a means of undermining or blocking future access of the pre-established power – that the purpose be to position oneself strategically, not to dispossess the other integrally.

In the *furor* over Soviet expansionist penetrations by military means into areas of (mostly already weakened or lost) Western influence, what is often forgotten is the extent of new Western economic involvement in – or penetration into? – areas of Soviet influence and vital interest in Eastern Europe. The asymmetry of method (but, surely, not of objective!) reflects endowments more than preferences; it does not cancel out the fact that as a matter of both maneuver and result there has been under way a reciprocal interpenetration of spheres. Barring a diabolical Soviet design to inherit world dominion by wedding capitalist contradictions to socialist inefficiencies, not all of the Western initiatives in Eastern Europe could be pleasant for the Soviets to witness – including direct US–Polish consultations about how to save Poland's Western-capitalized economy from the consequences of Polish management. At least some of the experience must surely be as much of a defeat and humiliation for the Russians as it is for the Americans to witness the Soviet infiltration into, say, Ethiopia (pending Iran?) following their failure to shield an emperor from the consequences of mismanaging the local sociopolitical system under US auspices.

Once basic parallels are acknowledged and asymmetries are taken into account, it is both possible and comforting to note that none of the conditions of tolerable or beneficial interpenetration has been seriously violated. With the rumored exception of their encouragement for the OPEC embargo in 1973 (itself preceded by Russia's exclusion from enforcing the Israel–Egypt cease-fire by Nixon's miniature replica of Kennedy's missile crisis), the Soviets have not used their influence (as distinct from propaganda) in the Middle East to assault vital Western interests, much as they have used influence with the radicals to gain access to a role in regional peacemaking and order maintenance. Would that the Western powers, and not least the West Europeans, be similarly reserved and reasonable. They would then use the leverage of their access to Eastern European economics and politics to encourage restraint of popular or elite demands for instant radical changes before rushing into public warnings against reactionary Soviet responses to system-threatening disorders. Evenhandedness is a virtue with manifold application in matters affecting victors and vanquished, oppressors and oppressed, in more than one region. It is a stance to adopt if deranged relations between rulers and ruled in smaller countries are not to destabilize relations fatally between the giant powers in critical regions of the globe.

Finally, Western access to Eastern Europe and Soviet access to the Middle East, Africa, and elsewhere in the Third World, have remained within the limits set by the stakes of the competition or the vital interests of the rival superpower and alliance. Nor is the balance of geopolitically-focused power anywhere near turning against the West globally. At the same time, however, as the permeability of the Soviet regional sphere is matched by the Soviet penetration into the global real estate, the progression to a new and more flexible equilibrium system is inevitably being purchased at the price of Soviet expansion. To wish and to argue for anything else is to plead for a strategy of dissolving only one of the interest spheres – plead, in effect, for a globalized 'rollback' and 'liberation' strategy (while adding the economic weapon to Dullesian psychological warfare).

It will take all the resources of genuinely conservative statecraft to ensure that the evolutionary process under way within Soviet Russia (despite setbacks) and in East–West relations (in Europe and, more precariously, elsewhere) not be set back frivolously, in ways fatally detrimental to the cause of East–West appeasement. Such appeasement, fitting moderate Soviet expansion into an international system which itself expands in the range of forces for order and disorder, is the priority item on any sensible agenda for the remainder of the century. It is a priority on the handling of which hinge the prospects for an all-Occidental alliance including Russia in the next century. Only such an alliance will be able to face jointly the challenges which the resurgence of the larger or global East will present to the Europe-derived West after the passing of the half-millennium of its dominance overseas and over the world's oceans. The alternative to alliance, it is possible to agree with the historically learned proponent of a different strategy,[5] is war within the Occident: not now, not soon, but sometime after the turn of the century; whether set off to purge ideological fanaticisms or to redress or resupply force structures, in either case fratricidal.

Either alliance or Armageddon will solve the problem of 'Russia and the West', through their fusion or the dispossession of both. It is easy to agree that much will depend on the evolution inside Soviet Russia. The crucial difference of opinion is whether 'liberalization' is to be sought by unvarying efforts to contain the Soviet Union as a rival military power and an alien political system or by efforts to co-opt Russia as a vital force and a both cognate and complementary spirit; whether the pursued aim is the conversion of one system into the other or their convergence, an integral adjustment of Soviet Russia to the West or the partial realignments of both. Much can be debated about a future impossible to predict and hazardous to project from the past. Yet what is to come must in the end be shaped, on the greatest of issues at the necessary high risk, with the help of nothing more reliable than a reasoned choice between competing prophecies.

Notes

1 See, among many instances, Joseph Kraft, 'What Secretary Haig has in mind', *Baltimore Sun*, 17 February 1981, p. A13.
2 See Selig S. Harrison, 'Dateline Afghanistan: exit through Finland?', *Foreign Policy*, Winter 1980–1, pp. 163–87, and the other sources cited therein. I accept Harrison's version of events as that of a serious scholar-reporter.
3 See the *New York Times*, 5 March 1981, p. B11.
4 See Ray S. Cline, 'A new Grand Strategy for the United States: an essay', *Comparative Strategy*, 1/2 (1978). pp. 1–11.
5 I am referring to the officially disavowed forecast by Richard Pipes, then of Reagan's National Security Council. See the *New York Times*, 20 March 1981, p. A2.

6

In the Place of Detente

We might well be witnessing now a penultimate phase in relations between the West and Russia, to be followed either by a lethal conflict or by convergence within an enlarged West. Specific crises – Poland and Afghanistan for the Soviets, and Iran and El Salvador for the Americans – have raised questions regarding American strategy: will it embrace the aim of reciprocal subversion, or will it explore the grounds for solidarity between the two empires? The present era is another of those proverbial last chances, though perhaps more final or terminal than most. Western and, in particular, American policy now has the opportunity to strike out in the right path at a fast-approaching crossroads, leading in one direction toward reconstruction of the international system, and in the other toward uncontrollable upheaval.

Strategic Doctrines and Dilemmas

After the triumph of public opposition to the war in Vietnam, the truth behind the American empire was revealed by the persistent efforts of both the Carter and the Reagan administrations to reinflate the national ego as part of rehabilitating America's role in world politics. Jimmy Carter's venture into moralizing ersatz-imperialism by way of a human rights campaign proved incompatible with the specific foreign interests of the United States and the domestic exigencies of the targeted regimes – Third World and communist. Ronald Reagan's attempt to substitute a muted variety of militarist nationalism in conservative clothing in place of Carter's spectacularly dressed-up liberal humanism was quickly imperiled by the public's preference for a welfare state over the warfare state. As projected budget deficits grew, so waned public readiness to pay even the material price for the easier, military substitute for moral primacy.

A controlled shrinkage of the worldwide empire, or its recasting through orderly devolution, seemed as uncongenial to the American political genius as did continued expansion and institutional consolidation. Nor was there an apparent will – or immediate need – to face the hardest choice: one between cumulative attrition and a manageable, timely association with the USSR in occasional efforts at restoring peace and maintaining order in regional theaters. Instead, real choices were obscured by the mirage of unilaterally managing the balance of power in a region such as the Middle East where the United States half-unwittingly had come to hold the higher cards. Paramountcy in a key region would nicely supplement playing only one – but big-power – card in the tricky game of trilateral global balance (signalled by a quasi-alliance with communist China). Yet, the longer-term implications of the equilibrium framework in its early phase were not understood any better than were those of the empire framework in its mature phase.

Spasmodic gestures in the direction of Beijing were hostage less to stolid fidelity to the Taiwan connection than to uncertainty as to how hard the Soviets could be pushed. Provisional success in the effort to exclude Russia from the Middle East, and the half-hearted strategy of tightening the encirclement of the Soviets through a US–West European–Chinese–Japanese grand alliance, stood in an uncertain cause-and-effect relationship with Soviet moves to counterencircle China via Vietnam and then the West through penetrations of the Persian Gulf and East Africa. As the curtain went up again over the traditional 'great game' (with the United States now in Britian's place), neither official nor expert-academic Americans were willing or able to deal with the consequences of conceding nuclear-strategic (and, in part, naval) parity to the Soviets. Should the United States tolerate a corresponding, if gradual, Soviet progression toward geopolitical parity, defined as comparable access to influence in the global periphery? If so, to what extent? If not, at what risk and cost?

The parity issue poses as acute problems for the differently situated and equipped US offshore–insular maritime power and Soviet heartland–continental power individually as it does for the relations between these powers. If a new era of equilibrium is to ease the current crisis of empire, and eventually supplant the imperial era altogether, even tentative efforts to redefine an asymmetrical inter-empire balance rule out a onesided stress on Soviet adventurism as part of a renewed emphasis on containment. Such a posture is liable to block significant progress toward making functionally meaningful the pronouncements, marking the high noon of detente, in favor of a joint US–Soviet stake in policing the outer limits of regional conflicts and disorders.

The once-again frozen perception of the Soviet Union as an aggressive–expansionist force, dating from events in Angola and bequeathed by Carter to an only-too-willing Reagan after Afghanistan, was the direct offspring of the flawed rationale behind the Nixon–Kissinger detente. Far from being able to practice restraint globally in return for grants of access to Western credits and technology, the Soviet regime had to behave externally like any other regime of an ascent-oriented great power if the Soviet system was to retain a vestige of legitimacy at home. That is to say, it had to make up for its economic inadequacy by utilizing its military resources for political self-assertion abroad. In the special Soviet case, moreover, making full use of Western economic inputs and being able to pay for them in the long run required an ideologically damaging move away from rigid planning toward a managed market economy in the Hungarian style. The doctrinal cost would have to be offset by evolving a substitute legitimation of a similarly ideological kind. It can be found mainly in promoting 'socialism' in the Third World. When so revised and adjusted, ideological legitimation would usefully reinforce the more widely significant source of regime legitimacy, mundane foreign policy gains. If the West desired either the means (Soviet economic dependence and diversification) or the outcome (Soviet economic and political liberalization), it had provisionally to accept their price in the form of a measure of Soviet geopolitical outreach. It could do so as long as countervailing Western power was effectively allied to the checks implicit in the extraideological Russian fear of and revulsion for the Third World and China – the real, Asian, East. Both types of constraints could be depended upon to make the price of greater Soviet leeway manageable by limiting the rate and scope of Soviet outreach.

Instead, however, American policy makers reversed the causal calculus. Accordingly, an unyielding denial of all Soviet geopolitical ambitions was perceived as a way to galvanize internal Soviet forces – both elite and popular – presumably committed to economic reform and craving material goods as their first or sole priority.

In this context, one fundamental recognition must precede all intelligent debate about the future directions of American foreign policy. Both from logical and pragmatic standpoints, a firm link between doctrine and strategy needs to be forged – between a set of premises (concerning the nature of the Soviet power system) and a set of precepts (suggesting ways of affecting that power's evolution). First, a relatively benign doctrine regarding the Soviet system must have a complementary strategy that differs more than faintly from one projecting a negative appraisal of past and likely future change in that system. Second, to be formally realistic and practically attractive, that strategy must be directed against something as well as be for something (or be keyed to a positive outcome). Third, the strategy must arguably unite international and domestic outcomes in ways potentially profitable to both of the principal parties. A conceptual statement of such a strategy, while it cannot immediately be translated into practical policy across the board, is necessary in order to confer intellectual authority upon even tentative and exploratory steps toward its application. National strategy is in place only when doctrinal rigor underlies and disciplines diplomatic flexibility, even as the latter works simultaneously to shield rigorous doctrine from the dangers of doctrinaire rigidity.

A good example of insufficient marginal adaptations in strategy is to be found in a recent analysis drawn from extensive professional experience in Soviet matters.[1] The author revises the negative and static image of Soviet Russia, but his suggested alterations in US policy remain superficial. Thus, in regard to the critical issue of competition in the Third World, the author recommends more sustained US–Soviet consultations and efforts to depolarize actors in Third World conflicts. Yet, to be more than cosmetic (as regards consultations) or fortuitous (as regards depolarization), both changes of current approaches require (1) enhancing the Soviet sense of being a coequal actor in the Third World as a basis for real and independent influence (consultations); and (2) reducing American fears of, and opposition to, any and all Soviet penetrations into the Third World (local depolarization). That is to say, more cooperation and control in the Third World require a prior US commitment to a strategy that breaks with the psychosis, the premises, and the precepts of reflexive containment. Lacking this disengagement from frozen patterns of thought and intended actions, US fears will inhibit bona fide consultation between the superpowers, while US opposition to Soviet 'expansionism' will encourage polarization on the part of competing local powers eager to exploit one or the other superpower and their rivalry.

A different argument, still only marginally or superficially adjusted, is no more helpful in opening up new vistas. This is the argument that the West or the United States can and should 'relax' because the Soviet inroads are, on unmistakable past evidence, the ineffectual efforts and fleeting accomplishments of a rival clearly unequal to its ambition in material resource as much as in cultural or any other appeal. Mastering the tendency to panic on the grounds of Soviet inability to cause pain may calm overwrought nerves, but it is not sufficient to improve policy. In fact, a Soviet regime hard-pressed domestically and regionally, running an asymmetrically rising-and-declining power system, is unlikely to gain greater legitimacy (and therefore unlikely to tolerate more social and functional pluralism within and more openness abroad) by adding global setbacks and failures to internal problems.

Nor is it useful, or even correct, to contend that there is no meaningful relationship between foreign success and internal regime stability on the grounds that external success is not satisfying, and failure offensive, to Russian national pride. It is equally misleading to argue that fulfilling through success or obstructing through failure popularly shared historic ambitions has no meaningful bearing on widespread conceptions of national entitlement. To disregard the foreign factor in the political economy of regime legitimation, and thus of the ability of the regime to relax internally, is to concede the fact of deep-seated Russian patriotism with one hand while with the other abstracting its dynamic implications by stipulating an all-absorbing Russian consumersim (laced with alcoholism).

In reordering a consistent national strategy, it is crucial, first, that it move beyond 'selective' containment excluding only areas of US disinterest or impotence. Only a more far-reaching revision of US strategy is a fitting counterpart of a more benign view of the Soviet system. Such a view will rate higher than is commonly done the system's ability to evolve into (Russian-style) authoritarianism from totalitarianism on the domestic front. In addition, it will credit the system's potential readiness, on the basis of enhanced capability and access, to inflect its external assertiveness (as distinguished from gratuitously attributed adventurism) toward actions supportive of a minimal world order – provided this order is not decreed in every detail by the United States. If this strategy is to promote intra-Soviet decompression, it demands deliberate relaxation of American constraints on Russian self-perception as a European world power.

And second, in a viable strategy third-party threats must not be considered less notable than the Soviets' just because they are diffuse or deferred. Accordingly, the decompression strategy aims to implement gradually the common concerns of the two superpowers with such third-party threats – concerns that will otherwise remain latent and without practical effect. It posits a joint stake in cooperating, rather than competing, for a margin of control over an increasingly chaotic world. In addition to the other assumptions supportive of this guardedly cooptative approach, the converging effect of the Soviets' economic shortcomings, plus setbacks on the periphery, might make them respond more positively to a more forthcoming American approach than they might have previously when they still followed the United States' view that the Third World was an ideal arena for a decisive breakthrough.

In this connection, it is relevant to ask which other major power is still capable of identifying with, or of exploiting, allegedly revolutionary forces and aspirations. In this perspective, too, it may no longer be reliably possible to deal with the ascendancy drives of major powers in neatly spaced succession, in which today's adversary becomes tomorrow's ally, and vice versa. More specifically, any policy that, in the current phase, increased dependence on China (less assuredly a balancing than a provocative counterweight to America's culturally cognate rival) constitutes a more problematic version of *Realpolitik* now than when the Most Christian King of France colluded with the Turk (against the Catholic Habsburg emperor) and the British allied with Japan (against Russia and in preference to Germany). Such textbook precedents are not automatically binding while the West as a civilization including Russia is organically retreating and more vulnerable to military and technological self-destruction than the East.

Decompressed Environment and Defense in Depth

Any credible attempt to alleviate and transcend the conflictual issue of hegemony in the international system will have to embody positive goals, attending to the causes of the emerging crisis of that system. It can do so if, in addition to laying the bases for a postempire world order, it aims to improve prospects for a durable social order within the two imperial powers. This requirement overlaps with the third criterion of valid strategy, which concerns a close interlock of domestic and international objectives and processes. A decompression strategy postulates one set of internal payoffs for the Soviet Union and another for the United States.

As regards the Soviet Union, foreign policy successes in the geopolitical arena, guardedly condoned by the West and thus relatively risk- and cost-free, are apt to feed back beneficially into the domestic Soviet arena on two counts. First, they add external inducements to internal pressures for enhanced economic efficacy, as a condition for stabilizing substantive gains; and second, they enhance internal regime-legitimacy as a result of increased prestige. The greater need for economic efficacy will compel greater functional diversification (i.e., pluralism) within the ruling elites, tending to deconcentrate the hold on power. Greater regime legitimacy should permit the elimination of the remaining totalitarian residue, while also extending the range of social pluralism. This ought to first contain and eventually neutralize the authoritarian biases latent in technocratic ascendancy anywhere and especially deeply embedded in Russia's national heritage.

Whether such trends are described as de-ideologization and pragmatization or liberalization, they only make the Soviet system more conventional, and ultimately ever more compatible with Western values – even if not visibly convergent with such values in areas other than those related to the formulation and management of foreign policy.

With regard to the United States itself, revising the Soviet security threat downward would permit the US military-security commitment to be redirected toward threats that are no less real, although they do call for less massive and sophisticated (and, therefore, less costly) military technology. This should ease the American version of social crisis, which has been fostered by a conspicuous conflict between security needs and welfare expectations. Essentially conservative, the revised strategy would facilitate a return to more traditional social values and more orthodox economic policies.[2]

The ideal – and not wholly unrealistic – global vision is that of a transition from two competitive empire systems (each by turns consolidated, strained, or rigidified by the competition) to an increasingly more dynamic inter-empire equilibrium. The equilibrium is loosened up by (1) cooperation in the face of third-party threats, and (2) the simultaneous but marginally disciplined emergence of these third parties. In turn, the emergence of such powers can be expected to (1) reduce the area of possible and necessary control by, and profitable contention between, the imperial powers, and (2) foster progress toward a postimperial, multipower equilibrium system. At peak effectiveness, such a system would be moderated by occasional concert among the greater of the powers which have arisen out of the process of relatively orderly change.

From the earliest stage, the objectives behind the strategy of decompressing the rival imperial power provide a justification for treating a range of peripheral positions as expendable from the viewpoint of US security and credibility. While such positions can be defined theoretically, what and where they are is in practice a contingent matter. Calculated detachment and qualified permissiveness are apt to enhance cohesion at the center of America's essential core empire (i.e., in relations with Western Europe and Japan). They reduce allied fears of unrestrained US–Soviet competition in Third World areas – areas that are excluded from effective inter-allied coordination. Greater US detachment might even foster active US–West European (and Japanese?) cooperation in Third World areas of truly vital and genuinely common interest. The same US posture changes the perception of stakes and mutual needs between the United States and key Third World actors. Making US involvement less automatically supportive is apt to enhance US control or influence over still-essential Third World attitudes and policies even before the effects of joint or parallel US and Soviet treatments of peripheral disorder have spread more widely. In short, the organization of the residual US empire will be made easier by a US policy that opposes a partially unilateral (American) strategy to wholly anarchic (Third World) unilateralism – one that responds to increased license with a somewhat freer hand, liberated from obsolete commitments embodying outdated concerns.

Moving from organization to defense of the residual empire, even the most tentative steps toward decompression in US–Soviet relations will entail a definitive abandonment of the static perimeter strategy in favor of an elastic defense strategy in greater depth. The former has induced reflexive responses to (Soviet-inspired?) local threats at the outermost frontiers of empire (or defense perimeter). It was peculiar to Democratic administrations including those of Truman, Kennedy, and Johnson. An elastic defense strategy 'logically' includes the willingness to depend on ad hoc combinations of US reserve power, primarily economic and hypothetically nuclear, conjointly with manipulation at the highest level of relations between the great powers, for limitation of hostile advances on the margins. This strategy was preferred by the more economy-conscious Republican administrations from Eisenhower to Nixon.

The practitioners of the static perimeter defense strategy failed to complete the objective of a liberal grand empire. The more elastic in-depth defense strategy also remained incomplete, because its proponents were not willing to involve the Soviets in the transition to an equilibrium-based conservative order of power. Whereas the first strategy failed because of US inability to either defeat or associate itself with extreme Third World nationalism, the second failed to overcome a cold war-related, ideologically colored evaluation of the strategic implications of even moderate Soviet globalism. In the process, its proponents perpetuated (almost as much as those of the static-defense school) an obsessive tendency dating from both world wars. They underestimated the various defensive, counteroffensive, military, political, and strategic options available to the offshore–insular power (currently the United States) relative to the continental –heartland power (now the USSR) at all levels of 'peaceful' or militant competition. Instead, both schools were discouraged by worst-case scenarios from seriously contemplating a dynamic strategy for mobile 'political warfare' that would test the possibility of evolving toward concord at acceptable cost and risk. They saw the Soviet potential and objectives as fully expressed in essentially physical and seemingly quantifiable resources and assets, such as raw materials, military materiel, or interior lines for projecting force. Even the more elastic of the two schools remained, also in the hands of a European-born historian–strategist, imprisoned with narrowly concretist, and congenitally American, thought patterns.[3]

When a strategy of defense in depth does not postulate a positive outcome capable of affecting future international behavior of the rival superpower through internal change, it lacks justification for sustaining calculated geopolitical withdrawals ('disengagement' and 'devolution') and corresponding concessions to the Soviet concern for geopolitical parity. Without such a rationale, the strategy is confined to an ultimately insufficient economic rationale (of lessened material cost albeit at the heightened risk of 'irreversible' advances by a putatively 'irreconcilable' hostile power). Lacking any theoretical confidence in a beneficent long-term effect on the rival power, the strategy rests on a fragile assumption that the cumulative impact of hostile advances at the periphery will elicit self-defensive responses from local forces. As a result, illustrated by the vacillations of the Carter administration, any would-be elastic strategy is doomed to relapse into static approaches to defense. As these falter or fail, they confirm a debilitating tendency to equate Soviet success with American setback.

Any strategy designed to compensate for the attrition of empire will be vulnerable to certain costs of transition to a revised ratio of (reduced) resource to (increased) risk that is essential to an equilibrium situation. A strategy of deliberate retreats and concessions will be even more vulnerable since it makes a virtue out of realigning perceptions of threats, targets, and objectives, while requiring the United States to make a major – but not unrecoverable – investment in a new hypothesis in advance of any flow of tangible dividends from the Soviet Union. The decompression strategy will also suffer with regard to Soviet perceptions and responses because of the difficulty inherent in executing all elastic-defense strategies, i.e., how to convey intent as to procedure and outcome without losing control over the process – its tempo and terminus. However, the difficulty of communicating the rationale for initiating the decompression strategy, the results expected from it, and the requirements for sustaining it must be set against the difficulty, perhaps even the impossibility, of articulating a less radically altered overall strategy that would still point to outcomes going beyond the results of the containment strategy achieved so far. Such a strategy must offer more than marginal revisions, and its advocates must suggest more than mechanical readjustments, of interest and capabilities in relation to threats, commitments, and objectives. It must hold out a substantive vision rooted in the organic factors that make up present reality and control future prospects.

Deadends Past and Potential

In the West, only a reassessment of the Soviet threat will help to ease and master the conflicts between short-term Atlantic priorities and long-term pan-European aspirations. It is these conflicts that increasingly beset intra-NATO relationships.[4] Within Europe, as well as globally, it will be necessary to expand the scope of analysis geographically (from the Atlantic West, or Europe only, to the Third World), temporally (projecting the present against the past and a putative future, or alternative futures), and conceptually (relating external goals to domestic efficacy, internal and external efficacy to regime legitimacy, and legitimacy to potential for liberality). Only then can one be released from futilely trying to square the circle of Soviet reform and East–West rapprochement: which is to come first and be given priority in diplomatic strategy.

To the same degree that less alarmist perceptions of Soviet power and intentions have prevailed in Western Europe than in America, all trans-Atlantic disagreements over specifics of organizing the defense of the American empire in its European core have become derivative. More than any particular deployment of theater nuclear weapons and delivery systems, differential perceptions of Soviet Russia in the Brezhnev and post-Brezhnev era have threatened to uncouple the two parts of the Occident. A corrective policy of guarded East–West appeasement could be phrased in one of two ways: in terms of a greater West including Russia, in the interest of keeping the West at the center of a restructured world order; or in terms of a likewise enlarged Europe (possibly minus much if not all of America's present involvement there) conceived in the interest of making the old continent a meaningful part of the new order. Failing both, the preferred and the second-best objective and outcome, the 'empire of the world' (signifying no more than the ability to shield the international system from the forces of chaos and from anarchy's drift toward tyranny) risks slipping prematurely out of the hands of a civilization rooted in Europe, without ensuring a safe evolution toward a less ethnocentrically defined order of things.

Not the least purpose or merit of applying the analytic categories of 'empire' to the American historical experience is to establish a formal theoretical basis for Soviet–Western convergence in international actions and function, if not at first in their dominant values. One may, therefore, run more than routine risks when testing the hypothesis that Russia's overt foreign policy continues to hide the ambition of becoming an integral part of the West – to share in its rights and duties on the world stage, and to that end, to either wed 'Europa' by mutual consent legally (as America did in due course) or, the rough suit rejected, move to regain self-respect by possessing her physically. If the botched Anglo-German scenario is repeated, American achievements of the second half of this century will be imperiled in the next century in circumstances that will not require a nuclear disaster to be fatal to a shared civilization.

A proponent of a strategy that takes such dangers seriously may confine himself to the central issue. The reasoning behind the decompression strategy is admittedly as optimistic about Soviet power as it is pessimistic about the environment in which it is asserted and about the consequences of attempting to restrain its dynamic in order to disrupt its structures. It frankly proposes relaxation in place of restraint, and decompression in place of decomposition. One thing it is not, however: it is not naive about Soviet power. To profess the immutable oppressiveness and hostility of the Soviet system is to oppose one ideology with another, and to overstate the effect of any ideology on politics and of the will to power on its ways. The only dogmatic point to be made about a coercive system of power is that it will change: for the better when not for the worse, for worse if not for the better.

Naivety about power is most common, and socially dangerous, as regards interplays within a larger field of forces. It may consist of the assumption that what we do unto others has no effect on their perceptions of us and their internal experiences; that a major change will or can leave the rest as before, and can therefore be meaningfully evaluated in isolation from its repercussions. This is the asystemic fallacy. It consists more widely still in the belief that either goodwill or adroit and patient policies can resolve all conflicts and tensions simultaneously. This is the liberal delusion. But, the shallowly realistic and falsely conservative self-deception is no less naive for posing as morally cynical or historically sophisticated. It holds that today, as to a degree in the past, the enemy can be safely defeated as a power and destroyed as a society and yet remain an intact and willing future partner, giving his unstinting all in a fight against the victor's past accomplice in bringing about the thwarted party's demotion if not destruction. The tacit assumption that a humbled Russia can be engaged in the defense of the West at some future date is the unrecognized error buried deep in the rational motives and the visceral instincts behind current US policies. It is the last, pathetic remnant of a specifically Western conceit, made worse by the hubris of a body politic which, issued from the New World, faces the outside without true insight into the lineaments of the centuries-long tragic chain of acts and events that had given it a brief mastery over the Old World.

As we endure the tedium of the contemporary turbulence in world affairs, the oppressive triviality of much that passes for high policy must not dull our capacity for choosing wisely at the crossroads – for the West as for Russia[5] – where a mistake would indeed be worse than a crime. It would mean catastrophe as the cause of equilibrium was sacrificed to a primitively realistic cultivation of the balance of power just as empire had been sacrificed, in the late Asian war, by a misguidedly idealistic subversion of the balance of wills.[6] Should the urgently needed new myth, positing a larger West, prove stillborn amidst mean divisions, the Soviet rulers would be united with the Russian people on behalf of rejecting for good what had not been offered in time. They might even bid successfully for reconciliation with their non-Russian Slavic kin, releasing them from present bondage. The reshaping of the Soviet-Russian empire in Eastern Europe is as unavoidable in the longer run as it has been ongoing in the short, so long as it was covered up by Soviet inchings toward greater influence globally and was unimpeded by feverish domestic lunges for sudden independence locally. A true 'Socialist commonwealth' implies placing movement toward greater corporate equality between its greater and lesser constituents above instant and complete individual freedom for all subjects. These are interchangeable values in terms of psychic gratification and rewards, even if not in terms of an academic theory of human needs and desires. A clear loss of value would take place only if an adverse turn of events deferred, perhaps permanently, the healing of the subordinate East–West cleavage within an Occident that faces, along with concrete, also an immaterial reality:

1 Just as in the wake of the French revolutionary and imperial epic in nineteenth-century Europe, so in the politics of the post-cold war/imperial era in our time: when reality becomes paltry while it secretes radically diverse potentialities, narrow realism is not enough.

2 When conventional realism suggests policies pointing to the self-destruction of a culture within the widest orbit it can be felt as

common, it ceases to cast a bridge across the actual to the desirable by way of the possible: its literal canons must be transcended as a condition of realigning the determining perception of 'necessities'.

3   America is too changed as well as aged to renew its energies by means of a nostalgically tribal nationalism, just as the conventional West is not only too weak but also unready to transcend nation- or state-centered realism through pan-human idealism: a higher realism for the era of intercultural politics dictates a reaching out for a pan-Occidental version of Westernism.

4   When American realists of the more literate brand contrast the subtleties of the Chinese with the boorishness of the Russian political style and culture, the fawning perception of the vaunted other mirrors the true Easterner's converse valuation of themselves: mocking the atavisms of the Russians is a way of confessing one's relative debility and the shared culture's inferiority at one stroke.

5   For a witness to wrest the sense of terror and pity from a catastrophic denouement to the age's renewed contest between Russia and 'Europe', and between cosmos and chaos at large, is unlikely to profit us directly. The territorial setting defines the current installment in the Europe-centered series of tripartite land–sea power conflicts as terminal, compounding the possible effect of the ultimate weapon. The two finalities are coming together in what may be the vanishing opportunity to seize a last chance for triumph over tragedy.

Notes

1   R. Buchanan Thompson, 'The Real Russia', *Foreign Policy*, Summer 1982, pp. 26–45. Buchanan's most recent Soviet assignment was as US Consul General in Leningrad.

2   On the economic issues see David P. Calleo, *The Imperious Economy* (Cambridge, Mass.: Harvard University Press, 1982).

3   These thought patterns and their implications for America's defense–strategic past and present are the subject of Michael Vlahos, *America: Images of Empire* (Washington, DC: SAIS Occasional Papers in International Affairs, August 1982). A related obsession with the concrete and tangible and visible – only reinforced by the electoral exigencies of the US political system – has favored focusing on bilateral negotiations producing

fixed and formal conclusions. This professional diplomatic bias is opposed to employing initially unilateral strategies keyed to an organic evolution susceptible of creating a more satisfactory or stable factual situation. While the negotiations mania has continued to predominate in the misnamed peace 'process' for the Middle East, it merged nicely with the concretist bias in placing SALT – or START – talks at the center of US–Soviet relations.

4 See Pierre Hassner, 'The Shifting Foundation', *Foreign Policy*, Fall 1982, pp. 3–20, as well as the Summer 1982 issue of *SAIS Review* devoted to 'The Tenuous Alliance'.

5 See Flora Lewis, 'At the Soviet crossroads,' *New York Times*, 28 September 1982, p. A23, reporting on the re-emerging cleavage between Westernizers and Slavophiles, now also within the Soviet–Marxist elite. But see also Dostoevsky: 'We Russians have two motherlands – Russia and Europe – even in cases where we call ourselves Slavophiles.' Cited in George Steiner, *Tolstoy or Dostoevsky* (New York: Alfred A. Knopf, 1959), pp. 31–2.

6 On the United States as 'empire' see my *Imperial America: The International Politics of Primacy* (Baltimore: Johns Hopkins University Press, 1967) and, more fundamental, *Career of Empire: America and Imperial Expansion over Land and Sea* (Baltimore, Johns Hopkins University Press, 1978).

PART IV

Communities and Civilizations

7

America against Russia

Shifting from the effort to contain Russian power at the center to rolling back its translation into influence at the periphery has implied a doubt about the value and viability of the basic approach. However, the more ambitious strategy, propelled as it is by the unavowed wish to do away with the Soviet system altogether, is likely to be revealed, possibly too late, as even more of an intellectually ill-founded and politically irresponsible gamble – and, as such, inferior to a more positively inspired and formulated wager.

Competing Premises and Projections

The expectation of success for the containment-plus strategy rests on the assumption that the United States can triumph by denying Russian ambitions in the Third World and Western Europe, while continuing to expose the Soviet Union to rising pressures in Asia and growing stresses in Eastern Europe, even as the regime faces the combined effects of economic shortcomings and politico-military exertions. Persisting in the strategy would, so the theory goes, bring about a revolutionary situation hospitable to the dislocation of Soviet domestic and imperial controls, or force the threatened political system to perform the improbable task of speedily reforming itself from the roots up. Buttressing these sanguine expectations has been the conviction that US-style societal pluralism would unfailingly withstand its innate vulnerabilities to win over the flagrant vices of statist authoritarianism; that the endemically crises-ridden continental–authoritarian way of constructing public order could not sufficiently draw upon a compensating resilience to outlast the grand cycle from take-off through apogee to the unraveling of economic dominance, peculiar to a long line of pre-eminent maritime–mercantile polities.

The wager contrary to that which underpins active containment and denial strategy rests on another possibility: that it might be more effective as well as safer to decompress the environment of Soviet foreign policy; that an abrupt revolutionary overthrow is less likely and might be less desirable than a gradual and orderly relaxation of controls and constraints on both sides; and that only a self-assured because also externally successful regime can safely implement its stake in improving internal efficiencies and thus meet the need for greater flexibility in the international arena. Implicitly denying that possibility, the seemingly lower-cost gamble in support of an all-round anti-Soviet 'democratic revolution' in fact risks not only a global war; it is also liable to replace the decreasingly repressive empire-type regional order managed from Moscow with one even less benign and less Western. Avoiding either pitfall – of a bigger war and more brutal or alien empire – warrants experimenting with return to an earlier posture. Then, the two superpowers' tacit cooperation in guaranteeing India against one of China's punishing expeditions paved the way for an important arms control accord (the 1963 Test Ban Treaty), without constituting the instant and full-scale condominium the Soviets were later to propound against Chinese 'expansionism' as the foundation for a since defunct detente.[1]

Apart from counterbalancing the intervening US–Chinese tie, staking out the areas of US–Soviet concert would remove a prime incentive for the Soviets' militantly anti-US self-assertion in the world at large. With the attainment of real parity, the number two power is tamed even as it is strengthened. It can now afford to forgo badgering the leading world power for admission to conservative partnership (a technique pioneered by Imperial Germany), and no longer needs to go about this with the aid of ostensibly unorthodox or nominally revolutionary means (an approach perfected by Soviet Russia). In the absence of real parity and the prospect of partnership, Soviet bidding for equality worldwide could not but narrow down to searching for leverage in areas of vital US interests in order to better protect Russia's continuing primacy in her own immediate orbit. In the absence of US–Soviet accord, moreover, the requirement to match China's support for Third World radicals has been a reinforcing incentive to Soviet 'adventurism'. Yet hidden in the ideological impulse is, again, as in the inter-regional bargaining, the more real fear that a mere residue of Chinese radicalism might, if unchecked or unmatched, ripen into serious revisionism aimed at the territorial integrity of the Soviet state itself. Thus, too, Germany's *Weltpolitik* was a facet of security concerns relative to France and Russia.

Once the Chinese became reconciled with the United States, it became even more onerous for the Soviets to remain inactive. The immediate cost in status of being placed on the same footing with China, as America's potential partner, prefigured eventual greater costs in security for Russia as the prime target of the actually emerging Sino-American strategic partnership. The costs could not be offset by benefits in trade and technology doled out by the rival superpower contingent on the Soviets' geopolitical self-effacement.

Thus, if the abortive Nixon–Brezhnev detente proved anything, it showed that (no more than Great Britain navigating between Germany and Russia) the United States could not achieve either of the coveted outcomes: one, enjoy alone world-power status without commensurately compensating Soviet Russia anywhere; or two, place itself at the head and effortlessly occupy the pivot of a great-power triangle by simultaneously improving relations with both Russia and China. Moving beyond the foredoomed version of detente meant locating instead a firm ground somewhere between US–Soviet collusion against China and US–Chinese conspiracy against Russia, while avoiding both a free hand for Soviet ambitions in the Third World and unqualified obstruction of all Soviet geopolitical aspirations. One or the other extreme was bequeathed by an earlier era as a missed chance or an unreal opportunity, a too eagerly embraced, all-too-facile option.

So long as the dominant premises prevail, US policy will be riddled with inconsistencies detrimental to its inner logic before compromising fatally its external efficacy. Chief among the inconsistencies is one between the secret wish to bring about the disintegration of the Soviet state and empire and the publicized expectation that the adversary exhibit a moderation out of keeping with the lot in store for him, if only (a related inconsistency) because the Marxist-Leninist ideology which is held responsible for the faulted 'adventurism' is fundamentally rational. Thus, as the Soviets watch the socialist wave of the future irreversibly recede, they are expected to display a prudence that conforms with the liberal-democratic ideal of the reasonable man, and the capitalist model of the rationally calculating economic man – both prone to viewing as irrational much of behavior mandated by the Reason of State.

Accordingly, at the bottom of the inconsistencies is an incongruity, which to grasp more than superficially exceeds the ability of the bureaucratic and wider culture that shapes US policy. It bears on the fundamental difference between the Soviet Russian statist and the American societal mindsets. The state-centered mentality, with its peculiarly idealist implications, inverts as much the presumption created by official Soviet ideology as the more materialist societal mindset contravenes the American civic belief system. However sincerely it may be idealized, the societal ethos implies an inescapably material thrust: society originates in and revolves around the functional underpinning of physical survival through material well-being; distributive justice within society is inseparable from the allocation of material satisfactions. In contradistinction from society, the state is about the perennial intangibles of power and prestige, role and status. The ideal connotation is reflected in that the critical issue of justice revolves around the abstract rights and duties of the state and its subjects, with the corporate prevailing indisputably over the individual interests under the stress of inner conflict as well as outer threat.

The preconditions of a Western–insular type of society develop conjointly with the accretion of major role and weight in power politics. By contrast, the statist bias of a continental polity will fade only with the role's passing. The latter fact combines with the difference to underline the significance of yet another phenomenon: the statist bias, characteristic of the European continent generally, deepens in proportion to Eastern developmental timelags, intensifying the Eastern Europeans' ambiguous compound of attraction and revulsion vis-à-vis the West. Thus the state–society and the East–West dichotomies are indissolubly linked in cardinal questions, wherein the imperative demand of the era's principal Eastern power confronts the near-insoluble dilemma of the day's pre-eminent Western power. Can the West be seen as inviting its historically separated part in the East to equality in power and prestige, complementarity in resource and mutuality of respect? Or must the West be finally scorned as foreclosing progress toward either form of satisfaction for the Eastern party and power? Hence, is it or is it not possible for the two powers to act in ways that would redress next to imbalances between states also the more elusive imbalances affecting the statist–societal amalgam within countries on both sides of the shifting divide?

It is this setting (made up of practically confusing logical inconsistencies and behavioral impulses emanating from a normatively incongruous blend of historically evolved state-centered Soviet idealism and theoretically postulated historical materialism, and its American counterpart) that augments the conceptual inadequacy of US policy. It reflects the American culture's tendency to pragmatism and an ideologically reinforced bias toward paranoia. If pragmatism places too great a weight on testing expectations against immediate results, paranoia perceives 'clear and present danger' in any apparent challenge to the culturally ingrained optimistic outlook; whereas the pragmatic outlook has affected especially the arms-related sector of US–Soviet relations, the paranoid proclivity has beset mainly the geopolitical dimension. The contrasting geohistorical conditions which shaped the Central-to-Eastern European political cultures, including the Russian, have produced a fundamentally different, pessimistic mentality. Pessimism goes deeper and resists disproof by contrary experience longer than optimism. It leads to anticipating and reacting to hypothetical future dangers, regardless of any favorable (equally long-term) prospects opened up by societal mythology such as, in the Russian case, the official Soviet ideology. Insofar as the other side of pessimism is fatalism, the psychological compound has a positive side: whatever may be the attendant persecution complex, the deeper-lodged tendency will be not to react to adverse developments hysterically because they belie – as they do for the American optimist – the ideal dreamworld projected forward from an unreally benign past experience. Instead, as a vague and remotely rooted dread turns into pressing danger, the pessimistic Russian fatalist's inner composure in the face of all-too-familiar adversity will be shocked into a resigned but also relieved, supremely defiant even if potentially suicidal, response to ordeal and acceptance of necessity.

It matters greatly whether a social and bureaucratic culture is, like the American, essentially present-oriented because it overlays innate pragmatism with a touch of paranoia; or is both psychologically and philosophically future-oriented with more than a touch of fatalism, such as the Russian. The predisposition will determine in what way and at what point in time the anticipation of potentially catastropic developments and outcomes begins to affect strategy, aggravating the ubiquitous worst-case thought pattern that weighs on all statecraft as it responds to the culturally neutral structure of the competitive state system. In swaying the neutral dynamic one way or another – sooner and relatively milder for the American, later but then drastically for the Russian – the cultural propensities that condition strategy-relevant premises and projections evolve organically. From this basis they foster operational transactions that issue in conflict while permitting occasional cooperation to reflect a secretly growing measure of convergence.

The dynamics of confrontation eventuating in the possibility of convergence bears on the prospects for a gradual confluence of Soviet and US foreign policy postures and perspectives extending to sociopolitical orders in due course. Foremost among the hindrances to narrowing the differences on either – the operational and the more organic – plane have been US and Soviet efforts to convert third countries to a particular model of sociopolitical order. The various means of persuasion and repression, inducement and constraint, deployed by primarily insular and more distinctively continental powers have been historically complementary mainly as unrealized possibilities. For the same reasons, the methods and techniques the contemporary rivals apply to bringing backward countries into the modern world have no more than a potential for being selectively combined for a superior aggregate effect. The more backward, economically hard-to-develop and socially polarized, the countries or areas are, the more the rigors of a Leninist-type party dictatorship may be the surer and shorter – although not the milder – route to 'modernization'. If only as a transitional phase, the single-party state may be more appropriate in severely reform-resistant cases than the alternative process of mediating institutional constraints on social mobilization through the agency of a comparatively free market and more or less genuine political democracy.

Competing efforts to convert Third World parties to rival sociopolitical ideologies is the contemporary version of the European wars of religion. As such, the attempts are likely to reproduce the defeat of both of the creedal fountainheads in favor of a middle ground of more or less fervent nativist adaptations to growing religio-ideological skepticism if not indifference. Meanwhile, as was the case in sixteenth- to seventeenth-century Europe, provisional outcomes in different places will depend on the kind and quality of a society's relationship to the established power center: presently US-centered West in particular, just as, before, the Roman papacy or

'German' emperorship and, in the still earlier phase of conversion from paganism to Christianity, Rome or Constantinople. Moreover, the issue of politico-military and now also economic hegemony – its attraction or a revulsion from it – will interlock with strictly local factors in both the wider global and the narrower regional arenas. Such factors bear on the legitimacy or just solidity of political regimes and the equity notably of the land tenure-related economic regimes and will, like the hegemony-related concerns, prevail over the intrinsic merits or demerits of the competing ideologies.

The intervening conflicts will, once again, distort the evolution of the encompassing state system. Retarding it for a time, the contentions may eventually promote evolution in the previously experienced ways if they integrate the more enduring post-ideological residues into variously institutionalized mixes of statist secularism (currently fostered mainly along the Leninist route) and societal materialism (the capitalist route). The main danger is that the ideological schism (socialist–capitalist as, before, Catholic–Protestant) will be intermittently revitalized by its correspondence with parties to the geopolitical (land – sea power) schism; and that the continuing acerbity will resuscitate (in the form of xenophobic nationalism) the equivalent of an earlier coincidence affecting Russia as much or more than her Byzantine predecessor. The parallel East–West and Orthodox–Catholic schisms cut confusingly across that between both branches of the occidental (Christian) politico-cultural universe and the wholly oriental (Islamic, functionally analogous at present to the Sinic). Such interlocks might again exacerbate the most utilitarian dispositions before ideologically extreme late-emerging wings of the contending creeds (lately quasi-Maoist and right-wing American) moved once more the previously moderated, older wings (post-Stalinist Soviet and liberal anti-Soviet Western) further to the center, with the final effect of de-ideologizing individual strategies long and widely enough to do the same for the international system itself.

The 'Unthinkable' War

Viewing the United States as pivotal in the US–Soviet–Chinese triangle has meant regarding it as free to explore the ranges from detente to confrontation along one side of the triangle and from virulent hostility to quasi-alliance along the other. That perception obscured meanwhile a less flattering image of the configuration. It is one that replaces the maritime–continental and the West–East dichotomy with a still older and, in ever-changing manifestations, persistent relationship between the 'civilized' core and its 'barbarian' circumference. In that optic, the United States appears no longer as the decisive insular balancer but as a receding imperial center.

The Nixon–Kissinger theory of detente amounted to offering the Soviet barbarians enough material tribute (via trade and technology transfers) to keep them quiet on the imperial frontier. Designed to purchase geopolitical 'restraint' with rewards qualitatively different from the expected return, the intended payoff represented 'appease-ment' in its most pejorative meaning – one different from appeasing a relationship by means of reapportioning qualitatively indentical, geopolitical, access conjointly with consequent responsibilities in a revised relationship of two comparably 'civilized' and essentially conservative powers. The formal roles were reversed, without changing the issue materially, once normalization with China began under the sign of the no longer confidently imperial Americans becoming in effect the barbarians called upon to pay a ceremonial tribute (the Kissinger and Nixon journeyings to Peking) to a superior political civilization and reascending empire.

As the crucial part of the strategy directed at the Soviets under the name of detente showed signs of failing, due to its lack of elementary realism and sense of history – both ruling out the proposed truck as unacceptable to a self-consciously ascending and geopolitically ambitious power – a more material content began to be poured into the established forms of the US–China connection. In keeping with tradition, trade and technology followed the preliminary prostrations (the notorious kowtow), without the Chinese surrendering their initial psychological advantage over the American side. In so doing, they drew with unusual ability on the strategically ideal position of a rear-continental power that automatically gives it a regulatory role relative to the offshore insular and centrally located amphibious powers, regardless of whether it is weak or strong or active or passive. The Celestial Empire was now despoiled of its former immunities, but also free of many past inhibitions; and the inheritors of the heavenly mandate were able to act along the lines of the Imperial German Chancellor von Bülow in the Anglo-Russian and Stalin in the Anglo-German setting. They could do more than anticipate, and could from time to time encourage, a warlike conflict between the major antagonists, to be arbitrated by the unengaged power to its advantage.

The closer the United States moved beyond exploring to exploiting the potential of the triangular setting in order to constrain Soviet 'adventurism', the more did applying strategy lopsidedly reinforce the imbalance in the US–Chinese relationship.[2] Granted, the reluctance of the Chinese to be too deeply involved with and indebted to the other of the 'social imperialists', together with US concern lest the military-technological aspect of 'normalization' provoke the Soviet side to rash acts, has provided a check on going too far too fast. The basic approach, however, remains in force. It has found reassuring sustenance in the thought that a major and especially a nuclear war is rationally unthinkable between the superpowers and can be safely discounted as a contingency relevant for devising peacetime policies. The cavalier attitude overlooked the real danger from the Soviet fear of dual encirclement, implicit in the miliary-technological application of scientific innovations that kept pushing out an ever receding frontier on the one hand, and, on the other, in the US-promoted alignments or complicities that were closing in on the Russian corelands in keeping with the classic precepts of traditional balance of power.

Any Russian regime would in the circumstances be under mounting pressure to break out of a tightening ring of strangulation, its choice confined to the one-time German option between a western and an eastern military strategy. Thus limited, the choice will favor the theater fittest to require no more than a limited military thrust, unlikely to trigger employment of the nuclear instruments if it is convincingly confined to reshaping only the psychological setting of a no longer endurable diplomatic logjam or arms-related stress. In such circumstances, and despite its poor historical record, the western strategy will remain the more attractive one into the early twenty-first century. It is then that the Russian need to do something may well have become urgent, not least because a more industrialized and better armed China will have ceased to be an easy target for a pre-emptive surgical strike.

Instructive in this connection is the shift in Germany from the post-1870 Russia-first strategic plan of the elder Moltke to the West-first Schlieffen Plan. It was primarily the result of intervening changes in military technology, which were not confined to the new ultimate weapon, the dreadnoughts. However, in the end it was not the arms race, intensified though it was by fears of a hostile surprise attack on both sides, that caused the war. It merely helped precipitate into warlike enactment causes inhering in unresolved geopolitical next to newly salient demographic issues. Once the war had been unleash-ed, moreover, essential equivalence in an untested and differentially perfected ultimate weapon, with only imperfectly understood utility for mutual deterrence, political leverage, or strategic employment, made both belligerents disinclined to use it either offensively or defensively.

For an example where impulses from the military-technological or vertical variety of encirclement match or outdo incentives embedded in the horizontal-geopolitical arena, one must shift from the Anglo-German scenario preceding World War I to a later one that also dramatizes more vividly the critical role of differences in political cultures. The operative parallel is then between Pearl Harbor, triggered by the prospect of a US naval buildup checkmating the prior Japanese effort, and a Soviet pre-emptive nuclear first strike inspired by a comparable turn in the arms race. Depending on the relative importance of conventional and 'revolutionary' military capabilities, the potentially war-precipitating asymmetries in technological prow-ess and material accomplishment, differences in political cultures, and divergent perceptions of geopolitical needs and threats will weigh somewhat differently on the dispositions of the rivals. But the choice facing the upthrusting – dissatisfied revisionist – party does not change fundamentally as a result. Such a party can drop out of the competi-tion and surrender all hope of parity or pre-eminence rewarding what may be an unrepeatable prior effort Or it can forestall an irreversible backsliding and strike out first, 'offensively', in the hope of defeating the odds (if it is the weaker side) or, at worst, reducing adverse disparities by mutually crippling blows – possibly as a preliminary to a rematch.

In either case, questions such as whether the apprehensions and expectations that motivated the choice were correct or not, and whether disregarding the underlying fears would have proven them unfounded, are retrospective considerations of little immediate help to the decision maker faced with a hard-to-avoid, and harder-to-reverse, choice. A context that is plausibly catastrophic for the Soviet Union in the triangular setting is made up about equally of geopolitical and military-technological features, with organic and operational dimensions. Implicit in the organic dimension is the prospect of adverse comparative economic growth rates relative to one or both of the other corners in the triangle, under strains from an increasingly taxing arms race. It is, again, of little immediate help – significant though it may become eventually – to assess unequal peacetime growths speculatively against estimates of relative rates of material destruction and social demoralization in a nuclear or conventional war. Operationally, the catastrophic pole moves nearer when the tempo of US – Chinese encirclement outstrips inchings toward US–Soviet accommodation. The situation worsens further when Soviet geopolitical gains have not been sufficient to compensate for a widening military-technological gap, notably in the strategically blocking defensive weaponry.

The potential of revolutionary weaponry to cripple politically the party unable to match the latest and the best technology reaffirms the traditional concern with preserving an irreducible minimum of (great-power) role and status. It raises that concern well above any more widely publicized fears of a militarily disabling first (nuclear) strike by the adversary. The direct consequence of the foremost political concern's primacy is to undo confidence in the invariably restraining effect of ultimate weapons on contingent behavior, and thus to restore international politics to its prenuclear, conventional mode. The incidental consequence is to dispel a seeming contradiction, that of nuclear weapons having little or no political utility (especially for ostensibly offensive purposes) while (presumably) radically changing international politics. One is thus forced to confront a genuine paradox of progress in state-of-art military technology undoing its supposedly progressive effect on policy.

The analogy from wars to religion finds yet another application when competitive conversion efforts raise the possibility of militarized conflict with a party whose political culture, as distinguished from ineffectually superimposed ideology, does not automatically assign the highest prized value to institutionally unmediated individuals. The statist outlook of the Soviet regime, and the 'average' Russian's, is the last in Europe to revolve around corporate values capable of filling the void opened up by religious skepticism or indifference. As such, the outlook represents a species of counter-reformation, damming in the energies and appetites let loose by individualist-societal emancipation from secular authority. Initiated by the seafaring Dutch and English, and perpetuated overseas by the Americans, the sociopolitical 'reformation' responded to the deterioration of feudal Europe's land–military sacral monarchy into an increasingly sterile continental absolutism, while entering in its turn yet another claim to universality and finality. In challenging that claim, the Soviet-socialist incarnation of Russian nationalism only follows on the heels of Imperial and National Socialist embodiments of the German. It, too, attempts to integrate the coercive-military and the acquisitive-maritime elements into a new format of continent-based power type under the aegis of a secularized 'faith'. If the updated continental–oceanic synthesis were to succeed in containing the appeals of materiality latent in the surviving values of insular polities while shedding its own coercive-military trappings, it could make more credible the claim to stand for necessary reform rather than staging a merely reactive counter-reformation: to represent a viable resurgence of hierarchically ordered authority for a larger and harsher world of the future, needful of a sturdier mix of order and freedom within and between communities.

This mark of continuity alone affirms the place of the Soviet state in a long line of evolution, on the whole productive despite its liability to vitiation. It overshadows the divergence that originates in an earlier Russia's having missed a key moment in the evolution of the European mind, one which finally released the medieval community of faith from any remaining urge to divorce itself from the earthly sphere in that it restored rationally generated power to its classic role within the compass of the secular territorial state. If much in the Soviet way of injecting the spirit of the Renaissance into the turmoil inhabiting the Russian soul was objectionable, some of it at least was the normal consequence of delays in catching up with a perennial view of man and the world – one which Western Europe is rapidly leaving behind as no longer befitting her current realitites and the United States resists making its own as contrary to an idealized perception of self. Remote as they may seem from the technologies that dominate and the technocratic mentalities that would direct nuclear-military strategy, such considerations do point to the location of real danger. The main peril does not lie primarily in either strategic miscalculation or accidental failure of the command–control mechanism on the Soviet side, producing a 'first strike'. It lies chiefly in the Western belief that a dual (horizontal and vertical) encirclement might insure foolproof strategic stability without entailing a political price unacceptable to the Russian mentality.

A touch of what might pass for madness has always inhered in responses to extreme predicaments, even when the maker of policy was clinically sane: thus Spain's Olivares long into the Thirty Years War, straining the last resources of the Habsburg realm at the risk of encompassing its dissolution; Napoleon throughout, when rationalizing severally the ambition to refloat France's faltering greatness on the full tide of his own; and Hitler until perhaps shortly before the end, when rousing the stressful *Land der Mitte* through a flawed resurrection of the Middle Ages for the sake of arresting history's time clock by enlarging the living space around a Greater Germany. It was the demonic impulse in these men that either set off or prolonged wars that were total by the standards of the age in which they took place. But it was also the policies of the eminently practical men at the helm of the maritime nations that made the aggressions appear defensive, and the wars just, to the continental peoples' yet unbroken spirit. Barring evidence to the contrary, the nuclear age operates under the same psychological laws of extraordinary behavior. It has not annulled the normative criteria of either strategic rationality or sentimental grievance by raising the level of physical destruction – its being acceptable depending more than ever on the perceived injury to the collective moral self as well as the growing capacity to reconstruct materially.

Thus it makes as little sense to prospectively discount, as it would to retrospectively damn, a Soviet resort to extreme force as either demented or delinquent, simply because it would be at variance with criteria of judgment inspired by demographic statistics and routine notions of sustainable damage. It would make no more sense than it does to impugn as devious the conventionally prudent Russian tendency to combine nuclear deterrence with civil and other limited defense. It is more profitable to note that all of the hegemonic drives in the past only followed upon the frustration of more moderate prior aspirations. What matters today is whether a likewise comparatively mild Soviet global outreach, following on the regional one by tsarist Russia, can be accommodated before thwarting it sets the stage for a climax. Under a worst-case hypothesis, conflating pressures from the two kinds of encirclement might eventually fuse also the traditionally escalating two phases of land–sea power confrontations into one with truly catastrophic consequences.

Tragic Ironies and Empty Triumphs

A nuclear or high-technology conventional war is commonly viewed as the ultimate tragedy. In fact, such a war would merely expose the more authentically tragic character of interstate relations – or its misapprehension, prompting competitive quests for onesided triumphs. It is the tragic dimension of statecraft that raises the underlying laws of politics, with their compulsions, to the plane of a moral law only hypothetically capable of constraining them as it arbitrates the tension between freedom and necessity. Just as force will tend to elicit an equal force in the action–reaction, attraction–revulsion, mechanics of interstate relations, so a vital force will strain to break out of the constriction as certainly as power flows into a vacuum, in order to eschew a static system's liability to deterioration. Moreover, a conflict that is (ultimately) exacerbated rather than (provisionally) contained by balance-of-power mechanics will intensify further if one or both sides wage it without taking into account the extenuating circumstances of the rivals' divergent situations and uneven stages of evolution along the space–time continuum. Ignoring the geohistorically conditioned propensities will also block out appreciation of the organismic properties that affect the movement of bodies politic by virtue of the strivings that an older physics accorded a central place in its cosmology.

Called upon to take definitive forms as it were overnight, post-World War II global American statecraft could not mature gradually enough to absorb the more elusive, including organic and evolutionary, aspects of international politics. Instead, the ardent converts from US-style idealism have willingly imprisoned themselves in the straitjacket of balance-of-power realism. Its minimalist rules implement a law of universal validity. But they also suffer from encompassing only quantitative inequalities among actors differentiated by nothing more significant than superficially applied attributes of 'offense' and 'defense'. The limitation creates a normative void that invites exaggerating the determinative influence of (American) civic myths and (Soviet) social ideologies largely extraneous to the constants that shape the process of world politics. One result is to link the quantitatively construed relativities of balance-of-power mechanics to the qualitative absolutes of 'aggression' and 'opposition to aggression'; the other, to view the latter as making operational radically different actor values judged in abstraction from their organic foundation. Though discrete, the two tendencies combine to preclude insight into the pervasive operational—organic duality in international relations as it bears on the tragic nature of interstate conflict. In keeping with the nature of the tragic, that characteristic resides in the ambiguity of the difference between (pre-emptive) offense and (assertive) defense, induced operationally, on the one hand and, on the other, the intrinsically equal relative worth of the contending parties, their values (moulding resources) and interests (maturing into rights), as geohistorically conditioned organic individualities.

In the last analysis, viewing interstate conflict as tragic requires acknowledging the essential equivalence of the parties to it — and the equivalence itself as ethically controlling. Accepting the equivalence depends in turn on laying bare and then fully appreciating the existential, geohistorical reasons for superficial differences in observable conduct — reasons which the presuppositions of the balance of power discount as irrelevant. Whereas actors caught up in the balance of power as quantifiable masses in motion are qualitatively interchangeable except for the distinction between offense and defense treated as value-based and -reflecting absolutes, in the tragic context the actors are interchangeable as bearers of values and upholders of interests that are relative to their evolving constitutions and functional roles. On the normative plane, the momentum that brings tragedy into the open overarches the conspicuous agitation of the conflictual mechanics. But, operationally, the tragic form and the implementing transactions can both be traced to the contrary thrusts of constraints and compulsions in a decentralized system of states. The two reciprocally checking tendencies make up all there is of order in such a system, which one or another actor will repeatedly try to break out of by means of hegemonic expansion.

Insensitivity to the tragic character of adversary politics at its most intense has not been confined to US-Soviet relations, but colors dominant attitudes to social upheavals connecting North America's own past to the South African present. It flows naturally from a culture that resists historically informed speculation leading to self-examination. The blindspot and its culture source are only partially explained by the absence from the nation's experience of 'tragedy' defined as the incidence of testing wars. In fact, America's sole genuinely tragic experience of the kind, the Civil War, has itself been trivialized into the preception of one side's unquestioned right fighting and conquering unqualified wrong. A reinforcing reason for the insensitivity to tragedy has been also its consequence, compounding the limitation. It has to do with the realistically inclined American pragmatist's commitment to removing from the ends of politics the least vestige of the romantic vision as it touches upon the shape and scope of the ideal community to be realized. It is this vision which, cast over the prudential calculations of *Realpolitik*, makes statecraft more genuinely realistic because more fully humane.

Combining a narrowly mechanistic view of politics with a sweepingly Manichean world view blots out in one sweep a totalistic – mechanical *and* organic – interpretation of an era's major conflict and a tragic perspective on such conflict. In the US–Soviet setting the collision of interests has reflected about equally the essential identity of the adversaries (as imperial core powers) and their existential diversity (as unevenly situated and evolved insular and continental powers), which in turn extends to differently deranged relationships between state and society. The Soviets have only superficially realigned the constitutents of the inherited tsarist conjunction of a flawed social structure and an overbearing state. America, for her part, has lacked a state consciousness that would channel contrary currents in a fluid and increasingly fragmented society. In consequence, resources for foreign policy have been generated inadequately, or not spontaneously enough, on the Soviet side; they were being mobilized and applied inadequately on the American side. For the continental power, the result was to shortchange mainly the means and slant the methods of a foreign policy closely attuned to the manifest and on the whole simple laws of power and power politics, mediated through the territorial state as both fact and idea. The means-related shortcoming clashed head on with the failure to sustain coherent aims and apprehend rival goals on the part of the insular polity, bemused by the difficulty of reducing complex societal dynamics to either prescriptively or predictively reliable guidelines for foreign policy.

Denying not only the fact of shared imperfections but also the inherent validity of the most basic values of the adversary (however 'tragically' misapplied) will inevitably debase a conflict. It has repeatedly lowered the US–Soviet conflict from the plane of tragedy to the platitudes of mere melodrama. However, adding the normative to the other facets of denied parity will eventually help incite a defensive bid for predominance. The aspirant to hegemony is the real tragic hero of politics, acting under a compulsion to transcend by acts of ultimately self-defeating defiance the constraints of a plural state system when they aggregate into an order perceived as not only imperfect but also inequitable. Challenging fate in the face of present denial and prospective decline is the last resort of despair just as often as the supreme sign of demonic arrogance. Therefore, the rebellion is properly an occasion for feeling pity for its causes, as well as experiencing terror at its consequence. It is a compelling reason for trying to understand, so as to overcome, the two sides of passion that, as heightened emotion or testing endurance, always threaten to invade the pragmatic pursuit of interests and then elevate it to a plane worthy of man's higher − if not necessarily better − nature.

Tragedy is most vividly present when unimpeachably rational strategic judgments translate into acts that fit the conventionally reasonable person's notion of criminal folly. The feeling of awe deepens and blends with disbelief when both the tragic context and the catastrophic climax are riddled with lightly overlooked ironies. Minor or major, the ironies of the US–Soviet conflict cast all the longer and darker a shadow over the future for being intensely illuminated from behind by their historical antecedents.

Relatively minor is the irony of a conflict induced originally by structural conditions at the center that is progressively exacerbated by intense contentions over minute peripheral stakes. The distorted emphasis was already present in the heyday of trans-Atlantic mercantilism, when it bred overseas priorities despite the primacy of intra-European economic exchanges. Deranging in the process the proportionate relationship between size of arena and scale of actor capabilities was only one of the consequences, although a seriously upsetting one for some. The distortion, with its harmful potential, has since migrated from economic stakes to military–strategic assets and supposed requirements. A protracted conflict will gravitate to areas combining lower risk with a higher profit margin relative to invested resource, when compared with conditions in a stalemated core of the system. However, when the two superpowers perpetuate an earlier error in only superficially different ways, they do so for reasons above and beyond any calculation of profit, or peril or prestige. Instead, they also revive the mythical quality which the Old World once attributed to the freshly discovered New. Then, too, the world beyond the core was idealized as a cure for domestic woes and an occasion for valiant deeds vindicating the claim to providential destiny. Only eventually were the peripheral fringes revealed as a source of draining conflict between the traditional centers and creeping corruption within each of them, due not least to misguided ways of converting unbelievers to one or another 'true religion'.

Much the same is true now when corruption assumes the form of lax banking practices in dealing with Third World debtors, temptations of easy victroy over vastly inferior parties in the military field, or relaxed standards of truth and widening chasms between rhetoric and reality in the political realm. Nor does corruption vanish for being indirect or deferred, as when Third World fundamentalism or revisionism, reacting with the terroristic weapons of the weak to alien values or resented Western policies, engenders defensively retributory or abjectly propitiatory responses on the moral level of the original offenses. The Soviets are implicated in like vicious circles, of which the Afghanistan imbroglio is only the most flagrant example. Each of the superpowers is led to propagate the latest version of a 'black legend' about the other, so as better to whiten itself. The unadmitted complicity does little to diminish the harmful effects of trying to bring the outermost world closer to oneself instead of containing its infectious disorders jointly.

More portentously ironic is the consequence of denying the premier land power both continental pre-eminence and overseas parity. The denial will defeat its object by forcing the frustrated continental state into a more extreme stance. And the ensuing drive – one not so much spontaneous as compulsive, less predatory than pre-emptive, so long as it grows out of the land–sea power schism only – will derive much of the positive emotion and energy that characterize it from a but fortuitously parallel cleavage.

The East–West schism is true to form when it too exhibits the overlaps that exacerbate conflict before they can be drawn upon to appease it. One or the other potential effect will predominate, depending on the ways of diffusing power. Means for enhancing capabilities can (and did) migrate from the West toward an East materially still unprepared and unproductive, in conditions of minimum sustained contact or conflict between the two: thus, in Russia's case near-exclusively up to and including the Petrine reforms.

Or, militant reception can merge (and has been gradually merging) with more or less imitative invention in conditions of intense East–West competition.

The contention-free kind of diffusion habitually spelled deformation, translating nominal convergence into effective divergence in such coupled spheres as military organization or technology and industrialism, nationalism and romanticism and Enlightenment and socialism, or constitutionalism and party politics. So long as the rate of transmission quickened in these conditions, the real or felt discrepancies could not but widen, postponing East's assimilation to West – let alone a converging movement on both sides – to the emergence of overtly or covertly waged competition. One way of fostering the positive trend, however perversely, has been through outflanking alliances meant to deflect the nearer-eastern power into conflict farther to the east. The strategy had been repeatedly tried in the West against the Ottomans (facing first the Mongols and then Turkomans or Persians on their eastern flank) before being more ineptly or less deliberately applied to Germany in relation to Russia and resurfacing in the US–Soviet–Chinese triangle. In actuality, the attempt to deflect the targeted power eastward mostly impelled it to direct its militancy westward, either (in the German case) to gain only time and space or (in the Ottoman instance) to improve skills and acquire techniques for dealing with the more dangerous and backward eastern enemy.

Assimilating East to West in capabilities or techniques by means of overt competition or covertly inimical strategy is benignly ironic, whether or not narrowing the gap undergirds any emergent sharing of concern with the rear-continental power. Differently ironic is a fact that might comfort US pragmatists but has not pacified the dogmatists. Diffusion from the West outward is henceforth worldwide in scope. It ought to create a basis for affinity between a not yet fully developed Russia and the underdeveloped world. But the uneven spacing of the distortions that will result from one-directional diffusion actually reduce the appeal of the Soviet model in peripheral societies: they defeat the feeling of solidarity without conferring on the Soviet Union a sufficient and sufficiently attractive superiority. Moreover, since the 'uneven development' Lenin was looking to for openings in revolutionary situations now divides the globally defined East at least as much as the East from West, official Soviet ideology can do little to help Russian policies deal with the handicap. It can at best ease instrumentally and legitimize doctrinally the kind of opportunistic support for peripheral revolts which the tsars provided routinely within a narrower sector to insurgents against British rule.

Compared with the feelings aroused by East–West peculiarities, a rationally analytical ideology such as Marxism-Leninism has perforce only the uncertain impact of a cerebral construct, notably on conduct unrelated to the underlying social impulse. Although self-consciously related to action, the ideology has demonstrably swayed no major foreign policy measure outside the Soviet imperium, itself subject to more evenly balanced tenets of the creed and imperatives of control. Officially embalmed sacred texts of a revolutionary dogma are better suited to impress radical aspirants to power (or critics of its actual exercise) than to retain dominance over behavior constrained by the responsibilities of power. Separated from Russian nationalism and statism, the ideology falls short of infusing the Soviet polity with the extra ingredient that Counter-Reformation Catholicism imparted to Habsburg Spain, secular Jacobin nationalism to revolutionary and Bonapartist France, and either Social Darwinism or Fascism to the two modern German Reichs. As an independent energetic impulse, Marxism's may actually compare best with the elan the French Third Republic was only supposed to draw from the Bergsonian philosophy in its heyday. The famed concept of the correlation of forces itself articulates too insufficiently the wide range of included factors to be as sharp a tool for analysis and guide to action in critical circumstances as its conventional model implementing an elementary law of power. Like the rest of the ideological apparatus, it helps rationalize policies for which the actual strategic *raison d'être* is more mundane, and the visceral impulse to which is saturated with myths more ancient and more deeply internalized.

Soviet reality illustrated the ephemeral nature of revolutionary ideology and policy even as Stalin made radical efforts to keep the revolutionary thrust alive by superficially reactionary means. As the agent, in his contest with Trotsky, of the influence that the art of necessary governance will exert on even the most self-consciously scientific ideology, Stalin practiced terror long enough to achieve a crucial material transformation. Thus also Mao, in trying to keep 'permanent' revolution in being at the cost of material retrogression, was to disprove its practicality definitively. Both revolutionaries from above left it to lesser successors to implement any revolution's fatal propensity to ripen into a thermidorian halfway house of the Directory type, built to shelter mellowed ex-revolutionaries from two calamities: relapse into the terror-shielded climax or extinction under quasi-Bonapartist reaction to its excesses preparatory to a full (rather than only partial and camouflaged) restoration of the old order.

The still vital Soviet ideology is one that celebrates state power triumphant in war and, so far as compatible with its maintenance, pledges continuing increase in social welfare in peace. The surviving trappings can be regarded as an insuperable barrier to internal evolution, and evolution itself as a process that could only be set back by US–Soviet appeasement. It is more useful, however, to distinguish the ideology's operative force from its declaratory facet. The former then appears as potentially less inimical to accommodation than is the operative rationale of a US detente policy viewed and applied as nothing more substantial than a cheaper and safer surrogate for militant containment.

The 'Last' Empire

So long as the governing Soviet pattern of beliefs continues to shift from the 'internationalist' to the nationalist end of the range, it harbors a dual implication for Soviet (and, thus, American) foreign policy. One bears on the fundamental ambivalence toward the liberal-materialist West. The perplexity, displayed also by the preceding globally ambitious polity east of the Rhine (Germany), serves to accent the insistence on genuine equality. Aim and attitude interlock in making it depend on progress toward such parity whether affinity prevails over antipathy or the other way round. The path of progress has been defined in lapidary terms by a great romantic realist (De Gaulle: '*détente, entente, coopération*'). It proceeds from reapportioning material and strategic assets, through admission of equivalence in basic communal values and partial convergence in foreign-policy principles and instruments, to a growing measure of partnership. The second implication of the Leninist ideology losing ground to Soviet-statist norms and the Russian-nationalist creed moderates the bearing of the first implication (involving parity) and reduces its cost for US and Western interests. It shifts prime concern from world revolution (and worldwide influence) to endangered national integrity.

The continental priority will not remove frictions with the more authentically global United States any more than Imperial Germany's disposed of the conflict with Britain. But it enhances the prospects for peaceably recasting world equilibrium even when foreclosing pat solutions for the narrowly Eurasian balance. Ages of adversity have forged the fundamental realism of the Russian body politic. They have made it stronger than any professed ideology of the ancient state's current incarnation. That is why the chief obstacle to accommodation may well lie in the more deeply ingrained American civic myths. Compensate as they do for inner uncertainties, the self-congratulatory myths breed a meliorist delusion about the world when they are doctrinally liberal, and foster a Manichean fantasy when they are dogmatically conservative. The salient fact is that the blessings of nature no longer translate effortlessly into special favors of history; that America has grown from a spoiled infant, thriving on quarrels among her elders, into a middle age tempted by the comforts of sanctimony. The fact that the mood has gained hold over the national psyche at a time when the testing choice may be rapidly narrowing to one between timely sharing and deferred (but, then, all the more painful) sacrifice may well be the ultimate irony looming within the tragic potential of US foreign policy.

If the makers of the policy discount the risks of war, because they deem war unthinkable in its new form, they run nonetheless willingly the implied risks to bring low a Soviet empire they consider the last of the old kind. Such hopes or expectations are not without precedents. In fact, however, the British had fought Spain and prevailed with French complicity, only to confront France twice with Germanic assistance before their winning over Imperial Germany spawned the Nazi perversion of the Prussian ethos and set the stage for bequeathing the struggle with the incidentally invigorated Russian ally to Britain's imperial successor. Nor is this all. The cost of success grows when each thwarted and reformed offender generates less societal energy for joining defense against the next and stronger challenger. Defeated Habsburg Spain fought French ascendancy willingly to the limit of her depleted resources, while the zeal of the French for containing Germany weakened from one world war to the next and the Germans' supposedly innate bellicism has been yielding to pacifism at the grass roots ever since.

In the circumstances, it hardly serves the cause of European stability and, by extension, global order to aim at the destruction of the Soviet empire and state. Breaking up the uncongenial system of controls instead of breaking new ground by integrating a Russia-centered aggregation of power with the Euro-Atlantic segment of a globally defined West would only re-enact similar past scenarios with equally or more questionable results. Extinguished Soviet power would have ceased to threaten American interests in Western Europe and her monopoly of influence in the Western Hemisphere, leaving in its wake little reason for the United States to concern itself with Eastern Europe. It suffices to remember that Britain's interest in that luckless region, too, had been wholly due to either Russian or German threats to the English stake in the then Near East on the route to India, and that no Western power (including interwar France) has ever found a workable basis for a productive or a profitable economic engagement with the area between Russia and Germany. With the dissolution of the Soviet political system, the West European community would face a refragmented Eastern European power vacuum exerting an irresistible pull on reunified Germany. A largely disengaged America would, however, no longer offer a counterpoise to the will of a resurgent German state to play a role in the East before being tempted to rule there.

The predictable consequences would be several. A 'free and independent' Ukraine would again seek German protection against the champions of Great Russia and Greater Poland. The Poles themselves would not know whether to try to dominate in one direction or fear domination from another, while the Czechs would be at a loss for how to earn forgiveness for having expelled the Sudeten Germans in retribution for their complicity with Nazi Germany. Whereas the Hungarians would be nervously on the alert against their lesser Slavic and non-Slavic neighbors, invitations to mediate the revived quarrels over territory along their borders and farther down in the Balkans would steer the Germans' policy toward the pitfalls of unsought management. The weakened Great Russians, now again isolated from the West, would be once more exposed to a stronger Asia, whether only externally or also internally. Retreating into a Solzhenitsyn-like xenophobia of the old-believer type would accurately reflect their being finally relegated to a rear-continental status. That status implied a key role when the position was occupied with respect to Germany and in alliance with England. This would no longer be true for an amputated Russia positioned behind a China correspondingly aggrandized and would-be amphibious, confronting an insular power bloc headed by Pacific-centered United States or Japan. Thus situated, the Russians would scarcely be fit or willing to use their remaining weight to distract pressures from remote Western democracies as they did in both world wars. They might well seek consolation instead in witnessing from afar the disarray of a West that freed itself from the bracing fear of Soviet power only to prove unprepared for either grander tasks or larger threats.

From the Ottoman through the Habsburg to the short-lived Greater German multinational empire, an ominous trend has been in evidence. Each power complex left in the wake of its dissolution a larger expanse of harder-to-manage fragmentation, opening wider the gates to assault on progressively weakening contiguous defenses in the West. Dissolving the Soviet empire attracts many as the prize of winning the equivalent of a third world war. Yet fulfilling such a wish would bid fair to undo the little that was positive in the consequences of the second global conflict. At the very least, the maritime–continental spectrum would be reversed into an east-to-west direction, on the ruins of what in spatial terms alone is the last such pattern that can center on the West. With its passing would fade immediate prospects, however tentative, for a more evenly diffused (multipolar) pattern of regional and global powers. Instead, the stage would be set for the supposedly last continental empire to be followed, as had been the war waged to end wars, by the next: the latest version of the Chinese imperial mode, properly updated in territorial scope, managerial style, and expansionist surge. It is doubtful that a fourth German Reich would be soon and firmly enough in place to offer sufficient counterpoise, and could under pressure afford to become a superior alternative, in the Eastern European marches of the Asian heartland.

The short- to middle-term prognosis is meanwhile for continued unrest migrating from place to place around the periphery while the center faces diverging lines of possible developments. One arises out of US–Soviet accommodation, promising deliverance from the consequences of disregard for the latent constituents of tragedy. The other inspires the premonition of doom, should a strategy arising out of the paranoia that is the dark underside of America's clinging to an inherited optimism trigger the latent fatalism of the Russians.

The priority of geopolitical givens over military–strategic and military–technological features of the present conflict dictates meanwhile that even more important than curbing arms is to check excessive alarms over Soviet penetrations and ambitions. So long as a congealed distribution of power is uneven, freezing nuclear weaponry on any level of parity is more unthinkable than nuclear war. Arms races do not cause wars: conflict is militarized when geopolitical configurations remain controversial too long and genuinely politic approaches to them are absent. But when arms issues monopolize attention, they do generate tendencies and tensions, give rise to mindsets and a momentum, that are conducive to war. Arms competition preceding a military conflict will influence more often its initial than its later phase and outcome; but it is the effect a prolonged arms competition has on social and political fabrics of the contestants that will determine the consequences of a rivalry in ways that transcend the incidence of war and its military result.

Rivals such as America and Russia will clash militantly over insubstantial peripheral stakes from their diverse points of departure in defense of pretendedly vital interests and universal values. A judicious strategy for timely concert between such rivals can help avoid war by fostering convergence and inflecting diversity toward complementarity. A thus developing concert can divert an only superficially peaceful competition from uniting the imperial adversaries in shared defeat, favoring the next empire, even in the absence of a still thinkable war.

Notes

1 On the Soviet 'official approaches' in the early 1970s and the immediate consequence for the Soviet activity in Angola of the US refusing to join in the 'adventure', see William G. Hyland, 'The Sino-Soviet conflict: dilemmas of the strategic triangle'. In The American Assembly and Council on Foreign Relations, *The China Factor: Sino-American Relations and the Global Scene* (Englewood Cliffs: Prentice-Hall, 1981) esp. pp. 138–9.

2 For discussion of alternative strategies see chapter 1, p. 34–8.

8

A West with Russia

Empires rise and fall and, outward appearances and changing political and economic orders notwithstanding, alter in style more than in substance. The disappearance of one makes room for another; openly coercive imperial systems built around continental core powers exist side by side with ostensibly consensual ones around insular–maritime powers; hegemonies within each are legitimated by the fact or prospect of hegemonial wars between the principals. Still deeply buried underneath the drift from the contemporary continental empire to the next is the conflict between the defining conditions of America and Europe: between the alliance leader, on the one hand, and the culturally as well as otherwise crucial part of the benign American version of empire, on the other. The former finds itself currently in stalemate, the latter in transition, along parallel ranges bounded by supremacy and parity, empire and equilibrium, mechanical balance and diplomatic pre-eminence. Failure to attend in time to the latent fissure between the two wings of the conventional West risks shifting westward to the mid-Atlantic the line currently dividing the European continent, without beneficially rearranging the politics of East–West differentiation on the global plane.

The American Stalemate

America's stalemate originates in the reluctance to assume the different costs of either empire or equilibrium. The reluctance, rooted in the nature of American society and culture, has made it as difficult to steadily implement as to adaptatively change US foreign policy. Equally deep-seated is the source of the dynamic tension between balance and pre-eminence that permeates Europe. It is reducible, by contrast, to basic concepts of statecraft distilled from the turmoils of a crystallizing state system. The differences in the governing modes of thought and action of America and Europe are sufficient to generate a chronically troubled relationship. The distemper is worsened whenever the rapidly shifting surface of American culture and society belies the firmly ingrained fundamental predispositions, and the compound of fickle moods and fixed mentality interplays erratically with the incrementally evolved (if periodically defied and deformed) norms of the informal public law of Europe.

The intra-alliance disparities in the formative and the currently favored time frames complicate the task of synchronizing medium-to-long-term responses to, and outcomes of, policies critical for the United States as a world power and for Europe as a regional political civilization. While the United States is frozen in the posture of 'anti-Sovietism', denying essential parity on the global plane, the thawing of the post-World War II ice-age in Europe means that the West Europeans inch toward, if not 'pro-Russianism', then accepting adjustment to the fact of Russia as the major European power. Reminiscent of the plight of the emblematic two-headed eagle of the decaying European empires, the strategic stalemate that ties down the single-headed eagle of the still-vigorous American republic results from the failure of clear vision in either of the two possible directions.

The post-World War II global American empire, growing out of the cold war in Europe, has fallen victim in the aftermath of a real war in Asia to the incompatibility between grand strategy and mass society, between a single-minded policy and a pluralistic polity. Society's normative values failed to nourish the spirit needed to implement a tentatively adopted role, while the vacuum of popular understanding grew imperceptibly underneath initially serviceable elite attitudes and practices of a mushrooming managerial bureaucracy. As a result, and before it could begin to formulate a sustaining mythology independently of the communist threat, the imperial establishment was summarily pulled down into the vortex of an adverse mass reaction to the first contact with unavoidable realities of empire. What mattered next was a creative rebound from a failed experience into a settled but flexible policy, unburdened of the fixation that had supplied the impetus to empire but not a foundation for holding onto it.

A two-power competition which does not overawe third parties will incite their self-assertion, feeding international anarchy. This fact alone points to the stake the established major powers have in world equilibrium. It also suggests that the greatest need for such equilibrium, as distinct from quantitative balance of power, is in intermediate areas that are incipiently crystallizing, but are unready to form on their own regional orders of constitutionally governed nation states, selectively mandated by conservative imperatives, let alone rise to the level of functionally integrated communities dear to the liberal imagination. If such an equilibrium can be defined as a standoff between pressures for coercive control and drift toward chaos, the corresponding US and Soviet postures and policies are those of inter-superpower solidarity and inter-superpower subversion: the first vis-à-vis disorders of common concern, the second within the powers' respective areas of special interest and ordering influence. Any real or potential benefit that can accrue from solidarity augments automatically the cost of its opposite, the urge to undermine the rival's dominion.

Movement from one posture to the other ought to parallel movement from empire to equilibrium. Neither was eased by developing rigidities in an institutionally aging (if physically ever younger) bureaucratic and affiliated intellectual apparatus. A popular predisposition in favor of easy-to-grasp nostrums for dealing with issues painted in black and white colors meshed nicely with the mentality of a foreign policy establishment whose political branch has been no more prepared than its professional arm to offer major revisions in perceptions and alternatives in policy. Sterility consolidated stalemate and the two entrenched policy ever more firmly in the strategy of containment. Conceptual immobilism made it possible for a strategy decried as 'static' to survive from one set of conditions into greatly changed circumstances. A stubborn possessiveness that might have been a strength for empire became thus the source of outright weaknesses or only ambiguities for the policy of equilibrium.

As part of efforts to come to terms with the consequences, the strategy for neither-empire-nor-equilibrium was rationalized on the 'realistic' side by self-styled conservatives invoking the balance of power in the interest of narrowly defined preponderance. It was legitimized on the 'humanistic' side by the same conservatives joining opportunistically with the liberals in stressing the primacy of the individual's right to freedom from coercion. The gradually waning liberal–utopian perception of the North–South, or center–periphery, issue helped reinforce dogmatic biases on the East–West issue commonly advertised as conservative. The 'typical' liberal will perceive Soviet Russia as a threat to either indigenously managed regional orders or the undisturbed exercise by the United States of a duty to correct North–South imbalances on the global stage. He forgets that if the regional balances are only emerging the sense of obligation has been patently fading, but not enough to disclose a realistic view of the North–South issues and their implications for the East–West relationship. It is not part of the liberal creed that order is instrumentally prior to justice; control is preconditional to orderly compensation for real or imagined injustices; and mechanisms for policing the process of change is a complement to redistributing wealth and relocating power. The 'typical' US conservative will more readily accept the onus of intervention on behalf of order, control, and policing. However, he will resist sharing the burden with the other imperial state even if it helped shed the restraints on the major powers and restrain the license of the minor parties, equally originating in the US–Soviet conflict.

That some sharing was in order became manifest when US retreat from world empire was attended by the erosion of the imperial formula for political economy, trading strategic protection by the hegemonial ally for preferential easements of the attendant economic costs. Within the US-led alliance, a historically non-existent ideal format of a liberal economic system that is not dominated by a core economy served as the screen behind which unevenly burdened and exposed allies could compete without politically disruptive consequences. Along the axis of East–West conflict, the inter-nation arms race performed its usual role as a short-term stimulus and long-term threat to national prosperity. It substituted for single-minded preparation for warfare as much as it inhibited widening the enjoyment of the several constituents of welfare. At the same time, no economic subgroup outside the American farmer has contributed the socially most congenial argument for muting the US–Soviet conflict, capable of reinforcing politico-strategic rationales. Big business has lacked the sophistication to combat anti-Sovietism with propositions that would match in persuasiveness and outdo in validity the widely advanced economic reasons for US–Chinese normalization. Big labor has been unwilling to fill the gap, because it lacked the conviction or the courage to part with the compulsory ideological orthodoxy of anti-communism uneasily coupled with anti-Japanese protectionism and ambivalence toward the 'military-industrial complex'.

An added responsibility fell in the circumstances on the principal beneficiaries of the change in the sociocultural profile of the top-level foreign policy elite, the social and ethnic marginals in the American polity, who, as part of the Vietnam fiasco, finally replaced the abdicating traditional ruling class in its last stronghold. They might have proceeded to affirm their right to succession by infusing America's imperial role with new esprit and fresh energy. Instead, they became the greatest single obstacle to a policy of US–Soviet accommodation for equilibrium. In the process, they proved on the whole more contentious than truly combative, antagonistic rather then positively assertive, eager to deny from instinct rather then defend at risk. They have imparted thus a predominantly negative thrust to their self-assertion as the new political class, while continuing to fragment into subgroups with ever narrower policy specializations, to be reaggregated, if at all, by ideological uniformity and orthodoxy. As, in keeping with a social law of universal application, increasingly competent second- and third-generation technicians were replacing the generalist 'founding fathers' of American post-World War II foreign policy, the question whether the change was for better or worse overshadowed many another quandary in US–Soviet – and US–European – relations.

The European 'Dialectic'

Matters have been different in Europe for reasons and in ways manifest so far mainly in the surface tremors of a rising groundswell, in a mere ripple above the crosscurrents which impel American and West European actors in diverging directions.

In their new-found fascination with the balance of power, the makers of American policy lack a taste for the complexities of equilibrium as much as they lacked the necessary constancy for empire. A Europe wedded by tradition to relating primitive opposites in a blend enriched by both was historically shaped – and is again beginning to be moved – by adherence to one-power pre-eminence in status as the modifier of multistate balance of power. Balanced power would insure the independence of viable states and plurality in the system's structure; diplomatic pre-eminence provided the system with a central focus. It also enhanced its essential coherence, rooted in the uniformity of stakes. Within a generally understood frame of reference for acting and reacting statecraft, the resulting tensions were for long less disruptive than many-sidedly creative on the whole. The principle of pre-eminence perpetuated the Imperial Roman ideal of unity, even as actual pre-eminence was passed on competitively from the Ottonian and the Hohenstaufen Emperors to a succession of continental monarchies (Habsburg Spain, Bourbon France, and Bismarckian–Wilhelmine Germany, with a mid-nineteenth-century interlude for Romanov Russia). The fact of power balancing stimulated the strengths before revealing the frailty of Greek polis-type individuality on a stage progressively enlarged from Italy to Europe in her entirety. The one thing no major European power would lastingly tolerate was that which America has since clung to as a means of avoiding both choice and movement: a permanent hegemonial alliance (as distinct from a temporary grand coalition in and for war) under the auspices of the insular or any other power in pretended defense of balance.

It was never easy to organize the European state system around two apparently contrasting but operationally complementary principles. However, the link between principle and practice began to wear thin only when an extra-continental state, Britain, took to impugning the exercise of diplomatic pre-eminence as tantamount to a drive for universal dominance. The imputation was first rehearsed against seventeenth-century France on behalf of coastal–maritime Netherlands, when the cause of England's religious–dynastic stability required grafting the interests of the weakened Dutch onto the rising trunk of English power. Thereafter, the method was perfected into the stock in trade of a strategy designed to forestall the successive bids of pre-eminent continental powers for oceanic parity. Equilibrium broke down repeatedly when the frustrated continentals proceeded seemingly to vindicate the charge of hegemonial ambition, if only to fend off the prospect or fight off the fact of a coalition organized by the insular balancer to defend its maritime near-monopoly by restoring the supporting continental deadlock.

As advertised, the policy was supposed to make the continental balance oscillate less widely and with greater fairness. In fact, it repeatedly disrupted the (self-regulating) operation of the system by impeding painful but less than catastrophic adaptations to the organic waxing and waning of collective energies and state power. Even as an expanding oceanic arena began to provide a potentially steadying backdrop, the insular power's concept conspired with the continent's configuration to first surface, and then institutionalize, a latent dichotomy: on one side, the maritime sphere, made resistant to balance by virtue of naval technology; on the other, the continental arena, uniquely suited for balancing by readily mobilizable military and financial resources. Thwarting repeatedly the extension of equilib-ruim worldwide made it all the more difficult to fuse balance and pre-eminence on successive plateaus of evolution reproducing stability on the continent. A national strategy wholly legitimate from the strictly British viewpoint revealed its full consequence when a chain of wars put an end to the sovereignty of Europe on the global stage.

Reinstituting the dichotomy under US auspices has meant that, for the time being, the European dialectic would not be adapted to the change in scale (if not in substance) of international politics. It also has meant that the two traditional wings of Europe – Western and East-Central – have been reduced to more or less passive weights in the continental deadlock now extending to Asia and presided over by the two Europe-derived superpowers. More spectacularly than the subjugated half of Europe, the semi-autonomous one has receded from being the principal subject of world politics to being one of its main theaters. It is also a potential trigger of the next and possibly last world war.

Such a triggering mechanism links the great wars fatal to the Europeans and to the Greeks before them. In both instances the trigger – to be distinguished from the fundamental or structural cause – was the fear of the major land power of losing a fractious ally vital for the security of its continental position and, in consequence, its sociopolitical order. What Corinth had been in propelling Sparta into the Peloponnesian War, Austria-Hungary was for Imperial Germany in setting off World War I. On the other side of the divide, the reluctance to forgo the navy of Corcyra (Corinth's former colony whose defection to Athens set off the fatal chain of events) was crucial to Athens' decision not to appease Sparta, and thus to go to war. Similarly, British concerns over the consequences which a French defection or defeat would have for the naval as well as continental faces of the balance of power were decisive in dissuading Britain from paying the price of accommodating with Germany in the two decades preceding the European War.

The West Europeans fear that US geopolitical and military–strategic initiatives might provoke Soviet Russia into a war that would originate outside while taking place inside Western Europe. Less manifest – but in the longer run as real – is the possibility that direct or indirect precipitants to a military conflict would be lodged in a declining, but for that very reason fractious and volatile, Western Europe herself. In straining the fabric of US–European relations, the dormant issue as to which danger is more real adds to the overt dissensions over routine policies and to the deeper divergences in diplomatic styles and political cultures. The fissures are ominous so long as it is US military presence in Western Europe that offers the last-resort insurance against any Soviet inclination to transform pre-eminence into dominance and hierarchy into hegemony – even as, ironically, this balancing military presence is among the factors susceptible of instigating a drastic Soviet reaction. Only if a global US – Soviet concert complements Russia's pre-eminence on the continent, and the two postures constrain one another in a complex global equilibrium anchored in military checks and balances, while transcending both, will things revert back to normal for Europe in particular. The public law of the European diplomatic tradition will then be restored by being adapted to the global dimension of managing a state system.

Meanwhile, the most even if so far only remotely plausible West European trigger for war will continue to lie in Germany. The Federal Republic could conceivably precipitate radically destablizing developments as a response to political or military opportunities: the former presented by either an accommodating or a dissolving Soviet system, the latter linked to China's or also Japan's resurgent might and revisionism, matching Germany's. In either case, for Germany's choice to be real and its initiative productive, they would have to effectively reopen the issue of German unity by way of a militant self-assertion or a diplomatically camouflaged abdication. Either prospect might induce the United States to try on its own to achieve the German objective by a 'vigorous' action toward Russia – in an effort, depending on circumstances, either to contain and control the drive or to pre-empt the impending desertion of the Germans. The feared price of inaction would be losing West Germany and, through it, Western Europe. The 'loss' of Western Europe would automatically enhance the triggering potential of a China indispensable henceforth as America's last militarily significant ally for anything approaching peacetime balance of power in, or a fighting chance in a war over, Eurasia.

However, in the nearer future, the pressure to support any one ally's aggressive or self-saving initiative, on pain of having to fight later with fewer supporters, is not likely to trigger military confrontation with Soviet Russia. The consideration acts instead as the spring hidden inside America's basic strategy for deterring such conflict. That strategy carries with it a temptation, readily translatable into apparent necessity, to intensify US–Soviet antagonism so as to counteract weakening cohesion in the Atlantic alliance, subject to military–strategic 'decoupling', or to forestall an accelerating West European drift toward a privileged 'detente' with the Soviet Union, encouraged by geographic propinquity. In either case, just as alliance dissension could take more serious forms than passing moods of disgruntlement, so the American reaction might then have to depart from the previous tactic of dispelling disaffection by re-engaging in arms control negotiations. On the American side, efforts to reawaken the sense of the Soviet threat would serve to remind the Europeans that the balance-of-power corollary to the pre-eminence principle continued to be relevant. However, if constraining intra-alliance dissension would entail escalating inter-superpower rivalry, European resistance to the rising costs of American insistence on waging the cold war as usual would point to efforts aimed at reducing the risks of balancing the military power of the adversary by conceding its diplomatic pre-eminence at the risk of interallied rupture.

In a tripartite sea–amphibious–land power setting, an essentially continental strategy for a grand coalition conduces easily to a maritime strategy implemented by an oceanic alliance. Thus, were an encircling US–West European–Chinese association to force the Russians to seek aggressive escape, forestalling its greater jeopardy might well induce a contiguous Western Europe to accommodate Russia pre-emptively and separately from the remote sea power. The normal inhibitions against co-hegemonial duopoly by foremost continental powers might be overcome if China, still weaker than Russia, then responded to the economic–technological attraction of the western wing of the Euro-Soviet complex, as the face saver for submitting to the military–political pressure from the eastern wing. If a Sino-Soviet complex came into being first instead, it might force Western Europe to follow suit into the Russian orbit, in an effort to elude the combined weight of the restored 'communist' bloc by loosening its cohesion. In either case, the United States would be left with only fellow-insular Japan to pit against the unified land mass. The association of the insular states would match in kind, if outmatching in scale and significance, a receding Albion's earlier (1902) alliance with emergent Nippon against the mere prospect of a Russo-German combine – or, more precisely, as a way out of the uncertainty which of the two continental powers Britain had reason to fear more and sooner, and then in Europe or Asia.

If there were to be instead a steady progression toward global US – Soviet accommodation, it would make the West Europeans look more seriously to their defenses than will a continuing antagonism between the two giants. A developing US–Soviet concert would be suspect of eroding further the West Europeans' residual diplomatic independence. The dampening effect on their collective self-respect should suffice to release incentives for shoring up the capacity for self-reliance more powerfully than will any abrupt threat to survival from an intensified US–Soviet nuclear arms race, to security from the race's repeal or a conventional-military US disengagement, or to security and unity from active German politico-military re-engagement. The upshot of West European renaissance would be to reduce the scope and the bearing of a US–Soviet condominium without correspondingly curtailing the Russian part in an all-European political community.

Many West Europeans will find it hard to accept a gradual reassertion of the classic principle of one-power pre-eminence in favor of Europe's last (and least European) great power. And many more may find it no longer congenial or meaningful to acclaim the implicit return to normalcy as a means to re-enhancing Europe's global role and standing. Nonetheless, such a distribution of power, role, and status within a greater West holds out the best and possibly the only real prospect for continuing and consummating Russia's Europeanization in relative tranquillity. For the United States to block this trend, as a result of its inner stalemate between strategies for empire (centered in a hegemonial alliance) and equilibrium (centered in US–Soviet parity) stifling capacity for creative statecraft, would only strengthen other, less auspicious, forces. These would inflect the course of international relations, the center of gravity in world power, and America's own strategic and economic orientation and eventually ethnic composition and culture, toward Asianization.

Such a shift, and the divorce from Europe that it would represent for the United States, could come about even under the best of American intentions for Western Europe. This might indeed be the case if the makers of US policies continued to distinguish insufficiently the overt fears from the secret needs of the two halves of Europe. While assessing exorbitantly the power and the ambition of one half, authoritative Americans fail to understand Europe any more than they empathize with Russia, and remain blind to the re-emerging sense of Europe's wholeness. If Europe is a single culture by virtue of contrast with other ways of feeling, it is even more one as a system of states tied together by the shared culture's diplomatic norms. These are no less vital for being formal, and no less sentimentally binding for being rational.

Realism's Speculative Dimension

Relating political cultures to statecraft means venturing into the realm of an elusive interplay between realistic tactics posing as instrument of strategy and romantic goals of strategy assailable as products of sentiment. Power politics is saturated with conflict and allows for cooperation only as a function of conflict. This being so, a key issue is whether the ensuing dynamic can be modified to promote a civilization's capacity to forge an enlarged community in order to elude deepening catastrophe. The contemporary significance of the alternative outcomes is underscored by the Western civilization's henceforth again precarious coexistence with politically resurgent other-world cultures. The juxtaposition suggests the need to widen the scope of analysis preceding policy, the more so as the maker of the latter will be invariably tempted – and up to a point obligated – to focus on transient palliatives in dealing with immediately pertinent factors and pressing crises. The dilemma is severe and calls out for a complete statecraft, one that integrates interstate competition into a design for accommodation within a civilization, as the preliminary to a viable *modus vivendi* among civilizations.

It is not difficult to demonstrate the foundation of the US–Soviet conflict in historically evidenced laws of great-power politics. It is even easier to seemingly validate the US (containment) response by appealing to the fundamental tenets of realism. The narrowly pragmatic realist can readily discern the specific stakes at issue between the two powers. He will tend to exaggerate their significance, and misjudge responsibilities for the attendant contention, when he fails to identify the conflict's basis in the disparities besetting the two powers and adds, instead, strategic raw materials to military bases as the geopolitically validated particular supplements to the structural, operational, and psychopolitical inducements to the conflict. He will play down the practical significance of the more speculatively inclined fellow-realist's stress on the role of more elusive drives and dynamics in a competitive setting wherein one side's means of self-protection is another's model of threatening provocation.

All of these features can legitimately be seen at work in the US–Soviet relationship. Since scarce desirable assets must be divided for safe possession, and their division cannot be negotiated in most instances, the resulting conundrums are a sufficient incentive to conflict among states. However, since rivals commonly agree on what the assets and consequent stakes are (agree on what they want, and what they want is intrinsically the same), conflictual interstate politics is basically coherent and can be managed rationally. By contrast, the fact that assets can be divided by consent only if the parties also share an overarching function in the international system is only a possible basis for cooperation that is not against a particular someone. Taken together, the partially contradictory facets of a reality to be addressed by statecraft make it hard for any one actor to arrive at the insight into the futility of a conflict in time and still harder for the contestants to arrive at the insight simultaneously and implement it concurrently.

In the concrete instance of US–Soviet relations, the dilemmas are intensified by several facts. One of them is that even if the geopolitician posits fundamentally correct basic structures, the prognoses he deduces from the analysis may be less reliably so, be they fearful or hopeful. The first was the case with the British geopolitician Halford Mackinder, when he located the source of Russia's salience within a perennial land–sea power cleavage. He made the related apprehensions hinge on a coming superiority of heartland over insular powers, and on the relative ease of combining the resources of continental neighbors (Russia and Germany). The second applied in the case of the Briton's more sanguine American critic. Asserting the superiority of heartland-adjoining rimlands, Nicholas Spykman predicated a peacetime continuation of the wartime US–Soviet alliance on the implausibility of the land vs. sea power cleavage being an unchanging cause of conflict (and, thus, obstacle to continuing cooperation against Germany). In a setting that corroborates inconclusively some of the premises of both analyses, but resists the fulfillment of either prediction, the Soviets are as interested in the acquisition of a role, and the status that goes with it, as they are in securing any particular geostrategic or geoeconomic assets and positions. Conversely, the United States is inhibited from conceding the role–status mix, and its minimal underpinning in geostrategic access, as much by a righteous sense of providentially conferred right and duty as by a rigorous definition and sober appreciation of truly 'vital' material and security interests.

There is yet another fact that impedes insight into the dilemmas of the US–Soviet conflict and thus impedes efforts to transcend its rigidities. It may well be that the need of the Soviet regime to perpetuate fear of the outside for the purposes of internal regime stability helps keep the conflict alive or, at least, at a minimum level of tension. Yet the rivalry is also intermittently fueled by the need felt by each successive American administration to offer the public a steady, easy-to-grasp interpretation of foreign policy while trying to differentiate its implementation from the predecessor's by either relaxing or reaffirming both conflict and strategy. The radical simplification and the surface fluctuation of policy are as much the attributes of institutionalized pluralism as the more evenly assertive stance is the requirement of a still evolving authoritarian political system.

If the reasons for US–Soviet conflict are self-evident, incorporating into the analysis the 'laws' of power and politics that affect large political and cultural entities, empires and civilizations, increases doubts that the contention is as valid as it appears to be inevitable. Two contending major powers will commonly bolster third parties in order to build up allies as counterpoises to each other. An imperial state is, in addition, more than commonly vulnerable to diluting its initial substance and constituent spirit. It dissipates economic, cultural, or administrative assets when it tries coercion to prevent dependents from defecting or diffuses the assets in the attempt to lock the dependents in by cooptation. The imperial state's precarious strength will become manifest when a protracted conflict with a comparably 'civilized' or, in the language of today, 'developed' power has eroded its material or moral base enough to make it succumb to much weaker forces from within or without. When a civilization encompasses two or more imperial states, their separate but broadly matching vulnerabilities will be consummated whenever the elevated third party or parties are from outside its boundaries, revealing the conflict's hidden identity as an intra-civilizational civil war. Just as the two world wars and the first in particular were such conflicts for the European West, so the cold war moves with its every revival closer to becoming a civil war for a Euro-centric greater West.

In an ideal world, insight into the laws of decline for imperial states and regnant civilizations would constrain impulses that impart momentum to debilitating particular conflicts. The insight would open pragmatic policy to the speculation that some of the basic impulsions for interstate conflicts – not least the operational relative to the organic ones – have been attenuated in their compelling force and causal impact, without abolishing the propensity for a conflict to continue once it was set off by a valid stake. Moreover, specific new conditions may have made particular conflicts, including that between dominant sea and land powers, more avoidable.

Thus, nuclear-powered seacraft and guided missile technology may well have decreased the value of uniquely specialized – and, as such, unevenly distributed – skills and supplies. If true, this fact alone impedes any single major state from dominating the seas, as England could and did in the era of primitive cannon-carrying sailing ships that were hard to maneuver and maintain and steamships dependent on coal supplies. If the built-in disparity between navally dominant and aspiring states stimulated conflict, so did the universally feared dependence on political control for commercial access overseas. That too has changed as the world economy evolved beyond the norms of both classic mercantilism and early, diffident capitalism. More generally, it has become possible as well as more profitable and politic for resource-rich developed states to attend efficaciously to internal tasks than to pursue elusive external acquisitions – a trend paralleling the shift from operational to organic factors as ultimately decisive in arbitrating relative positions of states. In their 'pacifying' effect, all these factors – military–technological, economic, and political – have been partially offset by heightened pressures to deploy strategic deterrents and counterdeterrents worldwide on both land and seas. Nonetheless, they have weakened the key stimulus to competition and conflict insofar as they have made maritime–commercial near-monopoly less necessary for the leading insular sea power as well as less possible. This fact alone has made sharing overseas access with a land power that is fundamentally conservative more tolerable – and, in the long run, unavoidable – even if not spontaneously attractive.

Hence, despite the utility of recurrent past analogues for directing and disciplining strategic thought, the present US–Soviet rivalry over the Third World periphery is less compelling than were earlier European conflicts in the Atlantic and Indian–Pacific sectors. It is even possible that the globe-encircling Anglo-French and Anglo-German conflicts themselves had already begun to lose the solid rationales based on vital material asset which characterized previous contests between the German emperors and the Papacy or, subsequently, the French and the Spanish monarchs, who had all one thing in common: the desire to possess the most of Italy. Before the new-found riches from overseas skewed the intra-European balances of power and trade, controlling key parts of Italy made eminent sense in terms of encirclement and counterencirclement maneuvers, imperial and crusading mystiques, and material self-enrichment. Today, by contrast, the US–Soviet conflict is becoming nearly as objectless in terms of geopolitical or geoeconomic rewards as it is senseless in terms of the lethal risks which it poses. To analyze fully the present conditions and the possibilities inherent in these conditions, it is necessary to marry elementary common sense with the most subtle and circuitous speculation; willfully suspend conventional thought to liberate the central insight and guiding instinct from accumulated patterns of assumptions, prejudices, and partial conclusions, each often valid in itself but distorting in the aggregate.

Realism's Historic Dimension

When one's perspective shifts from theory of international relations to the data of history, the distinction between the 'laws' governing the dynamics of conflict among states and the 'laws' affecting the survival of empires and civilizations parallels the contrast between two complementary kinds of historical analogy: one involving historically evidenced structures of power, the other evolutionary phases of relevant history. When dealing with the US–Soviet–Chinese power triangle in terms of recurrent structures, strategies, and alignments, it is proper to draw on the matured European state system for analogies and 'lessons'. But when the contemporary conflict is viewed in the perspective of a greater Western civilization embattled within an

international system modeled on Europe's, analogies to this civilization's early travail and the first stirrings of the European order are
more suggestive. The purpose of the inquiry into 'structure' is to
reduce and control the terminal (Russo-American) conflict within
Western civilization; the object of inquiring into 'phase' is to explore
the factors conditioning the emergence of a greater Western comity
(including Russia). Our inquiry focuses on factors that permit or
impede a new beginning after a chain of partial catastrophes, just as a
fresh start was wrested from a seemingly final catastrophe – the 'fall'
of Rome – in an earlier age.

Groping toward a new beginning involves first speculative and then
statesmanlike efforts to relate the fleeting present significantly to the
not-wholly-completed past. Consummating European history requires
reconciling Europe's East and West in depth, as part of reconstructing
and rehabilitating the European ecumene as a globally relevant entity.
The future to aim at is one that preserves an all-Western civilization as
a viable one amidst the resurgent other world cultures, and this within
an international system that is genuinely global because made up of
autonomous regional orders. To be vital, such a system cannot be
wholly free of conflict; and it may be hospitable to parity in role and
status among its most viable constituents even if it cannot be
indiscriminately egalitarian. But, most of all, the system must be one in
which a particular civilizaiton can recede from dominance without
being overwhelmed, give up supremacy without lapsing into either
political or moral subjection. Only in such conditions will a
consolidated West be able to go on contributing while again beginning
to receive, and cease trying to convert others without being either
subverted or perverted from the outside.

The postwar American empire stands a good chance of prolonging
Western ascendancy for a not much longer time than maritime Athens
had perpetuated the glory of Greece, and more briefly than Byzantium
carried on the majesty of Rome. A thus precariously deferred end of
the European era recalls the end of the Roman Peace in ways that
denote the current phase of evolution through the attendant structure
of the international system. Once again, in West and East and North
and South, a highly heterogeneous composite brings together but
keeps apart societies more or less political and organized into states:
some still battle-ready and -worthy, others fatally resigned and
declining, and still others only confusedly if aggressively emergent

The varied 'actors', spanning a volatile range of development, bestride a fluid line of division that separates a center from the periphery of a 'system' in revolutionary transition. They cover again a spectrum of political cultures and technological competences controversially 'civilized' and 'barbarian'.

There is, even today, no agreement on the event – let alone the general or specific cause – which finally displaced ripe antiquity's Roman with the early-Christian barbarian West. Similarly, it may never be possible to say with assurance which of the signal events already transpired – or yet to transpire – will have been crucial to the eclipse of the modern secular West. Has the key portent in both cases been a military setback announcing eventual collapse well in advance? If so, the defeat of the Roman legions by incoming 'Germans' at Adrianople (in the early fourth century) was replicated already at the very beginning of the present century by Russia's defeat in Asia or only by America's nearer the century's end. Or are chronic economic maladjustments, made worse by disruption and fatal by strangulation, to blame? In such a scenario, the Vandal seizure of the agrarian West's vital food supply from North Africa harbors omens only intimated by the industrial West's dependence on energy supplies from the Middle East. Or again, will the end come from a strategic misjudgment that replicates the late Romans' treatment of assimilation-prone and -ready barbarians at the center (the Goths), redounding disastrously to the benefit of more truly alien ones (the Huns and the Lombards)? If so, will a massive inroad from the east (as, before, of Islam) be eased by a mutually enfeebling contest between the age's major sea power (then Byzantium) and land power (then Persia) – the two surviving light-houses whose mere dimming threatened to consign the 'civilized' world to darkness?

Just as the chance for continuous renovation of the ancient West had been blocked, so post-crisis restoration of its early medieval replica was impeded, by the failure to fuse civilization with capability in ways that would infuse fresh energy into settled tradition. Aborting the condominial designs to harness the Goths by Byzantium and, subsequently, yoke together the Popes and the Holy Roman Emperors, eased the advance of unruly forces from the rear of the continent in the earlier instance and projected more narrowly territorial entities automatically into prominence in the later one. Creedal and instit-utional diversities, while only disguising power-political differences, made it in both instances possible to define the contests ideologically and, thus, formulate stakes and issues on a stage yet to be shaped and defined geostrategically. A like procedure has since been followed and fulfilled the same needs for the American and the Soviet newcomers to managing a larger uncrystallized arena, with effects already enabling lesser or newer actors to again challenge (so as to, eventually, supersede) the system's progenitors.

Subsequent shaping of the European system was as much the result of creative energy as of stalemating conflicts and disruptive tensions. They all were drained off into crusading assaults on the nearer East before an intensifying deadlock in the western half of Europe redirected energies farther across the seas, with the result of repeating (with respect to the Ottomans as, before, against the Mongols) the failure to coordinate resistance against an aggressively retaliating East. The lack of joint response left eastern Europe alone to absorb the impact of Asia while the western half kept moving toward global sway from its initial inferiority to the eastern (first Byzantine and then Ottoman) empires. The ensuing divergence in modes and rates of development was to bequeath to the most formal and mundane of activities, statecraft and diplomacy, the well-nigh sacerdotal office of healing the spiritual consequences of the political rift.

At the heart of classic West, a new beginning requires Western Europe to revert conclusively to her stillborn start in a Franco-West German association. The neo-Carolingian formula, firmed up in the interest of intra-European balance of power, precludes integral German reunification so long as it might disruptively reopen the issue of pre-eminence on the continent and make it impossible for liberalization in the East to progress conjointly with a continuing erosion of the fading division between Europe's West and East. Once the Russians are more demonstrably secure in the heart of Europe than they can ever be in the Asian marches, they will find it both strategically possible and diplomatically profitable to relax their hold on Eastern Europe in their capacity as a territorial great power. The additional, consummating requisite is that they will have won a compensating access to imperial role and status globally. The United States will more confidently concede and pace the compensations if scaling down expectations of Atlantic orthodoxy regionally revitalizes America's order-fostering with an evolution-promoting role globally. Reconstructing relations inside an enlarged West or, in relation to the global South, Northwest, will encourage outside powers to forgo engaging in the old game of playing the main rivals off against each other.

On the part of the 'new' China, this has meant invoking nominally constant principles of statecraft, while positing a largely fictitious fluctuation in superpower threats and capabilities, to justify abrupt changes in Beijing's policy alignments or subtler nuances in its biases. European history exhibits a chain of prematurely formed or activated polities, from eighth- to ninth-century Carolingian Empire through globally overextended (but internally undertaxed) eighteenth-century France. Proposing an uncertainly postrevolutionary and development-capable China as the prototype of globally significant regional powers has been part of projecting her into a prominent role in stabilizing relations between the superpowers. It is only the latest instance of bad phasing even in the perspective of China's true interests and a desirable trend toward multipolarity in the twenty-first century.

The True and Real West

Assessing the different costs and benefits of alternative approaches to East–West and North–South cleavages is at least as much a matter of intuitions influenced by culture-conscious social philosophies as it is of apparently more precise calculations of politico-military strategy and economic expediency. Of the leading European and Asian civilizations that populate the most critical sectors of the global stage, the traditional East is more markedly subdivided than is the West, with its two wings, one Catholic or Protestant and democratic–individualist, the other Eastern Orthodox and authoritarian–collectivist.

It matters whether Russia is finally Europeanized as a matter of enforced conquest, induced cooptation, or gradual convergence – or is thrown back upon Asia. Closely linked to Russia's deepening Europeanization is the issue of America's continued European-ness. Even if US posture tips toward Asia at first only strategically, chances are that the process will not stop there and will extend into internal dynamics based on shifts in demography. As an imperial mediator between the world's cultures, America might have usefully evolved a novel multicultural mix or synthesis from a stance of ethnic neutrality. However, a United States that has been reduced to only one – if major – component of an intercultural equilibrium, and is to play in it a

steadying role while exhibiting some consistency of internal development, is a country with a vital concern to safeguard and perpetuate its
European core. In this as in other respects, Soviet Russia with her
changing Euro-Asian ethnic balance and the United States are distant
reflections of one another. Whereas creating an ethnically neutral
'Soviet man' might have made sense for the undisputed leader of a
globally ramifying communist movement, the return to more conventional patterns of world politics has re-centered concern on preserving
the leading role of the European-Russian element.

It is a matter of legitimate contention, but also of covertly biased
interpretations, how European or Asian Russia is adjudged to be: by
the standards of religious tradition or contemporary ideology; as the
object of Mongol overlordship or self-styled successor to Byzantium;
as the expansionist into Asia or the last-resort guardian of balance in
Europe; as an alien oriental despotism or a standard eastern-European
authoritarian polity; in terms of peculiar and indefinable individual
'soul' or a readily classifiable political 'system' for managing society
and its material resources. In America, too, the elitist European
element has struggled against dilution and deterioration at the hands
of other cultural and inferior social forces. If Russia recalls in this
regard the 'second' (eastern) Rome unevenly bestriding the Occident
and the Orient, the effect of Europe on America replicates the impact
of Hellenism on an earlier, western Rome.

Thus, it was America's Europeanist upper-class elites that imitated
Europe's imperialist drive in the 1890s, spearheaded US succor of
Britain and (secondarily) France in two world wars, and assumed
eagerly the vacated imperial role beginning with the late 1940s. The
social base, after supporting the empire-generating wars, was quick to
reject the obligations flowing from both the imperialistic acquisition
(the Philippine rebellion) and the imperial assignment (the Vietnam
War). When the base bore up an increasingly professionalized foreign
policy personnel, the latter tended to re-enact the Hellenistic model in
that it showed preference for codifying over conceptualizing facts;
stressed technical expertise over imaginative exploration and inspired
improvisation; and schematized the manifold insights into interstate
politics that grew out of Europe's complex experience, reducing them
to textbook-like precepts for reflexive application.

Reducing reality to formulas is part (although not the whole) of the
scientific, as distinct from the humanist, branch of the notorious 'two

cultures'. In approaching international politics, the pragmatic practitioner of the scientific culture will look to step-by-step control of
interactions, whereas the speculatively and historically oriented
humanist will display greater confidence in the patterned spontaneity
of long-term evolution. Where the former would manage transactions,
the latter would merely nurture trends; where the former looks to
techniques for instant reassurance or avoidance of risk, the latter looks
to transformations in vaster stretches of time and space for clues to the
meaning and outcome of an unfolding drama. And where the former
deals with ostensibly interchangeable parts, the latter is more keenly
attuned to organic wholes. Whereas the 'humanist' bias is congenial to
the philosophical conservative, or conservatively inclined liberal, in
tune with the European tradition, America's utopian liberals and
hyper-realistic conservatives both gravitate toward the 'scientific' bias,
if from opposite ideological extremes.

The scientific culture favors some form of concretism in American
foreign policy. The stress is on military hardware (and rationally
calculable military strategy), on economic factors (and rationally
controllable socioeconomic processes), and on functional organiz-
ations and instruments (for managing competition and adjusting
cooperation). Diplomatic negotiations over specific issues are expected
to unfold in finite stages and achieve discrete and definable results as
they proceed. In the realm of economics, the believer in liberal utopias
would engineer a new world by way of economic development in the
'South'; the convert to neoconservative hysteria is concerned with the
Third World mainly as an endangered source of strategic raw
materials: instead of exaggerated hopes, he has unfounded fears lest
militarily or industrially vital resources be removed from control of
the older New World. In the military sphere, the self-styled US
conservative's obsession is with military hardware. It is easily matched
by the pristine liberal's equally compulsive singling out of the arms
race for blame and arms control for praise. However, when he severs
narrowly military issues from politics, on behalf of strategic environment made 'safe' (by arms control- or superiority-based deterrence) for
a status quo favorable to the United States, the conservative betrays a
fundamental tenet of his creed more unmistakably than does the
liberal when preoccupied with making the environment 'stable'.

Neither apprehensions nor aspirations in regard to the economic
factor, neither obsession with nor opposition to the military one, are

in either case linked properly to 'real' politics – one that mediates between safeguards or acquisitions focused on geopolitical space and historically conditioned psychological resentments or aspirations linking past to future time. The hyper-realistic conservative is in his way aware of the territorial plane of power politics, but misconstrues its bearing on statecraft when he ignores the psychological – broadly speaking spiritual – substratum. The obverse is true for the utopian liberal who stresses the moral over the material plane and places humane desiderata above institutional needs and determinants. If the liberal is vulnerable to the millenarian fallacy, the neoconservative apostate from too confident or naive liberalism succumbs to the fallacy's apocalyptic inversion. As for the votary of apolitical scientism of either or no ideological persuasion, he is suspended in mid-air when he isolates himself from historical time and geopolitical space and, in his headlong escape from discredited moralism, is prey now to economism and now to militarism.

The extreme viewpoints produce readily a radical opposition to any workable policy of accommodation with Soviet Russia. Each raises objections to some aspect of a policy that would relax resistance to Soviet 'outreach' abroad with the aim of expanding regime tolerance for more active societal and technocratic 'inputs' at home, liable to generate a positive political 'fallout' regionally. To reject both the premise and the promise of such a policy is to favor perpetuating Russia's burden of a historically accumulated sense of cultural and technological inferiority, calling forth a compensating insistence on ideological superiority if not also cultural exclusiveness. The American liberal, wishing for an easing of tensions with Russia while either misjudging or opposing the means to it, inclines to see in the Soviet system the last obstacle to worldly good; the conservative hoping for the final abasement of the Soviet regime, while unwilling or unable to run the risks of consistently implementing the means thereto, views the rival system as the foremost world evil. The liberal's reforming passion is the right-wing conservative's crusading compulsion; consistently presenting one side's rights and the other side's wrongs in the style of melodrama competes for public attention with intermittently pronounced anathema. Wholly lacking in both outlooks is the sense of the tragic which alone can mobilize compassionate understanding against the sense of inevitability and hopelessness.

While lacunae in both public and official mind are being filled with unchallenged conventional truths, in-depth reassessment is indefinitely postponed in favor of the diplomatist's abiding trust – and the politician's all-too-common stake – in negotiations for the sake of negotiations. The flaws have been glaringly evident in the two most critical regions, the Middle East and Eastern Europe. In both areas the anti-Soviet bias of particular subcultures within American society has helped train official sights at only the containment or also the expulsion of Soviet influence.

If it is to stop melodramatizing issues of this nature, the West will have to return to an understanding of the tragic nature of statecraft and its cost in human suffering. In that universe of thought and feeling, a sense of pity is evoked by the inability of mighty powers to reconcile contrary values and interests in ways that would enable them to elude paralyzing constraints upon themselves without inflicting maiming coercion on others. Possessing such a sense of the tragic is the gravamen of genuine Western realism dating back to Thucydides; it must be integrated into the instinctively easier sympathy for all who strive to wrest a measure of personal freedom from corporate necessities. Likewise essentially Western is to leaven rational calculations of means and prudent limitation of ends with a romantic impulse tied to a transcendent goal. The goal of mending an unfinished unity and community, which Machiavelli once sought for Italy, is now Europe's and the complete West's. The romantic impulse distinguishes Western political realism from the East's clinically dispassionate variety. Together with philosophical conservatism it is the necessary corrective of the scientific culture's inroads into statecraft.

A humanely historicist and traditionalist temper is by its nature conservative. It avoids the extremes of too simple (liberal) meliorism intent on all-encompassing conciliation, and too crude (pseudo-conservative) alarmism bent on shielding what is (including a conflict) from unsettling change. Thought and action coexist successfully when the feeling of unavoidably shared guilt surrounds the use of force, without paralyzing either the necessary will to power or impeding adjustments to the ways of power; when the necessary passion behind the reasoned pursuit of one's interests is tamed by compassion for the not wholly different plight of the adversary. He who meets such high criteria can usefully work for the political reconstruction of the real West. Our age can then look forward with some hope if no assurance to seeing the record of its thoughts and actions find an honored place, alongside the ancients of the modern West, in the library of a future Alexandria.

PART V

Patterns of Thought and Policy Prescriptions

9

Dual Geopolitics and Plural Pundits

The greatest threat to international stability – and thus, in the long run, to world peace – lies in the pervasive tendency to dilute concern for the real issues of politics by concentrating on nuclear weapons. The real issues continue to involve questions of territory, in the broad sense: control or influence over – or access to – geopolitical and geostrategic assets. The hard-won acceptance of the truism that arms-related issues, including arms races, are only the derivatives of, and thus secondary to, political conditions is again being overlooked without being formally repealed. For all practical purposes, the correct priority is forgotten under the pressure of the apocalyptic implications of a nuclear conflict and in response to a corresponding temptation for the policy maker: to seek heightened stature and popular approval by achieving a dramatic coup for 'peace' in arms negotiations and agreements.

It is only a supplementary factor that the American – and to a degree the official Soviet (as distinct from Russian) – cultures are inherently attracted by the tangible and instrumental aspects of problems. The predispositions of diplomatic culture, while ostensibly different, are in essence comparable in their tendency to focus US–Soviet relations on technicalities. Both sides are prone to equating the political side of the arms issue with uninterrupted dialogue and intermittent negotiations. In what is, in effect, an unholy alliance of seeming contraries, formal procedure and hardware technology are yoked together for dominance over substantive considerations; hypothetical calculations of deterrence and professional conventions of diplomacy take precedence over politically meaningful and strategically purposeful conduct.

The Conflict Summarized

To place the US–Soviet relationship firmly within the territorial framework where it belongs, it is necessary to acknowledge both the basic differences between the superpowers and their pursuit of fundamentally identical objectives, which the differences condition but do not control. The United States, being only the latest in the lengthy line of offshore–insular (or quasi-insular) major powers that seek or possess pre-eminence in the world while contesting a continental rival's claim to a comparable position on the adjoining land mass (then called 'hegemony'), is the product of nature and accident. It owes to nature its protective insulation from the main continental area and derives from this its pluralistic sociopolitical structure and peculiar societal mindset – one that resists reviewing critically the predominant attitudes and perceptions of self and rival which, bred by favors of space, are only reluctantly revised in light of changing times and technologies. Accident, in turn, has played a big role in America's rise to great-power status. Insofar as this ascent is based on economic strength, it is the fortuitous result of a favorable conjunction: of increases in productivity from a range of technological innovations with the needs and opportunities implicit in the evolving structure of the world economy. The political power and role the United States derived from this was, typically enough, the product of a mutually enfeebling contention and stalemate among major, mainly continental, military powers. The configuration is one which, beginning with the Venetians and the Dutch and continuing with the English, periodically attended the principal maritime – mercantile power's rise to pre-eminence.

The continental rival – currently Soviet Russia – is compelled by its emplacement among actually or potentially threatening other continental powers to contrive, by art or artifice, that which nature bestowed upon, and accident confirmed, as the privileged condition of its more fortunate counterpart – and 'natural' rival. Contrivance will mean erecting an artificial insulation by developing an inner-zone security belt of dependent lesser states, and it will entail safeguarding that inner-zone security and stability system through offensively enacted defensive strategies. Actually pre-emptive – if ostensibly provocative – such activities are keyed to either support or subversion of outside parties in the surrounding zone(s) within or outside Eurasia. The control/coercion mechanisms that implement the inner-zone security system will be involved in a mutually reinforcing interplay with an authoritarian Soviet political structure, which only the requisites and consequences of activities directed outside the inner zone can counteract and reverse. Such authoritarianism is an improvement over the totalitarianism latent or manifest in a polity prone to isolating itself from the outside and capable of self-isolation – descriptive of imperial China and Stalinist Russia. But only in a favorable global environment will the milder mode of coercive governance be receptive to liberal tendencies of the kind that natural insulation permits and accidental endowments foster in an insular sea power. In the absence of specially favorable conditions, the authoritarian pattern will be fostered, if not also necessitated, by external pressures impelling the continental regime to match, through contrived and unavoidably imperfect imitation of spontaneous processes, the economic and technological accomplishments of the rival power type. Only contact – peaceable or violent – with the better-equipped society will provide the necessary means for, as it is an incentive to, such imitation.

Compared with the disparities between insular and continental polities, East-West differences add only an aggravating ideocultural dimension to the institutional and attitudinal effects of situational diversity. It is, however, a dimension capable of introducing irrational elements into the inherently pragmatic and rational conduct of a conflict based on the narrowly defined geopolitical contrast and cleavage. Thus, East-West polarity is, on the whole, a secondary – though original – factor. More markedly deriving from differences in situations are the ideological corollaries of the land-sea power conflict. The essentially liberal ideology of an insular–maritime polity consists of formulas for universalizing both the instinctual biases and reasoned preferences conditioned by its natural–accidental constituents. The averred objective is to extend the ideological values of the privileged community to less-favored environments. The implied one is to weaken resistance to the liberal values and to the political system they support. This would result from establishing in unassailable logic the equation of affirmed universality and inherent validity as the foundation of unique and exclusive legitimacy. Conversely, the ideologies of continental (Central-to-East European) powers represent rationalizations of particular handicaps or deficiencies. These and the related remedies are held to require and justify as necessary either forceful control/coercion mechanisms (glorified in right-wing to fascist ideologies) to defeat anarchy, or efficient as well as equitable organizational and other contrivances (favored by left-wing to communist ideologies) for matching the products of free spontaneity.

The Issue Restated

Thus stripped of secondary features and derivatives, the divergence in methods observed by the two power types shows itself to be compatible with an essential identity of shared concern for status through role and security through superiority. Such essential identity and consequent moral–political equality are the normative basis, if one is needed, for the naturally disadvantaged continental state's pursuit of geopolitical or geostrategic parity with the naturally favored offshore–insular power. Defining concrete conditions – or asset distribution – that constitute overall parity and, consequently, equilibrium between asymmetrically situated and unequally endowed powers is extremely difficult. However, the difficulty is not an insurmountable obstacle to developing, in good faith, concerted approaches to such parity, once the principle has been admitted. The contest over the validity of the principle (historically defined as mandating the extension of the balance of power from the continental to the oceanic theater) and its practical implications constitutes the one continuous theme in the modern (post-sixteenth-century) Euro-centric international system and has occasioned its catastrophic wars. It intermittently characterized interstate or inter-empire relations in earlier periods from remotest antiquity forward as well. The contest reflects the urge of each of the two power types to simultaneously (1) establish secure pre-eminence in its special habitat and (2) intrude upon the other's sphere to secure material goods, politico-strategic or military - strategic assets, or (based on either) diplomatic leverage for effective bargaining over the scope and modalities of the converging intrusions.

It is in these terms that Soviet control systems in Eastern Europe and Southwest Asia must be viewed, as well as Soviet interference with the innermost control system of the United States in Central America and its spatially or otherwise graduated inner to outer zones, extending from Western Europe and Northeast Asia to increasingly peripheral positions in the Third World. The Soviet emphasis on the insulating inner zone, on the adjacent zone (a militarily and ideologically threatening, if diplomatically and economically tempting, Western Europe), and on the peripheral outlets as bargaining chips, is not a fixed constant. It will alternate as contingencies develop and opportunities change, influenced by American responses, with repercussions on internal Soviet developments. However, the Soviet grand strategy will invariably treat these theaters as interlocked, irrespective of local successes and setbacks, in a global strategy. Ultimately, however, wide-ranging strategy is as much a key to safeguarding the integrity of the Soviet political system (as one to evolve autonomously) and Russia's territorial security (as one repeatedly infringed) as the matching US policies in these concentric zones are to protecting analogous values.

If it is to underpin the degree of stability attainable through an arms balance, US–Soviet political accommodation must reconcile the schematically parallel and operationally conflicting needs of the two powers. Such a reconciliation will entail a redistribution of points and areas of access that productively implements a parity-evolving process encompassing geostrategic concerns as well as nuclear-strategic capabilities, and can be plausibly represented as an acceptance of such a process. Negotiations may be a way to implement the process and ratify progress in some areas (currently in the Middle East, in particular) at favorable junctures. However, the willingness of the better-endowed US party to adopt the principle of geopolitical parity by appropriate conduct (implying concessions in the initial phase) will be the more significant touchstone of a will for accommodation.

The failure or reluctance to grasp this fact – and the failure of US policies to allow for situational differences between the United States and the Soviet Union, reflected in radically different conceptions of the state, its basis and function – underlies both the frustrations of detente during the Nixon–Kissinger era and the fallacies of the policy's critics. For detente to be a 'two-way street', as the critics argued, both the essential identities and the existential differences of the two superpowers must be integrated into a coherent strategy. And if the strategy is to be one combining competition with cooperation, as they conceded, it must assign as viable a meaning to cooperation in promoting system stability (or 'world order') as it does to competition over individual stakes. The governing assumption of the Nixon–Kissinger conception of detente was that affording the Soviets economic–technological favors or easements could entrap them into abandoning or only distract them from pursuing gains abroad. The premise of a simple trade-off between power and prosperity fitted closely the economic values-centered ethos of a Western liberal society and its conception of the state as an inherently valueless, supportive machinery. Moreover, it conformed with a rudimentary notion of diplomatic linkage. However, the offshore–insular tradition is wholly alien to continental Europe's essentially immaterialist, political concept of the state as both an organic entity and a value transcending society. The conceptual difference is only enhanced by the ideocultural biases and complexes of Central-to-East European societies, leading them to negate the essence of the Western model while they eagerly anticipate its fruits. Finally, in regard to both criticism and conception of detente, treating it as containment by other (safer and cheaper) means meant pretending to political realism while pursuing an illusion under cover of diplomatic–strategic sophistication. It is more realistic to view individual constraining acts as but intermittently necessary in a process of transition from the existing US–Soviet 'balance' to a stabler world equilibrium.

It is not for this summation to spell out again where and what kind of geopolitical concessions, at the various stages of a necessarily prolonged process, might be feasible in view of prudently construed US interests and necessary as well as sufficient in view of legitimate Soviet interests. Further, specific illustrations (advanced in chapter 2) can neither prove nor disprove the plausibility of replacing 'detente as containment by other means' with a strategy of decompression that might consummate the effects of containment (not least as regards the 'mellowing' of the Soviet system). Instead, the points to be made are general.

Just as the costs of Soviet expansion into remoter outlets can be compensated for by the benefits to the Soviet political system and the East European control system (based on functional diversification implicit in the outreach, and its sociopolitically liberalizing repercussions), so continued or intensified US denial of such external gains is apt to have negative consequences internally as well as potentially catastrophic consequences externally. As to the temporal dimension of a more flexible geopolitical policy, two additional points may be made. One is that the United States ought to periodically engage in conduct that reflects recognition of Soviet Russian needs; conduct that, through both symbolic resources of diplomacy and real-political responses, recognizes the Soviets' entitlement to effectively participate in regional- and world-order maintenance on the strength of an assimilable extension of Soviet influence. Testing Soviet willingness and capacity to respond in the desired, and *ex hypothesi* anticipated positive, ways will require the United States to show itself, over a decent period of time, ready to barter specific 'territorial' concessions for changes in the overall 'systemic' conditions. The latter are internal to the Soviets and external to both parties alike, affecting US–Soviet relations and international stability. Only by conveying an unmistakably and fundamentally altered official US mindset, and not by any more direct attempts at manipulation, can an evolving US policy affect the evolution of the Soviet polity as well as Soviet policy. The risks of the exploration can be borne so long as the United States not only preserves the ability to reimpose retaliatory restraints on the Soviets but actually strengthens the capacity to do so at home and among the allies by demonstrating US reasonableness and Soviet intractability. The fact that no US policy maker in the post-World War II era has ever willingly ventured upon such an experiment undermines analyses and assessments postulating an incorrigible Soviet aggressiveness and adventurism in the world at large.

The other point to make is that, while any accommodation process is bound to extend well into the twenty-first century (wherein the potentially catastrophic consequences of an opposite policy are also located), the generational change in the Soviet leadership imparts special importance to the more immediate future. Just as the older Soviet leaders were naturally content to live in the present on the ambiguous basis of contrasting assumptions about US dispositions in general, so a younger leadership is obligated to look forward to the result and record of its own stewardship when it departs from the scene two or more decades hence. Therefore, in a relatively short term the 'new men' will be naturally inclined to seek conclusive evidence as to the kind of basic US posture they may or must take into account as the fundamental premise by which to govern their own posture. The basic question is whether the United States is prepared to deal with Soviet Russia as an equal in terms of politically significant facts and acts; or whether it will continue to adhere to the power type it represents and refuse to grant such equality to the premier continental power as of Russia's right (and as a matter of considered American conviction, as distinct from a momentary convenience relating to intra-Western contentions).

The Regnant Policy Reviewed

The policies of the Reagan administration could be best understood as having demonstrated the classic US isolationist–regional imperialist syndrome. They have not offered a favorable climate for experimenting with a constructive approach to US–Soviet accommodation, outside the sphere of opportunistic public rhetoric. The more reliable indication of the motivating impulse behind administration policy has been its commitment to erecting an impregnable strategic defense for the continental United States capable of recreating US insulation from Eurasia by reversing the effect of prior military technologies. Complete success or, worse, the appearance of unmatched progress toward foolproof defense, would create the worst conceivable environment for an auspicious exploration of alternatives to either cold war or containment. Instead of furthering a remote goal of geopolitical parity underpinning nuclear-strategic parity, 'perfect' defense would insulate the United States from effective Soviet reactions to the consequences of onesided vulnerability. This would instantly create a finite time zone of acute danger for Russia's political standing, if not security, and thus for international stability. In contrast to such specific perils, geopolitical parity is conveniently ambiguous. It is unlikely to be and does not need to be accomplished in either literal or exact terms of 'equality' before the international constellation of a US –Soviet competition–cooperation mix is altered – as it is certain to be, in due course – by emergent third major powers modifying the context to the disadvantage of the two superpowers, even if not immediately in ways equally threatening to both.

The issue of geopolitical parity does not confront either the Soviet or the US leadership with an impending choice between accepting irreversible role/status demotion and staging a defensively inspired if offensively implemented armed reaction. The same, however, cannot be said of the Strategic Defense Initiative (SDI). Irrespective of the enhanced deterrent potential its proponents postulate, SDI carries within it a challenge. The challenge is an acute one to a government acting in the spirit of the continental-European statist tradition. Any such government will be expected to defend, at the moment of an undeferrable decision, the indissoluble link between the legitimacy of an inherently change-prone and -capable regime and the inalterable requisites of great-power status for the state. In the Soviet instance, this means the historic Russian state. SDI thus either compounds or replaces and exceeds the delayed risks implicit in the geopolitical encirclement of Russia by the US–Chinese quasi-alliance.

A Russian regime's failure to react forcefully to an unmatched manifest US success in deploying strategic defenses would entail the risk of incurring public revulsion of the kind some US observers of the Soviet reality regard as the imminent penalty for economic misman-agement. Such an estimation, however, ignores that such mismanage-ment and its social consequences have always been the commonplace features of nonetheless enduring continental authoritarian states and empires like the Soviet. To build US policy on the delusive assump-tion that the Soviet state and political system are experiencing irreversible decline, while discounting the fragility historically eviden-ced by the political economies of maritime– mercantile (insular) powers, is worse than a mistaken view of the present. It is a crime against the future of a civilization of which an evolving Russia and Eastern Europe, although currently alienated, are an integral and increasingly indispensable part.

Finally, to dismiss – as an intellectual construct unworthy of practical consideration – a strategy based on abstract structural analysis and historical antecedents will continue to mean (not least in the American setting) surrendering to policies devoid of conceptual content at both the bureaucratic and the political levels. Since the Reagan administration has been marked by an unprecedented degree of conceptual vacuity, its 'historic' task may well prove to have been to do no more than prepare the soil by its negative example for invention and innovation by the next administration. Unfortunately, a policy-making process hostage to two- to four-year electoral spans is unsuited to generate strategies whose elusive long-term dividends depend on more conspicuous and immediate outlays of assets cheris-hed all the more jealousy for not being always resolutely defended. The one possible corrective to the liability is one which the US electoral system and, deriving from it, the standards for selecting principal foreign policy makers are least likely to produce: a political class willing and able to cease projecting bureaucratic routines into the management of isolated crises through diplomacy-simulating tactics or arms-related technics, and disposed to start evolving a geohis-torically validated strategy for the long pull. Without such a conver-sion the institutional weakness (not shared by the oligarchical regimes typical of earlier insular–maritime powers at their apogees) may well outweigh in time all of the natural and accidental advantages the United States has enjoyed over its continental adversary. The advantages do not guarantee that a power even less tractable than the Soviet, and a culture even less congenial than the Russian, will not be the eventual recipient of any ensuing opportunities and benefits.

Alternative Frameworks and Assumptions

Creating the intellectual basis for such a new political class or only a better foreign policy is the ever-receding purpose behind academic writings on US–Soviet relations. Arranging the various facets of three representative recent interpretations and prescriptions along continua comprising conceptual frameworks, basic assumptions, and policy-relevant implications will help contrast them systematically among themselves and, more often implicitly, with the positions argued in these pages.[1]

Most fundamentally distinctive is the extent to which the geopolitical setting of the conflict, engendering interests, is made explicit or, instead, mainly the conflict's domestic sources and related values are emphasized. The geopolitical framework is integral when it consists of factors deriving organically from space as they are nurtured historically. It is only formally controlling when it infuses the spatial setting with only accidentally or operationally related features. Such an analysis and prescription are then geopolitical in form (or strategic bias) and either value-ideological or military-technological in content (or substantive thrust).[2] The formally geostrategic approach differs nonetheless, if not as fundamentally as the geohistorical, from one that is ideological in form as well as substance in that it fails to relate the implied primacy of values over interests to an explicitly delineated geopolitical setting.[3] Intermediate between the two – but also different from both because largely non-conceptual – is an approach that is eclectic in method and pragmatic in bias.[4] Deliberative rather than doctrinaire, it derives interests from values in the last analysis and is inherently reasonable where the others are in different ways and degrees rationalist.

Basic assumptions about the nature of the conflict, with effect on policy, follow directly from the overarching framework of analysis. They narrow down into interconnected beliefs about the relations of offense to defense in conduct and of the two behaviour modes to a revolutionary or a conservative cast of fundamental dispositions. The dogmatically ideological view opts unequivocally for defining the conflict in terms of Soviet Russia as an offensively revolutionary party in terms of the polity or, at least, its policy. The typically noncommittal pragmatic approach suggests a compromise: the Soviet system is internally conservative but revolutionary aboard; its policies even if defensive in their cause are offensive in the consequences. Both geopolitical schools of thought – the geostrategic and -historical – treat the offensive–defensive distinction as largely fictitious – with a difference. The geostrategist echoes the pragmatic view in disclaiming interest in causation: a defensively motivated Soviet advance, too, will reduce American access or presence. On the practical plane, he thus discounts any difference in the modes of exploiting differently motivated gains: only for security or also supremacy; and he minimizes the extent to which a US counterstrategy inspired by contrasting assessments is apt to sway Soviet conduct toward the more limited or the more extensive goal. On the speculative plane, stressing the tendency for a successful thrust to be self-perpetuating as it compels the forward defense of the new asset at the margin has a like effect: it obscures the significance for diplomatic (as distinct from military) strategy of the practical–normative as well as operational – implications of the fact that the impossibility to clearly differentiate offense from defense constitutes the root cause of a conflict's tragic character if not inevitability.

As regards the revolutionary character of a foreign policy, it can be identified in technically precise terms – as entailing radical change in the conventional norms of international politics – or be construed loosely – as implying the pursuit of major changes in the distribution of power. Since the ideological approach locates its diagnosis of Soviet foreign policy closer to the first than the second definition, it is internally coherent when impugning that policy as revolutionary. The same is not the case for the other two approaches, thus when the eclectic analyst identifies the characterization with the Soviet aim to expand the number of left-oriented dependents, and the geostrategist with the objective to bring to the Soviet side one or another of the critical 'linchpin' countries. A Soviet policy that aims at revising the ranking between the two superpowers (toward parity?) while being committed to a hierarchical, great-power-dominated, international system more strenuously even than the United States, is conservative–revisionist; it is not revolutionary, least of all in the stricter and only meaningful sense. In fact, the latter description is better reserved for China's posture whenever it veers toward declamations against 'hegemonism' or 'great powerism'. Far from being revolutionary in substance, Soviet policy is at its worst revolutionary only in form, as part of ideological self-legitimation by means of tactical measures in pursuit of conventional role- and status-related strategic objectives.

In a related matter, it follows more naturally from the geohistorical than from any other approach to resolve the tension between the innately doctrinally (Marxist-Leninist) 'internationalist' and the innately (Russian) nationalist determination of policy-relevant interests and values in favor of the latter. The henceforth widely agreed upon assessment of the two determinants being compounded veers toward the ideological component as the analyst moves along the pragmatic-to-dogmatic continuum. However, the policy implications are not fundamentally altered so long as the geostrategist echoes the ideologue when he equates Russian nationalism with an unqualified, unalterably expansionist imperialism – the difference between them, and with the pragmatist, being then reduced to uneven emphases on small-scale encroachments at an expanding core's periphery and larger-scale pre-emptive thrusts against established states closer to the center of the international system as evidence of innate Russian expansionism.

Controversial Facets of Key Dynamics

Sharper differences reappear with respect to the domestic factor and its relation to foreign policy as the prime determinant or malleable object thereof. Integral to the ideological approach, the causal primacy of the domestic structure and values is most starkly at variance with the thesis of developmental coincidence of domestic structure and basic foreign policy posture, resulting from the geohistorical perspective. In keeping with the latter's spatio-temporal orientation, as the identity of the premier continental power moved eastward in geopolitical space, the temporally staggered evolution of the successively resource-sufficient authoritarian domestic orders coincided with the strategic challenge to insular sea powers evolving concurrently from a liberal–oligarchical to a liberal–democratic regime. The result has been a closed circuit of spatial and temporal, internal-political and foreign-policy cum external-systemic factors. It does not lend itself to representing foreign policy in general as the outgrowth of the domestic order, and that order's dynamics as the efficient cause of particular policies – and, therefore, rules out treating Soviet foreign policy as due to a political system that is uniquely *sui generis* rather than typologically generic. The issue is less clearly drawn with the two less markedly ideological treatments, when the eclectic approach leans on the whole toward the domestic derivation thesis and the geostrategic one assigns greater weight to the systemic or environmental context, articulated in terms of the oceanic–continental dichotomy, without making the preference unmistakable or arguing the reasons for it explicitly.

When the issue is the effect of (US) foreign policy on (Soviet) domestic order, the pragmatically inclined analyst questions its very possibility. He impliedly considers the issue in terms of the direct or immediate effect of specific US foreign-policy moves on a spectrum of empirically ascertained or speculatively hypothesized Soviet interest- or opinion-upholding (official) groups or cliques. When the more conceptual approaches postulate the effect as a possible one, they do so in more broadly defined terms. They assume the potential or capacity of the operational setting in its entirety to co-shape the organic makeup of the Soviet polity, while the makeup itself is operationalized in terms of policy priorities that reflect changing assessments of Soviet opportunities and risks and are implemented through differing allocations of resources – all representing or entailing more or less deliberate and controllable transformations over a variably long run.

The above-mentioned crucial distinction coexists with differing assessments of the kind of Soviet domestic change that might relate to US–Soviet accommodation and in what sequence. At one extreme of the range is the doctrinaire ideological postulate of accommodation as contingent on near-total Soviet change, to follow upon radical structural reform induced by the US policy of strict denial of both prior and future Soviet geopolitical gains. The contrary extreme is the geohistorically inspired scenario placing US–Soviet accommodation in the lead as a critical trigger of, and continuing stimulant to, internal evolution and its beneficial convergence with the changed environment. While they clearly lean toward the first-mentioned extreme, the pragmatic and the geostrategic analyses shade off none the less to unequal degrees away from its innate radicalism on this as on other issues.

Somewhat related to the divergent assessments of the reciprocal impact of external and internal conditions, their respective primacy as determinants of policy and elasticity as policy mediums, is, next to the directly entailed relationship between operational dynamic and organic factors, one between economics and politics. The differing evaluation bears now on the actual – as distinct from the doctrinally affirmed – extent to which politics is conceded primacy over economics in Soviet practice. This will mean the extent to which the uniformly affirmed Soviet economic crisis is deemed capable of being directly acted upon by US foreign policy so as to precipitate sociopolitical change. Subtle differences, ranging from an outspoken skepticism of the pragmatist to the ideologue's affinity for economic warfare and advocacy of economic sanctions as part of a comprehensive strategy package, exist between the three schools. But neither replicates the crude linkage between economics and politics implicit in the belief once acted upon the American side and disproved by the record of detente, that an operational entanglement of Soviet policy-makers in the administration of resources that had been expanded by US economic–technological infusions would or could lead directly to uncompensated (geo-) political abstinence; that the functional web of interdependent material interests would or could neutralize the political effects of the tragic knot entangling the two geopolitically disparate powers in structurally conditioned conflict.

The domestic cum economic factor points to the issue raised by the current Soviet crisis. It bears by way of the larger rise–decline phenomenon directly on the aim and desired outcome of US foreign-policy strategy. The tendency to overestimate the scope and/or single-mindedness of Soviet objectives, and to underestimate the regime's capacity to deal with any possible-to-probable domestic crisis without facing a major internal upheaval or yielding before external pressure, diminishes along the spectrum from the radical, doctrinaire–ideological, through the military geostrategic to the pragmatically eclectic, reasonable approach. As a result, whereas the ideologue and the geostrategist can and do look toward eliminating Russia as a significant competitor – the first through the destruction of the Soviet Union as a totalitarian-imperial system, the second by way of 'pacifying' it as an expansionist power – the pragmatist's more modest recipe is for an indefinite management of the rivalry.

The apparent aimlessness of the latter's favored strategy highlights the fact that neither approach projects the significance of the Soviet crisis against US liability to a different kind of vulnerability, implicit in a one-time rise–decline cycle as distinct from multi-phase ups and downs. Consequently, dwelling on the ways and means of out-competing the Russians ignores the implications of the possibility that the endemically crisis-prone continental power may nonetheless out-last the insular society as an equally competition-capable party. By downgrading the time dimension, all three approaches sidestep the issue of timing of conflict resolution, critical in relation to third parties as regards not only the most desired but also the most feared process and outcome. The latter range from an all-out Soviet triumph by means of a many-faceted subversion strategy (the ideologue), through specific breakthroughs on one of the main fronts with support from a first-strike nuclear capability (the geostrategist), to an all-destroying nuclear war (the pragmatist).

One Man's Realism, Another's Utopia?

Shortchanging along with the time dimension also the spatial one of the total environment in which desired or feared outcomes might occur is as relevant as any for the quality of 'realism' in a policy stand. The proponents of all three approaches would differentiate themselves from prescriptions for far-reaching accommodation within a finite period as naively utopian. In fact, they suffer from their own brand of utopia, lodged in either an insufficient or a biased grasp of power dynamics. Paradoxically, least utopian is the maximalist, doctrinaire-ideological, approach. Its advocate avoids the figment of a cost-free demotion or outright destruction of the Soviet system by accepting major war as the attendant risk if not probability. The ostensibly more sensible pragmatist conceals in his peculiar kind of *Realpolitik* the utopia of an indefinite management of the rivalry, to be sustained within an uncontrollably changing international setting, but without a determinate outcome, by the presumptive capacity of the American political system to orchestrate suitable policies: while practicable in terms of the institutional limitations of the US political system and prudent in terms of the latitudes offered by the international system, the policy would (ideally) be at once non-provocative in mode and productive of specific measures required to 'stabilize' US–Soviet relations indefinitely in purpose. No less – though more elusively – utopian is the geostrategist's confidence in the feasibility of minutely calibrating material constraints on Soviet power with nominal concessions to appearances of US moderation and self-restraint. He would apply the mix along the different fronts and facets of a strategy oriented at bottom toward denial and rollback, in regard to the regional Soviet imperium on the western front (see below); the eastern front (i.e. by mobilizing China and Japan to 'block' Soviet expansion, but without incurring the explosive consequences of the encirclement); and the southern or central front (thus by admitting the Russians to institutional role without conceding them real influence in Middle Eastern peacemaking).

Most fundamentally unrealistic, however, is the disposition of all three analyses to address US–Soviet relations in isolation from a dynamic setting of third parties. Being asystemic, the analyses are in this respect one-dimensional even as that quality is ascribed to the Soviet Union as either a single-mindedly ideological or a single-factor military power. Neither approach explores the implications of alternative US strategies and their outcomes for the position, capabilities and ambitions, of either major or minor third parties, and thus for the total environment – be it defined as conflictual international system or conflict-moderating world order.

Neither, in the same vein, does any of them meaningfully relate the Soviet domestic to Russia's regional-imperial, and the latter to the larger Euro-global, theater. Thus the geostrategist, who comes closest while remaining true to the formalism intrinsic to the approach, would transform the 'political realities' in the region without 'formal political changes.'[5] However, he does not pause to consider the conditions that might make evolving readjustments of both the form and the substance in the relationship between central authority and client autonomy (critical for any empire) acceptable to the Soviet core power, because – equally important – sustainable by liberalized client-state regimes without spilling over into pressures for degrees of independence reopening the issue of defection. Consequently overlooked is the possibility that stabilizing a beneficial evolution at its successive stages requires that both repulsion from the proximate Eastern (Soviet) center of control and attraction by the differently remote West be neutralized in a supportive Euro-global setting.

Therein, an increase in effective political-diplomatic deterrents to Western encouragement or exploitation of strains in East-central Europe would have to dovetail with conditions apt to reduce the Soviet fixation on total control and enforceable stability in the region, viewed decreasingly as the indispensable bulwark of politico-military stability in an either hostile or inaccessible environment.

Three Faces of Reason in History

In the final analysis, the issue of realism vs. utopianism in dealing with the US–Soviet rivalry revolves around fundamental questions such as these: does the contrast if not contradiction between domestic (and regional) crises, pointing to Soviet decline relative to recent past, and continuing Russian global expansionism, constitute an either significant or genuine paradox (one that subsumes a likewise paradoxical relationship between narrowly military and wider economic factors and between these and the sociopolitical expectations of the public or goals of the regime)? Or are these apparent contradictions a commonplace of the domestic and foreign politics of continental powers, increasingly pronounced as they move eastward, that has no unequivocally self-evident implications for the Russians waging and the United States managing the rivalry?

Consequently, is tightening, only maintaining, or actually relaxing external geostrategic and economic constraints on the Soviet system, especially when it has become engaged in efforts at internal reform (for greater efficacy only or, also and implicitly, gradual mitigation of the authoritarian mode) the more realistic or utopian, stabilizing or catastrophic, way out of a conflict that over and above any actual or imagined paradox constitutes a predicament for both sides? And is one of the approaches to be embraced because relaxing external constraints risks equipping the Soviets for a more effective assult on western interests and positions at a later date and stage of development, in keeping with either a persistent ideological rationale or an unchangingly expansionist geostrategic rationality? Or else, is a different and contrary approach to be favored because, thanks to the workings of the cunning of Reason that presides over intricate interplays of internal and external structures with developmental stages and political strategies, relaxing the environment bids fair to facilitate sociopolitical changes that would make it practically infeasible to resume the mode, let alone expand the scope, of Soviet expansionism even if it was initially intended in some elite quarters?

Since no one's opinion on this vital core issue will or can be either wholly convincing or universally shared, the question as to what is 'realistic' in US–Soviet relations and what 'utopian' must be addressed in terms of a general theory (or, at least, typology) of both intra- and inter-state politics that has been reinforced by historical considerations of some depth and scope.

The historical dimension is confined to the prerevoltuionary Russian background in both the doctrinaire-ideological and the formally geostrategic analyses. Whereas the main emphasis in the former is on the specific nature of the Russian state, the latter's is on the peculiarly Great Russian imperialism. Failure to treat historically also the wider configurations and longer-term time spans contributes to slighting the comparative dimension of analysis while obscuring thus also the factor of dynamic evolution. As a result, with only pro forma qualifications, Russian expansionism is indicted as uniquely virulent as well as unchanging, one that is neither schematically nor substantively comparable with any other (including the American). The bias is understandable in the case of the historian of Russia abiding by professional distaste for speculative generalizations from particular historical phenomena; it weakens the claim to incorporating the historical dimension into the geostrategic analysis when referring to the conflict itself, or America's prevailing in it, as 'historical' substitutes for relating the spatial dimension explicitly to the temporal one. It conforms to the preferences of the American political culture to compensate for the omission by elevating the military-technological and strategic factor to undisputed salience in an analysis focusing on the present and the near future. But it also weakens the ability to correct the culture's myopia with a history-aware Europeanist approach, perpetuating thus the foibles inherent in a quasi-Hellenistic reception of the older culture's insights and intimations.

When, by contrast, the methodologically eclectic pragmatist explicitly discounts the relevance of an 'abstract past' for the present characterized by the new specifics of nuclear weaponry in particular, he is faithful to his premises – as he is, *qua* Sovietologist, when confining the historical background to the Stalinist and post-Stalinist era.[6] The cost of divorcing oneself from the larger past and its potential to guide the present and thus shape the future becomes evident when the aim of policy is then formulated in the ambiguous terms of a 'normalization' of US–Soviet relations. This implicitly ignores the fact that the conflict is eminently normal as one between insular and continental powers, while only a historical insight that has been deepened without being buried by the awareness of military-technological innovations can point to unprecedented – i.e., abnormal – diplomatic-strategic alternatives to repeating its commonplace traditional resolution in mutually weakening war.

Two Kinds of War and Rival Wagers

The conceptually eclectic pragmatist is no less true to form when he makes avoiding a nuclear war the priority objective of managing the conflict, to the detriment if not exclusion of any more positive purpose. The other two, more rigorously conceptualized, approaches face instead the possible-to-probable outbreak of military hostilities as part of waging the conflict in the preferred mode. In so doing, they assimilate a US–Soviet military engagement to any other war – conventional or not – between any other contending parties. They do not regard or identify it as qualitatively different on a different plane of discrimination from the conventional vs. nuclear: as intra- vs. inter-civilizational. The bias is sufficiently pronounced to obscure the true meaning and message of a passage one of the authors quotes from Toynbee's *Study of History* about the effects of militarism on the lifespan of civilizations. It is, in this connection, a secondary if significant consideration whether the militarism potentially responsible for the 'suicidal process' that engulfs civilizations in 'fratricidal' conflict is currently only its crude Soviet or also the more elusive but also insidious American version – the latter illustrated by the military-technological emphases of the geostrategic approach.[7] It is more to the point that the foredoomed civilization contemplated by the philosophizing historian is without question wider in scope than the centralized–militarized Soviet, as the approvingly quoting author suggests.

The certainly unintentional misreading of a statement with an unmistakable intent points to a larger failure: that of a strategic game plan to integrate into its intellectual underpinnings a considered prophetic guess about its ultimate implications repeatedly evidenced in history.The issue narrows down to the choice of one's principal fear or, differently put, the main scare one propagates to make others fearful: Russian power and purpose, or American persistence in denying their expression within historically legitimated limits. This core difference expands naturally into the choice between a strategic gamble and a strategy embodying a wager: the gamble predicated on the ability of the United States – and the conventional West at large – to 'prevail historically' in an intra-civilizational conflict at an acceptable cost to both national interests and the civilization's potential for survival; the wager predicated on the possibility to strengthen a regenerated civilization by cooperating with the historical process of convergence between its complementary parts. Much of the rest, elaborately argued as it may be, is but academic sound and partisan fury producing little of value for the body social and politic in both its narrowest and widest delimitations. Barring a greater degree of consensus, neither of the rival interpretations and prescriptions is likely to 'educate' either the public or the power holders, any more than it is likely to sway actual policies from their fixed course, either at all or in time, when departing from it more than microscopically.

Notes

1 'These pages' meaning the ones preceding what follows in this essay, but also, and for the willing reader mainly, the book as a whole.
2 Zbigniew Brzezinski, *Game Plan: A Geostrategic Framework for the Conduct of the U.S.-Soviet Contest* (Boston/New York: The Atlantic Monthly Press, 1986).
3 Richard Pipes, *Survival Is Not Enough: Soviet Realities and America's Future* (New York: Simon and Schuster, 1984).
4 Seweryn Bialer, *The Soviet Paradox: External Expansion, Internal Decline* (New York: Alfred A. Knopf, 1986).
5 Brzezinski, *Game Plan*, p.234.
6 Bialer, *The Soviet Paradox*, p. 376.
7 Brzezinski, *Game Plan*, p. 129. The fuller extract from the quote is as follows: '. . . militarism . . . has been by far the commonest cause of the breakdowns of civilizations during the last four or five millennia . . . Militarism breaks a civilization down by causing the *local states* into which the society is articulated to collide with one another in destructive fractricidal conflicts.' (Italics added).

10

Collective Mind and Individual Mindsets

The time has come for the United States, as it faces the advent of the twenty-first century, to develop an authentically American outlook on US–Soviet relations. If and when this happens, the outlook will fill a vacuum and place a distinctive imprint on the blank now existing in the collective mind of the leader of the West. To be realistic, the outlook will have to reflect an existential fact and meet an intellectual criterion. The fact is that the US–Soviet rivalry is positional, rooted in space. It does not extend far back in time, and has acquired even less than the comparable Anglo-German contention the poisonous attributes of a 'hereditary' enmity along the lines of centuries-long Anglo-French, Franco-German, and Germano-Slavic antagonisms. Intellectually, the policy outlook must cease being manichean and mechanistic and become tragedy-conscious and (as previously defined) 'totalistic'. Total diplomacy was once called for as part of building situations of strength for negotiations with a still totalitarian Soviet Union. This time, however, diplomacy must be total in terms of its conceptual foundation and not primarily in the range of implementing instrumentalities, and must cease reflecting an overemphasis on internal-political factors and ideological determinants.

Such is not the case presently. It is not as regards either the conception, the implementation, or – last but not least – motivation of US foreign policy. The reasons are to be found in limitations affecting both concept and conduct of affairs, and have to do with partisan biases. If the limitations make it difficult to define and implement the 'national interest' correctly, the biases carry with them the unchecked pretension to codify that interest authoritatively.

The Official Dyarchy

Neither of the two main arms of the US foreign policy establishment has satisfactorily performed its function and lived up to the public trust. The elective political branch has failed to perform either of the key tasks of leadership: to periodically offer meaningful policy alternatives and to engage at all times in the public's incremental education in regard to both the goals and the means of policy. Only partially to blame have been the short intervals between elections, adding brevity to instability of official tenure. A short and uncertain incumbency militates most of all against a new policy that can have only delayed benefits to set against the initial cost of real concessions and apparent setbacks. The predicament of the professional experts was the almost obverse one of a vested interest in the long-lasting utility of laboriously acquired know-how, not least of the military–technological and military–strategic kind. Least attractive is then a policy that places a premium on innate qualities of political judgment by only a few in the highest policy-making authority, within a dynamic diplomatico-strategic setting.

Given the conjunction of mutually reinforcing sources of paralysis, with idea-men keeping the power-brokers on a lean diet, the general public was starved of choice between alternative strategies for dealing with the conflict and bereft of hope for eventual exit from the conflict. It remained unnoticed that even an only intermittently attentive public was more amenable to basic policy changes (witness the turnabout in opinion on China) than the managers of its consciousness (and, occasionally, directors of conscience) have been inclined to posit, let alone act upon. Untapped remained the subterraneous source of public longing for release from the lastingly unbearable tension of an unnatural hostility; and absent from American politics was a 'dark horse' candidate for high office prepared to stake all on taking the aspiration seriously, leaving the field wide open for the standard politician eager to capitalize on the animosity.

On the strictly intellectual plane, the failure of the elective political and expert professional dyarchy to fulfill its public role was reducible to the incapacity to relate seemingly opposite terms to one another in a way more dynamic than would result from treating them as mutually exclusive; to match contradiction with compensation any better than to relate previous outcomes meaningfully to subsequent evolution.

Thus, the partly provisional and partly lasting diminution of material and moral resource attending America's regression from empire, far from excluding, rather demanded the acceptance of the greater risks attached to a flexible equilibrium (one entailing an enlarged diplomatic role in Europe and greater access to desired strategic or material assets in the Third World periphery for the Soviets). Similarly, it was too simplistic to hold that an enlarged access would elicit no internal or external Soviet response other than recidivist repression and escalating expansion, and at the same time to treat the bestowal of American or West European economic or technological bounties as incompatible with Soviet global self-assertion (and an enlarged Western tolerance of such self-assertion). To postulate a contradiction meant ignoring the role Soviet geo-political achievements play in compensating and partially covering up for economic and technological dependence in a society as deeply desirous of national prestige as of material prosperity.

It has been no more convincing to extrapolate the reasons for and the outcome of one instance of 'appeasement' (in the 1930s) into a differently circumstanced antagonism, while failing to consider the consequences of a 'denial' strategy in vastly more comparable (pre-World War I) conditions. Nor was it, finally, helpful to draw in fact (as distinct from rhetoric) a sharp line between competition and cooperation as if they were unrelated dynamically in either their milder forms or their ultimate shapes as confrontation in total war and condominium for minimum order. Relieving an implausible dichotomy with the prospect of a competitive–cooperative mélange did little good so long as both of the constituents were not underwritten with equally potent practical reasons and analytically rigorous rationales. One must isolate reasons other than a spell of peculiarly understood 'detente' to explain why the United States should adopt and foster a cooperative line also outside arms control; similarly, a rationale is needed beyond the abstract call for an undefined but all too precisely envisaged 'world order' to demonstrate why the Soviet Union should collaborate in upholding a shared stake in stability.

The experts have further set back the education of the public by treating Russia's pursuit of 'destabilizing' gains abroad as mutually exclusive with political stability inside the Soviet Union – i.e., by representing the rival foreign policy as the outgrowth of radical regime instability, and as both an intended and the 'objectively' vital remedy for the regime's illegitimacy. The logical consequence has been to treat the policy as adventurous, implying (as the condition of the term's appropriateness) that it was prompted by considerations unrelated to objectives traditional with great powers and vastly exceeded available Soviet means. Actually, in the Russian no more and no less than in the American or any other case, a foreign policy is successful domestically when it does, and a successful foreign policy will, usefully enhance the legitimacy or only popularity of a regime or administration, on either near-universal grounds (such as citizen patriotism) or country- or regime-specific grounds (i.e., official ideology or mythology). However, the greatest success in either the domestic or foreign arena cannot fully or lastingly substitute for radical failure in the other sphere, regardless of whether the touchstone is political liberalization in the Soviet case or economic and fiscal stabilization in the American one.

It only compounds the simplistic character of thinking oblivious of the 'dialectic' at work within the phenomena and processes relevant for foreign policy when it fails to reflect their institutional setting by being itself 'systemic'. It is one thing to apprehend the proposition that any substantial change within an interlocking system automatically entails far-reaching changes within and between parties to it. It is another to actually think that way and apply the defining property of a 'system' creatively to policy, until the geometrically expanding range of causes and effects forces one to stop anticipating possible or likely future contingencies. Thus, as a simple but also critical example, little or no concern or forethought has been spent on the consequences of achieving moderate or extreme goals of a containment/rollback strategy in Europe or Asia or worldwide, and the ways and means of dealing with them. By the same token, thinking and acting has proceeded as if altered policy behavior, producing, say, geopolitical adjustments for extended US–Soviet parity, kept everything else constant, and a cost did not entail offsetting benefits as a 'second' consequence or vis-à-vis 'third' parties. If one shortcoming will near-inevitably result in staying with a policy too long, the other will lead to rejecting any policy change that entails incurring fresh risks for potentially unprecedented rewards.

The Decisional Dialectic

A simplistic thinking that misses the 'dialectical' interplay of (partial) opposites for an integrating (provisional) outcome will derange decision making, not least in the triangular US–Soviet–Chinese setting.

Superior strategic thinking will consider the effect of any initiative or response not only on the immediately targeted 'second' but also or especially a 'third' party. It will then also weigh equally the impact of that effect on the positions or relations of the principal 'two'. More generally, such a thought pattern will anticipate not only the immediate effects or consequences of a policy but will address from the outset also the problem of how to deal with them – to wit, parry or lessen any ensuing damage and exploit or augment likewise hypothetical benefits. A thus enlarged mode of policy thinking is likely to produce a more continuous and coherent strategy than one that does not consider the third party (or, ideally if not always practicably, a set of 'third parties') any more than it encompasses (as the practicable maximum?) the three-part chain from an initial policy act via its intended or possible-to-probable alternative consequences to the range of responses which the newly created situation is apt, in principle predictably, to elicit from the several concerned parties. Strategic reflection that proceeds in keeping with a multifaceted pattern that is triadic in regard to both parties and process, actors and action, is broadly speaking dialectical. It will implement best the moderating constraints and stabilizing tendencies that come together in a complex equilibrium, as contrasted with more primitively reflexive balancing.

Strategic thinking can proceed instead by way of discrete units of action and reaction, involving only one other party or immediate effect at a time. When it does, it is (in literal contrast to the dialectically triadic mode) incrementally dyadic. It suits best and accentuates further a lack of consensus on longer-term policy objectives. To say that it is congenial to the pragmatic US political and institutionalized bureaucratic culture is not to affirm that the procedurally triadic mode of policy thinking has not been applied to the US–Soviet–Chinese triangle. The difficulty is with how this has been done. By and large, US policy makers have considered only the effect of relations with China on Soviet policies, and that in the short run. Downplayed or even ignored were both the long-term effect on the Soviet polity and the effect of alternative forms of US–Soviet relations on China and her development in any time span. Inasmuch as so lopsided a thinking procedure reflects exclusive preoccupation with containment through encircling coalition, it shortchanges the more substantive issue: the basis for which of the available alternative strategies is to be laid by what kind of interactions with which of the other two parties preferentially?

In this connection, seeing US–Soviet relations in strictly antithetical terms of radical opposites will obscure the significance of the overlap which differentiates a schism from polarity (and leaves open the possibility of synthesis). The schism comprises the attributes of powers such as Russia and America, primarily continental and insular or Western and Eastern, which, unevenly distributed between the two, make them no more totally different than exactly identical in all respects. The overlap area comprises the makings of complementarity in functions and convergence in behavior and institutions. It is a basis for accommodation as well as conflict. Combining instead the dogmatic conviction with a pragmatic bias leads naturally to stressing the more superficially constituted US–Chinese overlap, in 'parallel' interests, as a basis for tactical cooperation and (outside the realm of illusive Sinophilia) little else. In fact, the pragmatic mindset responsible for promoting cooperation with China will fit readily into a dogmatic repudiation of a more substantial community of longer-term interests and cultural affinities with Russia. A casualty is the concern lest the favored mode of thinking about strategy foreclose US–Soviet convergence beyond the extent already manifest in the area of conventional principles and basic techniques of foreign policy.

So long as the more complex thinking mode was not applied evenhandedly, much could be said in favor of the contentious pluralism manifest within the American Executive and between it and the Legislative in the making of US foreign policy. In that the pluralism compounds the effect of pragmatism, and accentuates thinking that proceeds incrementally, it has precluded a pro-China tilt from degenerating into a hard-to-redress lurch. It has also hindered geopolitical constraints on Soviet foreign policy from deepening into compulsion to respond aggressively. The offsetting weakness of the pluralist–pragmatic combination is that it tends to produce sporadically only tactical rationales for US–Soviet cooperation, mostly in congenial areas such as arms control. It leaves the field free and open to ostensibly strategic or covertly dogmatic reasons for conflict, and fails to generate convincing credentials for combining conflict with cooperation.

It will be impossible to produce a compelling rationale for a mixed approach to the Soviet Union so long as particular US interests are unfailingly perceived through the dogmatic postulate of a generalized competition. Nor will it be feasible for the pluralist–pragmatic decisional mode to integrate into current policies the consideration of hypothetical future developments and the range of available responses to them. Thus, to illustrate from earlier arguments, the immediate (or 'first') consequence of a two-front containment policy will be its provocative effect on the Soviet Union. It is liable to generate as an ulterior (or 'second') consequence a situation to be anticipated before creating the first effect. The situation can consist of a deepened military–strategic US dependence on China as the key if not only or last significant ally; or, if the Soviet response is forcible or the strategy has succeeded to the point of disrupting the Soviet system, the ulterior consequence can be the movement of Chinese power into the resulting vacuum. Either of these consequences would comprise the effect of contentious US–Soviet interactions on China as the third party; it would be made more likely or serious by a policy that had been limited to anticipating only the constraining effect of US–China collaboration on Russia. And it would create a more difficult situation for the United States to deal with than it had to face before. One part of the worsened situation – the policy's 'systemic' effect – would be the center of gravity shifting toward China (or Asia generally) in one way or another; its other part might well be a marked increase in global and regional instabilities in the Third World and Eastern Europe, reducing the capacity of any major power to affect events. That is to say, the effect of the policy would not be confined to the sole intended one of eliminating the Soviet threat concurrently with Soviet power from the international system, making it correspondingly easier for a thus relatively strengthened United States to achieve its objectives.

Thinking along such lines means integrating the adverse implications of containment, validated by historical antecedents and plausible in terms of realistic theory, into the formulation of strategy from the start. The alternative is to have to deal with the effects only as they surface and, having become obvious, are also all the more onerous. The inclination, prompted by the simpler mode of policy thinking and making, will then be to discredit any effort to anticipate ulterior consequences of a range of hypothetical strategies with multiple third-party implications. The prevision will be treated as impossible, because it exceeds the capacity of a multicentered bureaucratic apparatus to conceptualize policy; or it will be disowned as unnecessary, because a catastrophic outcome is implausible or its extent and context unpredictable. It becomes easier – and may by default become necessary – to take eventual triumph over the single adversary (perceived in isolation from other threats) for granted, without the policy maker being necessarily prepared to deploy the required means and incur the costs of either success or failure.

When the dogmatic strain is absent, a more purely pragmatic mode will tend to favor, rather unrealistically, a different scenario: of the conflict gradually subsiding into a stable plateau of limited rivalry without either its bases or the strategy changing fundamentally. In the real world, a major conflict is likely to test with more determinate results the strengths and weaknesses of the alternative modes of policy thinking, roughly coincident as they are with the difference between state- and society-centered political cultures. The balance will most markedly tilt in favor of the anticipatory over the reflexive thought pattern when the need for a conceptualized grand strategy dwarfs the utility of tactical conventions for dealing with immediate contingencies. In a protracted major-power conflict that will create the need sooner or later, the party with a political culture stressing pragmatically implemented societal values also in the international arena risks paying a high price for proving the superiority of incrementally deployed flexibility and spontaneity. The cost will rise if the proof is to be administered against the longer-term policy perspective of a more self-consciously state-centered political culture that encourages dialectically conceived planning of strategy keyed to climactic-to-catastrophic contingencies.

Dual Allegiances and One National Interest

Throughout the emergence of the United States to world power, it has been the more or less conscious intention behind the pressures exerted and the influence sought by the ethnic and religious groups constituting the nation's composite physiognomy to invert the effect of the American political culture on the ways of thinking about and making foreign policy: i.e., expose instead the culture itself to the cumulatively shaping impact of the directions actually taken by foreign policy. If, at the peak of the initial US foray into overseas imperialism British-style, the Irish had forced the Anglophile foreign policy elite to 'twist the lion's tail' so as to remain electable locally, later-wave German immigrants tried to prevent that same ruling group from rushing to the succor of the British Empire before taking its place. With the threat shifting to communism and, upon reconsideration, the Soviet Union, the critical mass of directly interested ethnic elements shifted from Western and Central to Eastern Europe. Their impact grew with the waning of the traditional elite, largely unequipped for the growing technicality of the military–strategic and economic instruments of policy and finally discredited by disproving in a minor war the validity of its compensating claim to superior political wisdom and judgment.

For individuals directly victimized by Soviet power and policies, the principled absolutism and emotional drive of émigré politics as it expands into the void of practical tasks of governance spilled over readily into the larger vacuum of an authentically American policy toward Russia. For others, with a less immediate personal link to the directly affected countries or faiths, the main impulse came from their status as sociocultural marginals in Anglo-Protestant America, to be mended by so refashioning the American polity and policy as to move the marginals closer to the society's center. Once the social barriers against them had been lowered by the socially mobilizing effects of World War II, Catholics and Jews among others could gravitate from religious to secular political commitments centering on Eastern Europe for some and Israel for others. Consolidating radical anti-communism or -sovietism as the other face of integral Americanism in the process meant disposing of the dual-allegiance issue at one stroke, and not a moment too soon, as the brightest of the ex-marginals advanced to the foreign policy making front office. Once entrenched there, they have shown little inclination to keep reassessing the issue of US–Soviet confrontation and convergence on either organic or operational grounds so as to relate it to America's escalating ethnic fragmentation, before their new-found centrality was diluted in the expanding kaleidoscope of a multi-cultural United States.

Compared with the domestic, the outside influences emanating from the multilateral Western alliance have been weaker and mostly indirect. They could carry over into an altered scene diplomatic traditions ranging from extreme antagonisms, activating latent Russophobia, to one-sidedly slanted or profitable alliances, giving rise to sporadic enthusiams for things Russian (Great Britain, Prussia–Germany). Or, finally (France), the needle on the policy compass could oscillate uncertainly between the appeals of the nostalgically recalled past formula for foreign policy independence, anchored in Russia, and its ruefully tolerated if not resentfully endured historic and present 'Anglo-Saxon' alternative.

An authentically American outlook and policy cannot but automatically reduce specialized viewpoints, born of peculiar histories and particularist concerns, to their properly limited role in fashioning democratic consensus and demonstrating strategic utility. Until then, the partisan visions will go on battling with unequally potent persuasiveness for the unshared possesion of American consciousness. In so doing they can be only anti-Soviet or deep down also anti-Russian. Representatively extreme among the biases have been the national mindsets of two geographically most Western of the Eastern European and most Eastern of the culturally Western Slavic countries. One of the mindsets has been inspired and formed by the desire of an insecure small people for safe protection by a kindred protector. The other is fired by a more ambitious nation's haunting sense of need to recover the once-possessed equality (if not superiority) of power with respect to an oppressor no more endurable for being ethnically related (and having once been the weaker party).

Consciously or not, the Poles look backward to conditions of greatness between the Germanic neighbor to be held at bay in the west and the Great Russian one to be reduced to its corelands in the east. The diametrically opposite prescription of the historically Slavo- or Russo-phile Czechs has been for the full inclusion of a 'liberalized' Russia, first tsarist and later Soviet, in a receptive European and latitudinous world order. Only briefly forgotten in favor of the gradually revealed unreality of a liberal–nationalist shortcut to instant individual and corporate freedom under exclusively Western auspices, the prescription for gradual evolution was reaffirmed immediately after the interwar illusion had given way to the wartime nightmare of a Pax Germanica. The more realistic vision was not wrong for being again premature in unready conditions, when a small country unwilling to revert to the position of an expendable appendage of the West could be neither strong nor stable enough to serve as a bridge across too wide a chasm between West and East, and could at the most betoken the plight of small – and, subsequently, also not so small and

not only *East* European – countries groping for a practicable measure
of independence as states, and a satisfying degree of renewed self-
respect as nations, within an order comprehensive enough to effectively cancel an obsolete distinction and division.

When Otto von Bismarck described the possession of Bohemia as
the key to the control of Europe, he wrote the script for the scenario
implemented by the founder of a later German Reich. Hitler had
plucked the Bohemian thorn out of the side of Greater Germany so
that he could proceed undistracted to erect the walls and garrison the
moats of the *Festung Europa*. Neither would Stalin let go of a
Bohemia that, if not needed to serve as the anvil upon which to
hammer asunder a diminished Germany, became all the more critical
as the strategic underpinning for Germany's separated eastern half.
With communism going down in defeat in Western Europe, Russia
would all the more resolutely protect at the center of the continent her
ancient ambition to add an effective role to her henceforth uncontes-
table identity as Europe's greatest power. Just as Munich a decade
earlier, the particular event implementing that resolution helped rouse
the West to the need for self-defense. The pursuit of the role has since
gained as much in refinement as the claim has in substance. The task of
easing the ambition without submitting to arrogance is not one that
can be safely left to either manifestly inadequate or covertly biased
patterns of thought – and action.

The time available for decision about fundamental options is never
indefinite. The present is marked by a new generation of Soviet
leaders. Russia's twisting road toward the light has traveled from
Stalinism through an ultraliberal (by Soviet standards) Khrush-
chevian reaction, and just recently emerged into a more prudent and
realistic reformism from a corrective Brezhnevist regression. Even as
the new men in the Kremlin ponder this legacy and assess the outer
latitudes for socially unsettling and politically risky change, they will
need to consider what external conditions they have to take into
account when shaping the projects and pursuing the achievements
they would wish future judges to measure them by.

As it nears its own maturity as a society and a power, America may
yet be blessed with a matching fresh impulse. If so favored, the United
States will make true on an enlarged scale the boast of the nineteenth-
century British statesman George Canning. It will redress with
something new the balance of the Old World by lifting from an

Occident that was made whole again the curse of an unbridgeable division between land and sea, last united after Rome by the continental–maritime empire of Spain at a like transition between eras. But if it is not, America will have deserved losing the unifying task to the Russian heartland power, closer to the ascendant East and nearest to imperial Spain in kind. In such a case, the projection of the United States onto the world stage through participation in World War I might well strike a future historian as noxious in its delayed consequences, because premature; an evolutionary aberration that deflected more seasoned polities from tackling the linked problems of Germany and Russia within traditional frameworks unaffected by the inconsistencies of a remote and capricious mass democracy.

If it is to avoid so harsh a judgment of history, that same democracy must learn from England's mistakes and move into the future by retracing backward into the twenty-first century the course of Britain between the nineteenth and twentieth: from multiple but manageable preoccupations with a range of problems created by France, Russia, and the fledgling United States to the submersion of all concerns in one with Germany. If the United States is to meet its first test as a world power better than the United Kingdom met its last, it will have to tone down a like fixation, on the Soviet 'danger'. Only then will it be free to tackle the emergent variety of tasks and threats that easily match the earlier challenge of the non-German parties to the fellow-insular realm, even as East Asia replicates for Britain's successor many of the contradictory features (other than cultural familiarity) that aroused fond hopes only to cause irate frustrations when inhering for the ex-metropole in emancipated North America.

For a no longer confidently imperial United States to call instead upon the unsettled and potentially unsettling power and resource of East Asia to 'right', with one stroke of policy, an imaginary imbalance within the Europe-centered and -derived segment of the world system, somewhat as barely consolidated France had once been invited to do in its Italian antecedent and an unready United States in the European phase, would again entail a certain cost in the centrality and autonomy of the 'restored' system segment. It might also curtail the independence or well-being of some or most of its parts, regardless of whether China and Japan were involved divergently or in unison because the latter had either retained free access to the Western markets or its material prosperity had given way to political crisis and its adopted Western to the more authentic Asian identity and orientation as a result of seeing the access sharply reduced. In an international system inching toward regionally articulated coherence on a global basis, a purely offensive bid for one-power hegemony is about as obsolete as the defensive recourse of a self-destroying 'civilized' core to the 'barbarian' intruder–savior from the periphery. The task of responsible policy combining progress with conservation is then to implement the military-technologically enforced prevalence of the evolutionary-organic over the interactive-operational factors by merely trying to mediate – space in time and soften in impact – inevitable fluctuations in potency and precedence between unevenly maturing – advancing and receding – parties.

When a policy keyed to moderating the rise–decline rhythms not only between powers but also among intermittently dominant and dominating civilizations has absorbed both the full range and the limiting conditions of historic precedents, it will be positioned to transcend those precedents into an effective anticipation of the attendant pitfalls; its shapers will have begun to creatively rethink also US–Soviet relations even as particularistic biases are being absorbed within a 'collective mind' more comprehensive than America's alone.

Index

Index